Advance acclaim for

En la Lucha
In the Struggle

◪

"*Mujerista* theology is emerging as a major expression of feminist theology from the context of the lived experience of Hispanic women in North America. Ada María Isasi-Díaz is undoubtedly its major spokeswoman, although she consciously seeks to speak for women as agents of liberation in the context of a community of peoples (Cuban, Puerto Rican, and Chicanos) in North America. Her new book *En la Lucha* brings a systematic methodological reflection to the doing of what is and must remain very much the grassroots praxis of Latinas whose native tongue is neither academic theology nor English."

— *Rosemary Radford Ruether*
Garrett-Evangelical
Theological Seminary

"Ada María's book is an affirmation of hope in our struggles for justice. She shows the motives of our journey toward liberation rooted in Latina cultures and our condition as *mestiza* women. A *mujerista* theologian, Cuban-born, with the Third-World women theologians Isasi-Díaz sees theology as a radical element in our struggles for life. With Latina women, and with the academic community at large, she challenges our understanding of theological knowledge by addressing the structural connections between praxis, ethnicity, theology, and ethics. Isasi-Díaz provides a crucial point of reference for advancing a womanist discourse congruent with the beliefs, expectations, and identity of Latina/Hispanic women. Her insights will creatively influence both academic and religious communities."

— *María Pilar Aquino*
University of San Diego

Elaborating a mujerista theology –

En la Lucha
In the Struggle

A Hispanic
Women's
Liberation
Theology

ADA MARÍA ISASI-DÍAZ

Fortress Press   Minneapolis

EN LA LUCHA / IN THE STRUGGLE
A Hispanic Women's Liberation Theology

Scripture quotations from the Revised Standard Version are copyright © 1946, 1952, and 1971 by the Division of Christian Education of the National Council of Churches.

Cover design by Patricia Boman
Interior design by Peregrine Publications

Library of Congress Cataloging-in-Publication Data

Isasi-Díaz, Ada María.
    En la lucha–In the struggle : a Hispanic Women's liberation theology / Ada María Isasi-Díaz.
        p. cm.
    English text with chapter summaries in Spanish.
    Includes bibliographical references and index.
    ISBN 0-8006-2610-9 (alk. paper)
    1. Theology – Hispanic American Women. 2. Liberation theology. 3. Women's Studies. 4. Christianity and culture. I. Title II. Title: En la lucha–In the struggle.
BR563.H57I82   1993
230'.082 – dc20   93-9220
                                                                        CIP

The paper used in this publication meets the minimum requirements of American National Standard for Information Services-Permanence of Paper for Printed Library Materials, ANSI Z329.48-1984.   ∞ ™

Manufactured in the U.S.A.   AF 1-2610
97   96   95   94   93   1   2   3   4   5   6   7   8   9   10

"A mi vagabunda y desmembrada generación,"
to my vagabond and dismembered generation the world over,
particularly to my generation of Cuban sisters and brothers,
deseándonos ganas de un mundo liberado
y fuerzas para la lucha para lograrlo,
wishing us a deep desire for a liberated world and
the strength to struggle to accomplish it.

Pero Nueva York no fue la ciudad de mi infancia,
no fue aquí que adquirí las primeras certidumbres,
no es aquí el rincón de mi primera caída
ni el silbido lacerante que marcaba las noches.
Por eso siempre permaneceré al margen,
una extraña entre las piedras,
aún bajo el sol amable de este día de verano,
como ya para siempre permaneceré extranjera,
aún cuando regrese a la ciudad de mi infancia,
cargo esta marginalidad inmune a todos los retornos,
demasiado newyorkina para ser,
—aún volver a ser—
cualquier otra cosa.

Lourdes Casal, *Para Ana Velford**

But New York was not the city of my infancy,
nor was it here that I grasped truth for the first time,
not here the corner of my first fall,
or where I heard the whistle that cuts the night.
That is why I will always remain marginalized
a stranger among the stones,
even under the kindly sun of this summer day,
just as I will always remain a foreigner,
even when I return to the city of my infancy,
I carry this marginality immune to all returns,
too much a New Yorker to be
—even to once again be—
anything else.

*Originally this poem was published in a literary magazine called *Areíto* (New York) 3, no. 1 (Verano 1976): 52. Later it was included in the posthumous volume, *Palabras juntan revolución,* (La Habana: Casa de las Américas, 1981).

CONTENTS

Preface

I AM A *mujerista* theologian, an activist theologian committed to the struggle for justice and peace. The poor and oppressed of Lima, Perú, where I had the privilege of living for three years, taught me that without liberation there is no justice and peace and that no one can be liberated at the expense of others or isolated from others. The struggle for liberation is the struggle to be self-determining within the context of community and in view of the common good, and to have the material conditions needed to develop into the fullness of our capacity. This fullness of being to which we are all called cannot become a reality if we cannot do according to what we know. For at the core of our being lies our conscience, our moral consciousness, demanding from us responsible decisions in accord with reasonable judgments. Fullness of being requires a commitment constantly to check, expand, and deepen our understanding of the values according to which we choose, and constantly to strengthen our resolution to decide according to those values at no matter what cost. And for me, to do *mujerista* theology is one of the key ways in which I contribute to and participate in the struggle for fullness of being, for liberation, an indispensable preparation for the coming of the kin-dom of God.[1]

For me to do *mujerista* theology is a vocation: it is the best way I can at present live out who I am and what I believe I am called to do. I do *mujerista* theology not to promote myself, but that fact does not take away from nor contradict the fact that doing *mujerista* theology is fulfilling and life-giving for me. It is a way of responsibly living my Christianity, struggling for survival and liberation as a Latina in the U.S.A.

1. Two reasons compel me not to use the usual word employed by English Bibles, *kingdom*. First, it is obviously a sexist word that presumes that God is male. Second, the concept of kingdom in our world today is both hierarchical and elitist. The same reasons hold for not using *reign*. The word *kin-dom* makes it clear that when the fullness of God becomes a day-to-day reality in the world at large, we will all be sisters and brothers—kin to each other. This terminology was suggested to me by Georgenne Wilson, O.S.F.

In doing *mujerista* theology I struggle for liberation because religion is an essential and integral element of Hispanic culture. For a Latina, religion does indeed provide or influence many of the understandings and motivations of daily life. I believe that religious understandings likewise are part of the ideology of the U.S.A., an ideology that grounds and supports societal institutions. I believe that *mujerista* theology, by providing a platform for the voices of grassroot Hispanic Women, can be an effective means of challenging (and, I hope, changing) present ideology and societal structures because they effectively exclude and oppress Latinas.

I come from a hard-working middle-class family with certain privileges that money can buy but with no monetary wealth. As a middle-class woman I am always two or three months away from not having enough money to pay my bills—including my mortgage—but with a certain degree of confidence that such a thing will not happen. As a Latina I have often experienced ethnic prejudice and sexism: in educational institutions both as a student and as a professor; in women's groups and in organizations where difference is neither understood nor valued; in many diverse situations and places such as stores, conferences, government offices, Latino businesses and organizations. For me to do *mujerista* theology is an effective way to struggle against the prejudices that oppress me and my Hispanic sisters.

As a *mujerista* theologian I straddle the academic and the Latino worlds. Hispanic Women are indeed my community of accountability. But I am an academically trained theologian, and part of my praxis has to do with attempting to impact academia, to bring Latinas' religious understandings and practices to bear on the academic world and on academic disciplines, particularly theology. My writings reflect these two worlds, between which I move constantly. Some of the language I use in my writings is certainly alien to the majority of grassroot Hispanic Women, but I am confident it does not betray who they are, their beliefs and expectations. Though I do not speak for them, I speak with them and on behalf of them. *Mujerista* theology is an effective way of doing community advocacy. I also hope that *mujerista* theology's method and insistence on the validity and importance of Latinas' religious understandings and practices will impact not only theology but also the churches and, through them, society.

This self-revelatory statement, as well as the acknowledgments below, are meant to make obvious my subjectivity and my social locality. Who I am, where I am coming from and where I wish to go shapes the method and content of my theological work. Though such self-revelation is always dangerous I have entered upon it because I believe that the pretense of objectivity by theologians indicates complicity with the status quo, a status that for me and my Hispanic sisters is oppressive.

Acknowledgments

"HONRAR, HONRA" — to honor others honors one — is a saying of José Martí, one of the literary greats of Latin America, the soul of Cuba's independence at the end of the nineteenth century and of its revolutionary struggles ever since. Although the length may seem extravagant to some, these acknowledgments are my way of honoring those who have blessed me with their friendship and love, and those who have shared with me their experiences and knowledge through the years. It is a way for me to say that I cannot do theology and will not do theology apart from a community of support and accountability. It is also a way of giving the reader a sense of who I am.

My first debt of gratitude is to the Hispanic Women who have in many different ways been my sisters in the struggle. I particularly wish to thank those who have given me so much by sharing with me their religious understandings and practices. I thank Inez, Adela, Marta, Lupe, María, Olivia, Margarita, Esperanza, and Caridad, who speak from the pages of this book. I thank all the other women who participated in the reflection weekends at which Yolanda Tarango and I gathered the material first used in our book, *Hispanic Women: Prophetic Voice in the Church*, material which is also reflected throughout this book.

I want to thank my *mujerista* community, particularly Yolanda Tarango, Carmen Villegas, and María Antonietta Berriozabal, whose support has been unswerving. Our friendship was birthed by the struggle, and the struggle is indeed one of our friendship's main sources of nourishment.

For the last ten years I have been a member of the Women's Liturgy Group in New York City. The group has persisted through the years in gathering once a month to celebrate our lives, to explore and deepen our faith. In the process many of us have become good friends, we are *familia*, and we know we can depend on one another. I thank all of these wonderful women for their support and encouragement. Particularly I am grateful to Mary Ragan, who listens to me and shares with me when I am fit to be tied; to Cindy Derway, whose affirming praise always nourishes me and spurs me on; to Janet Walton, who every single time she sees me affirms my ability to be a theologian; to Eileen King, who first introduced me to her beloved city of New York and who has shared generously with me through the years. Finally I owe a major debt of gratitude to Ann Patrick Ware. We worked together at Church Women United while I was writing my doctoral dissertation, from which this book draws extensively. Ann Pat helped me at work time and again during those years so I could have time for my studies. She has edited all of my written work during the last six years, always insisting on clarity of thought as well as precise and effective use of the English language. I am most appreciative of her ability to make my English correct without making it sound "non-Cuban."

I want to thank a scattered feminist community that had Union Theological Seminary, from which I graduated in 1990, as its initial point of reference. In particular I want to thank Angela Bauer, Pam Brubaker, Liz Bounds, Hyun Kyung Chung, Marilyn Legge, and Serinity Young. Their friendship has confirmed my belief that the creation of feminist communities is an effective survival strategy.

To all of these sisters I say those wonderful words of Marge Piercy, "Give birth to me, sisters, in the struggle we transform ourselves. . . . This morning we must make each other strong. Change is qualitative: we are each other's miracle."

I am grateful to my doctoral dissertation committee, who guided the work on which this book is based. Beverly Harrison was my adviser at Union Theological Seminary, and her trust enabled me to follow my theological insights and experience as I worked on the initial formulations of *mujerista* theology. Margaret Farley helped me keep in touch with my Roman Catholic roots. Her clear and methodical thinking and her vast knowledge of Roman Catholic theology kept me on a firm footing. Victoria Erickson has been enormously helpful to me regarding the use of social sciences in my theological method. I am particularly grateful to her for teaching me that I am not alone in my convictions regarding the need to have the voices of Latinas in my writings, that there is a whole school of sociologists whose theories back me. Larry Rasmussen became one of my theological dialogue partners through his written work before I met him personally. Larry is a true gentle man always willing to spare a moment to help me clarify ideas and concepts. I am deeply grateful to all of my committee members for their willingness to work with me and to embrace me as a colleague.

I am grateful to my large family for their loving support and care, which is so intense and has such actuality that although I am the only one of us who lives in New York City I feel that, after all, I do *not* live alone. I especially want to thank the three little ones, Alexandra, Javi, and A.J., who repeatedly give me an opportunity to be concerned about important things like diapers, peanut butter and jelly sandwiches, and learning how to swim and to ride bikes. These three little ones, because they con-cretize for me the future in a very personal way, always offer me hope and refresh me.

I am grateful to Michael West and Lois Torvik, my editors at Fortress Press, and to my copy editor, Sydney Merkel, who also edited the Spanish in this book. Without their support and help this book would not have been possible.

Finally, a word of explanation about the dedication of this work. I finished high school while my country, Cuba, was going through earth-shaking events that have radically changed the course of its history and of mine. My generation, whether we came to *el exilio* or stayed in Cuba, was the one that had to struggle to find who we were and how to give meaning to our lives—the task of all teenagers and young adults—in the midst of great turmoil. Those of us who live in the U.S.A. are part of the genera-tion of the 1960s that saw racism challenged by the civil rights movement and the myth of U.S. invincibility challenged by the movement against the war in Vietnam. It was my generation that welcomed the Spirit-filled winds of Vatican II in the Roman Catholic Church and had to learn how to accept and nourish its challenges in our personal lives. This is the genera-tion that has been a key element in and a great beneficiary of the women's movement of the last twenty years. This is the generation that has been so instrumental in the unbelievable unfolding of events the world over—what was the U.S.S.R., Eastern Europe, South Africa, China, Central America, Latin America—during the last few years.

I believe all these experiences, benefits, and challenges have been given to us, whether we have been active participants or not, to prepare us for the task that still lies ahead. They have been given to us to prepare us to move our world to be a life-giving world, one in which liberation is a possibility for all if we are willing to struggle passionately for it instead of believing that justice means only equality for a few at the expense of most others. Our lives up to now have been a preparation so we can work without rest to stop the destruction of our world by ecological devasta-tion even as the threat of nuclear destruction abates.

I dedicate this book especially to my generation of Cuban compatriots called to build bridges between the Cuban community in exile and the community on the island. The future of our country will depend on our ability to understand the depth of Martí's *"la patria es ara, no pedestal,"* the mothercountry is an altar, not a pedestal, and to live accordingly. It will depend on our ability to dream dreams and see visions—to look forward and think of new possibilities instead of trying in vain to bring back what was or to maintain what is. Let us indeed be willing to forge ahead, convinced that to struggle is to live: *la vida es la lucha.*

Prólogo

SOY UNA teóloga mujerista, una teóloga activista comprometida con la lucha por la justicia y la paz. Los pobres y oprimidos de Lima, Perú, con quienes tuve el privilegio de trabajar por tres años, me enseñaron que sin liberación no puede haber justicia y paz y que nadie se puede liberar a costa de otros ni sin contar con los demás. La lucha por la liberación es una lucha por la auto-determinación de la persona, miembro de una comunidad la cual entiende lo que es el bien común. Es una lucha por las condiciones materiales necesarias para el desarrollo pleno de nuestras capacidades humanas. No se puede lograr esta plenitud de ser a la que todos estamos llamados a no ser que podamos actuar de acuerdo con lo que sabemos ya que en el centro de la persona se encuentra la conciencia, el sentir moral que nos exige decisiones responsables de acuerdo a nuestros juicios. Plenitud de ser requiere que constantemente comprobemos, ampliemos y profundicemos los valores que guían nuestras decisiones, y también requiere que cada día nos comprometamos con mayor firmeza a actuar de acuerdo a esas decisiones, no importa cual sea el costo. Para mí el hacer teología mujerista es una manera de contribuir a y participar en la lucha por la liberación, preparación indispensable para la llegada del reino de Dios.

Para mí el hacer teología mujerista es una vocación: es la mejor manera de vivir hoy día de acuerdo a lo que creo Dios quiere de mí. Yo hago teología mujerista no para promoverme a mí misma, pero eso no quita el que el ser teóloga mujerista me satisfaga y sea vivificante para mí. El hacer teología mujerista es una forma responsable de vivir mi cristianismo, de luchar por sobrevivir como latina en los EE.UU., de luchar por mi liberación.

El hacer teología mujerista es luchar por la liberación porque la religión es elemento integral de la cultura hispana. Para las latinas la religión provee o influencia muchos de los entendimientos y motivaciones de la vida cotidiana. Yo creo también que lo religioso es parte de la ideología de los EE.UU. Y yo creo que la teología mujerista, porque da a conocer las voces de mujeres hispanas de la base, puede ser una manera efectiva de retar y cambiar la ideología y las estructuras sociales presentes ya que éstas nos excluyen y oprimen.

Yo vengo de una familia de clase media muy trabajadora; de una familia con ciertos privilegios que usualmente están relacionados con tener dinero aunque por ser seis hermanas y dos hermanos nunca tuvimos mucho dinero. Ser mujer de la clase media quiere decir que si me quedo sin trabajo sólo tengo dinero para vivir por tres meses pero, a la vez, vivo con un cierto grado de certitud de que siempre voy a poder encontrar trabajo. Por ser latina he sufrido prejuicio étnico y prejuicio por ser mujer en instituciones educacionales mientras fui estudiante al igual que ahora que soy profesora; en organizaciones de mujeres en las cuales el ser diferente ni se entiende ni se valoriza; en muchas diversas situaciones y lugares como tiendas, conferencias, oficinas gubernamentales, negocios y organizaciones hispanas. Para mí el hacer teología mujerista es una forma eficaz de luchar en contra de los prejuicios que me oprimen a mí y a mis hermanas hispanas.

Como teóloga mujerista me muevo entre el mundo académico y el mundo latino. Yo considero que son las mujeres hispanas a quienes tengo que rendir cuentas. Pero soy una teóloga con entrenamiento académico y parte de mi praxis consiste en tratar de impactar a la academia, de hacer que las prácticas religiosas y manera de entender la fe de las latinas tengan peso en el mundo académico, sobretodo en el campo de la teología. No todo el lenguaje que empleo es conocido por las mujeres hispanas de la base, pero creo que lo que digo no traiciona lo que ellas creen y practican, quienes ellas son. Aunque yo no hablo por ellas, no me proclamo voz representativa de las latinas, sí hablo con ellas y en favor de ellas. Mi quehacer teológico es una manera efectiva de abogar por las hispanas. Y espero que mi método teológico y mi insistencia en la validez e importancia de la manera como las latinas entendemos nuestra fe impacten no sólo a la teología sino también a las iglesias y a la sociedad.

Digo todo esto sobre mí para hacer explícita mi subjetividad y situarme socialmente. Quién soy, cuál es mi perspectiva, cuál es mi meta, informan el método y contenido de mi quehacer teológico. Aunque hablar de uno mismo siempre es peligroso, corro este riesgo porque creo firmemente que el pretender ser objetivo de los teólogos tradicionales es señal de complicidad con el *status quo* el cual es opresivo para mí y mis hermanas latinas.

Reconocimientos

"Honrar, honra" dijo Jose Martí, uno de los ilustres literatos de América Latina, el alma de la independencia cubana y de todas sus luchas revolucionarias. El reconocimiento de muchas personas que hago a continuación es mi manera de honrar a quienes me han dado su amistad y amor y por años han compartido conmigo sus experiencias y conocimiento. Este reconocimiento es una manera de decir que yo no puedo hacer teología y que no haré teología sin una comunidad de apoyo a la cual rindo cuentas. Y este reconocimiento es también un modo de compartir con el lector una noción de quién soy.

Mi primera deuda de gratitud es con las mujeres hispanas quienes son mis hermanas en la lucha. En particular quiero darle las gracias a quienes han compartido conmigo sus creencias religiosas y prácticas de fe. Gracias a Inez, Adela, Marta, Lupe, María, Olivia, Margarita, Esperanza, y Caridad, quienes hablan a través de las páginas de este libro.

Le doy las gracias a mi comunidad mujerista, en particular a Yolanda Tarango, Carmen Villegas, y María Antonietta Berriozabal, cuyo apoyo ha sido constante. La lucha le dió a luz a nuestra amistad y es la lucha su alimento principal.

Durante los últimos diez años he pertenecido a un grupo de mujeres el cual ha perseverado en reunirse una vez al mes para celebrar nuestras vidas, para explorar y profundizar nuestra fe. Hoy en día somos amigas, somos familia, y sabemos que podemos depender las unas en las otras. Les agradezco a estas mujeres su apoyo y estímulo. En especial le doy las gracias a Mary Ragan, con quien hablo cuando necesito entenderme a mí misma; a Cindy Derway, cuyos elogios me sostienen y animan; a Janet Walton, quien cada vez que nos reunimos me anima en mi papel de teóloga; a Eileen King, que fue la que me introdujo a su amada ciudad de Nueva York y que tanto ha compartido commigo todos estos años. Finalmente, mi mayor deuda de gratitud es con Ann Patrick Ware. Trabajamos juntas en Church Women United mientras yo escribía mi disertación doctoral. Ann Pat me ayudó repetidamente durante aquellos años para que yo tuviera tiempo para mis estudios. Ella ha corregido el inglés de todos mis escritos durante los últimos seis años, insistiendo siempre en claridad de pensamiento tanto como en un uso efectivo del inglés. Lo que más aprecio es su habilidad de corregir mi inglés sin hacerme dejar de sonar cubana.

Quiero darle las gracias a otro grupo de feministas que aunque disperso geograficamente forman una comunidad de apoyo para mí. Nos conocimos inicialmente en Union Theological Seminary, de donde me gradué en 1990. Angela Bauer, Pam Brubaker, Liz Bounds, Hyun Kyung Chung, Marilyn, Legge, and Serinity Young: amigas que confirman mi convicción que la creacion de comunidades feministas es una estrategia efectiva de supervivencia.

A todas estas hermanas digo esas palabras maravillosas de Marge Piercy, "Dénme a luz, hermanas, en la lucha nos transformamos nosotras mismas. . . . Esta mañana tenemos que fortalecernos. El cambio es cualitativo: somos un milagro las unas para las otras".

Gracias a mi comité de disertación doctoral, el cual guió la obra en la que se basa este libro. Beverly Harrison fue mi consejera en Union Theological Seminary. Su confianza en mi capacidad como teóloga me permitió seguir mis discernimientos y experiencias y así pude llegar a las formulaciones iniciales de la teología mujerista. Margaret Farley me ayudó a mantenerme en contacto con mis raíces católicas. Su pensar claro y metódico y su vasta sabiduría de la teología católica me mantuvieron sobre una base firme. Victoria Erickson me ha ayudado enormemente en el uso de las ciencias sociales en mi método teológico. En particular le agradezco el haberme enseñado que no soy la única que cree en la necesidad de incluir voces específicas en mi trabajo, que hay una escuela entera de sociólogos cuyas teorías apoyan mi pensar. Larry Rasmussen fue uno de mis compañeros de diálogo teológico a través de su obra escrita antes de que lo conociera personalmente. Larry es un verdadero hermano siempre dispuesto a ayudarme a clarificar ideas y conceptos. Agradezco a todos los miembros de mi comité el estar dispuestos a trabajar conmigo y a aceptarme como colega.

Agradezco a mi familia su apoyo tan cariñoso y su atención tan intensa y tan sincera que aunque soy la única que vive en Nueva York me siento como si no viviera sola. Quiero darles las gracias en especial a los más pequeños de la familia, Alexandra, Javi, y A.J., que me dan la oportunidad de interesarme en cosas importantes como pañales, leer cuentos infantiles, y aprender a nadar y a andar en bicicleta. Alexandra, Javi y A.J. concretizan el futuro para mí de un modo muy personal y eso me da esperanzas y me anima.

Gracias a Michael West y a Lois Torvik, mis editores en Fortress Press, y a mi editora del manuscrito, Sydney Merkel que también redactó la mayor parte de las secciones en español de este libro. Sin la ayuda de ellos tres este libro no habría sido posible.

Quiero terminar aquí con una explicación de la dedicatoria de este libro. Terminé mis estudios secundarios mientras que en mi patria, Cuba, sucedían acontecimientos de importancia mundial que han cambiado radicalmente el curso de su historia y de la mía. Mi generación, tanto los que vinimos al exilio como los que permanecimos en Cuba, tuvo que luchar para descubrir quiénes éramos y el significado de nuestras vidas–el deber de todo adolescente y jóven–en medio de un gran tumulto. Los que vivimos en EE.UU. hemos formado parte de la generación de los 1960 que vivió la lucha en contra del prejuicio racial y que vió el mito de la invencibilidad de EE.UU. desafiado por el movimiento contra la guerra en Vietnam. Fue mi generación la que recibió con alegría los vientos llenos del Espíritu del Concilio Vaticano Segundo en la iglesia católica, y que tuvo que aprender a aceptar y nutrir sus retos en nuestras vidas personales.

Esta es la generación que ha sido elemento central y que se ha beneficiado grandemente con movimiento feminista de los últimos veinte años. Ésta es la generación que ha sido tan instrumental en el desarollo de increíbles acontecimientos mundiales en lo que fue la Unión Soviética, en Europa Oriental, Sud Africa, China, América Central, y la América del Sud durante los últimos años.

Creo que todas estas experiencias, estos beneficios, y estos desafíos se nos han dado para prepararnos para la tarea que todavía queda por delante. Tenemos que mover a nuestro mundo para que sea un mundo vivificante, un mundo en el cual la liberación es posible para todos si estamos dispuestos a luchar apasionadamente por lograrla en vez de creer que "justicia" significa igualdad para unos pocos al costo de la mayoría. Hasta ahora nuestas vidas han sido una preparación para que podamos trabajar sin descanso para parar la destrucción ecológica de nuestro mundo la cual se acrecienta a la par que la amenaza de la destrucción atómica disminuye.

Dedico este libro especialmente a mi generación de compatriotas cubanos llamada a construir puentes entre la comunidad cubana en el exilio y a la comunidad en la Isla. El futuro de nuestra patria depende de que comprendamos profundamente lo que dijo Martí, "la patria es ara, no pedestal", y que vivamos de acuerdo a ello. El futuro de Cuba depende de nuestra capacidad para soñar sueños y ver visiones–de mirar adelante y pensar nuevas posibilidades en vez de esforzarnos inutilmente en hacer que el pasado retorne o de mantener estaticamente el presente. Tenemos que estar dispuestos a abrir brecha convencidos de que la vida es la lucha.

Introduction

THE APPEARANCE IN 1988 of the book *Hispanic Women: Prophetic Voice in the Church* brought to public attention one strand of theological work that Latinas had been doing in the United States. In that book Yolanda Tarango and I began the work of writing *mujerista* theology. Theology at large, it seemed to us, was lacking a key element that has since become the core of our work: providing a platform for the voices of Hispanic Women. For years we had been personally enriched by grassroot Latinas' religious understandings and the way those understandings guide their daily lives. We firmly believe that those religious understandings are part of the ongoing revelation of God, present in the midst of the community of faith and giving strength to Hispanic Women's struggle for liberation. Having been educated in theology, we believe we are responsible for gathering the voices of Latinas because of their value for our own strategies for survival. We believe we also must present the voices of Hispanic Women to the public at large so they can be taken into consideration by all who do theology and thus be reflected in the life and teachings of the church.

This book pushes further and deeper the ideas and methods presented in the earlier book. Like the first one, it is a platform for the voices of Latinas because their lived-experience is the source of *mujerista* theology. To pursue this task I went once again to speak with each of the women whose voices are in the earlier book as well as with two other Hispanic Women.[1] As I spoke with these women, who live in different areas of

---

1. Initially I was not able to locate one of the women, Adela. She had moved and nobody in the community knew where she was. Eventually she got in contact with me and I was able to visit with her. But by then I had already interviewed Esperanza and what she shared with me was so rich that I could not but include it. I also include the material from the interview with Caridad. The circumstances in her life seemed to me to be so different from those of the others that I felt that her understandings would greatly enrich this work.

1

the U.S.A., who are from different national backgrounds and from different socio-economic strata, who have different degrees of formal education, different ages, different ways of looking at and practicing their religious beliefs, I became all the more convinced that as Latinas we have a significant contribution to make to the society of the U.S.A. generally and to theology in particular.

I also became convinced that *mujerista* theology, because it is a liberative praxis, must be mainly about the moral agency of Latinas—how we understand ourselves as agents of our own history, how we create meaning in and through our lives, how we exercise our moral agency in spite of the oppression under which we live.[2] Years and years of talking and reflecting with Hispanic Women throughout the U.S.A. had made me aware of my own experience and practice regarding the use of the word *conciencia,* conscience. One of the reasons for this book is the need we have to go deeper into these understandings and examine how they operate in the lives of Latinas in order to strengthen our struggle for liberation. This book examines the links between Hispanic Women's understanding and use of *conciencia,* moral agency, and praxis. This examination demands that we further elaborate *mujerista* theology: how is it a liberative praxis, what is its role in the struggle for survival of Latinas, what are its key understandings?

Naming Ourselves

Two initial challenges confront those of us who understand the importance of a name. To name oneself is one of the most powerful acts any person can do: Should we call ourselves *Latinas* or *Hispanic Women?* And should those of us who struggle for our liberation call ourselves *Hispanic feminists* or *feminist Latinas* or something else? Should we call our theology *feminist Hispanic theology* or *Hispanic Women's liberation theology* (as we did in our earlier work) or something else? Because a name is not just a word by which one is identified but also provides the conceptual framework, the point of reference, the mental constructs that are used in thinking, understanding, and relating to a person, an idea, a movement, we need to address this issue.

In addressing whether we should use *Latinas* or *Hispanic Women* to identify ourselves, the first thing to note is that among ourselves we hardly ever use either of them.[3] Most of us use the national adjective that refers to the countries where we were born or from where our ancestors came:

---

2. I was delighted to find one other person who insists that she is concerned with ethics in order to enable moral agency. See Sarah Lucia Hoagland, *Lesbian Ethics* (Palo Alto, CA: Institute of Lesbian Studies, 1989), 1–23.

3. Some now are proposing that we use "Hispanic American." See Fernando Segovia, "Introduction," *Listening* 27, no. 1 (Winter 1992), 3–6.

Cuban, Puerto Rican, Colombian. The only exception to this, in general, are Mexican-Americans, who refer to themselves in a way that indicates both their ethnic-national roots and the fact that they are citizens by birth of the U.S.A.[4] I believe that unless we are clearly grounded in our own country of origin or that of our ancestry, we will not be able to link arms with those who come from other Latin American and Caribbean countries, and we will not be able to survive in the U.S.A.

Perhaps the difficulty in agreeing on a given word to name the different groups in the U.S.A. has to do not only with how disparate we are but also with our suspicion that by putting us all under one "name" the dominant culture is trying more easily to control and assimilate us. There is also the fact that we cannot be defined racially since all races are part of our peoples. We have no monolithic characteristic except, perhaps, the Spanish language; but we cannot identify ourselves as Spaniards since that is the national adjective used by those born in Spain.

In this book we will take turns and use *Hispanic Women* in chapters 1, 3, 5, 7 and *Latinas* in chapters 2, 4, 6. In other sections of the book we will alternate the two terms. I do this not to avoid choosing but because I think that deciding on one term is premature. I believe that only as our communities gain power will we see the need to decide on one of these terms. The time for this is not yet at hand but might well be upon us sooner than the dominant groups of this society believe.

When it comes to those of us Latinas who feel the need for a name that would indicate the struggle against sexism that is part of our daily bread, a name that would help us identify one another in the trenches as we struggle for our survival within Hispanic communities and U.S.A. at large, what should we call ourselves? Some of us have called ourselves *feministas hispanas,* Hispanic feminists, though it has been an appellation riddled with difficulties because it has meant giving long explanations of what such a phrase does not mean.[5]

Feministas hispanas have been consistently marginalized within the Anglo feminist community because of our critique of its ethnic/racial prejudice and its lack of class analysis. Though Anglo feminists have indeed worked to correct these serious shortcomings in their discourse, in my experience

4. Of course it is important to point out that a significant number of Mexican-Americans refer to themselves as "chicanas," many from New Mexico call themselves "Spanish-Americans" and some simply refer to themselves as "*mejicanas.*" To understand the differences implied in each of these terms see Earl Shorris, *Latinos—A Biography of the People* (New York: W.W. Norton & Company, 1992), chap. 7.

5. Ada María Isasi–Díaz, "Toward an Understanding of *Feminismo Hispano* in the U.S.A.," in *Women's Consciousness, Women's Conscience,* ed. Barbara H. Andolsen, Christine E. Gudorf, and Mary D. Pellauer (New York: Winston, 1985), 51–61.

their praxis continues to be flawed in this regard.[6] The phrase *feministas hispanas* has also been rejected by many in the Hispanic community because they consider feminism a concern of Anglo women. Yet Latinas widely agree with an analysis of sexism as an evil within our communities, an evil made into a touchable reality through the different ways in which Hispanic Women are repressed and exploited. In spite of our understanding of sexism and its role in our oppression, however, Latinas have not had a way to name ourselves until recently when some of us came up with the word *mujerista*.[7]

A *mujerista* is a Hispanic Woman who struggles to liberate herself not as an individual but as a member of a Hispanic community. She is one who builds bridges among Hispanics instead of falling into sectarianism and using divisive tactics. A *mujerista* understands that her task is to gather the hopes and expectations of the people about justice and peace and to work, not for equality within oppressive structures, but for liberation. A *mujerista* is called to gestate new women and new men — Hispanics who are willing to work for the common good, knowing that such work requires us to denounce all destructive sense of self-abnegation. A *mujerista* is a Latina who makes a preferential option for herself and her Hispanic sisters, understanding that our struggle for liberation has to take into consideration how racism/ethnic prejudice, economic oppression, and sexism work together and reinforce each other.

Mujerista Theology and Traditional Classifications in Theology

Mujerista theology has always insisted on the intrinsic unity between what has traditionally been referred to as systematic/dogmatic theology and moral theology/ethics. The exposition of *mujerista* theology as a liberative on praxis in chapter 5 of this book will clarify why *mujerista* theology sees ethics and systematic theology as going together. As we studied the history of "conscience" we came to understand why Catholic moral theology degenerated into a "science of guilt and sin" in the sixteenth, seventeenth, and eighteenth centuries and remained almost exclusively preoccupied with the training of priests as judges until the Vatican II Council in the 1960s: moral theology was "cut off from its speculative roots as well as from dogmatic and spiritual theology."[8]

---

6. Ada María Isasi-Díaz, "A Hispanic Garden in a Foreign Land," in *Inheriting Our Mothers' Gardens*, ed. Letty Russell, Kwok Pui Lan, Ada María Isasi-Díaz, and Katie Cannon (Philadelphia: Westminster Press, 1988), 91–106.

7. Ada María Isasi-Díaz and others, "Roundtable: Who We Are and What We Are About," *Journal of Feminist Studies in Religion* 8, no. 1 (Spring 1992): 105–25.

8. Charles E. Curran, *Directions in Fundamental Moral Theology* (Notre Dame: Univ. of Notre Dame Press, 1985), 221–22.

Another reason why we do not separate moral theology/ethics from systematic/dogmatic theology derives from the fact that the source of *mujerista* theology is the lived-experience of Hispanic Women, and one of its central preoccupations is the enablement of our moral agency. This means that we do not strictly follow standard procedures of ethics but are developing our own. Finally, the common understanding that, in general, moral claims should not be deduced from religious ones or that ethics should not be dependent on theology does not apply here for this reason. In spite of the fact that we live in a secularized society here in the U.S.A., Latinas' culture is not a secularized one. As will be explained later in this work, religion is an integral part of who we are and, therefore, what we do is intimately tied to what we believe.

Another traditional distinction that *mujerista* theology does not embrace is the one between moral theology and ethics. In traditional Roman Catholic theology, moral theology seems to parallel what in Protestant ethics is called *theological ethics.* These terms are used, usually but not exclusively, when referring to the accumulated body of moral teaching or knowledge based on doctrinal teachings, in the case of the Catholic church, and accepted theological teachings, for the Protestant churches. The term *ethics* seems to be used most often when referring to questions of actual behavior and decision making; often it means the application of moral theology or theological ethics to a specific issue, for example, euthanasia or the death penalty. But Christian ethics in most cases does not accept being set apart from moral theology or theological ethics because it often includes theological understandings. Since the distinction is not clear, probably because it is not tenable, in *mujerista* theology we use moral theology, religious ethics, and ethics interchangeably.

In *mujerista* theology ethics is always understood as social ethics. This follows from the centrality of community in our culture and from the fact that *mujeristas* denounce the split between the personal and the political as a false dichotomy used often to oppress Hispanic Women.

The Written English of a Cuban

This book bears the burden of being a work done in translation. I say this not to excuse my writings from the rigor of grammatical correctness but rather to explain the "sound," the "turn of phrases" I use, which, I am told, strikes some dissonance in the Anglo ear. My insistence on my writings' not "sounding" Anglo is because language not only expresses but is an intrinsic element of human understanding. I wish to try to communicate how the world is seen and understood from a Hispanic perspective. Because I am Cuban, my language is full of what others consider exaggerations, hyperboles, repetitions. What seems hyperbolic to the English reader is to me nothing but a needed emphasis; what seems repetitious is a way of connecting ideas and constantly building on what I consider central in the argument. Repetition also has to do with my concern that I may not be understood because English is not my native language and because what I say refers to a world not known by the majority of my readers.

My insistence on sounding in English like myself, and not like someone for whom English is her first language, is a way of preserving my identity, of insisting that to contribute to the theological enterprise Latinas do not need to forget our culture or our language. It is also necessary so that my primary community of accountability can resonate with what I write. It is of utmost importance for me that Latinas who read my work be comfortable with it, find themselves in it.

◧ INTRODUCCIÓN

La publicación en 1988 del libro *Hispanic Women: Prophetic Voice in the Church* hizo público una de las vetas del quehacer teológico de las latinas en los EE.UU. Ese libro, del cual somos autoras Yolanda Tarango y yo, fue el primer escrito sobre la teología mujerista. Nosotras considerábamos, y todavía lo creemos, que en general a la teología le faltaba un elemento vital el cual se ha convertido en eje principal de nuestro quehacer teológico: ser foro para las voces de las mujeres hispanas. Por muchos años las bases religiosas y prácticas de la fe de la vida cotidiana de las mujeres latinas han enriquecido nuestras vidas. Creemos que esas prácticas y bases son parte de la continua revelación de Dios, quién está presente en nuestras comunidades de fe dándonos fuerzas para la lucha por la liberación. Es por eso que estamos convencidas de que las voces de las mujeres hispanas deben de ser tomadas en consideración en toda labor teológica y en toda enseñanza y práctica eclesiástica.

Este libro desarrolla los conceptos religiosos y métodos teológicos presentados en el primero. Este libro, al igual que el otro, es un foro para las voces de las mujeres latinas porque sus experiencias cotidianas son fuente de la teología mujerista. Para continuar desarrollando esta teología fui de nuevo a hablar con cada una de las mujeres cuyas voces se escuchan a través de las páginas del primer libro. Al hablar con todas ellas me sentí más convencida que nunca de que como latinas tenemos una contribución importante que hacer a la sociedad de los EE.UU. en general y a la teología en particular.

Estoy convencida también de que la teología mujerista, por ser una praxis liberadora, tiene que tener como meta principal el desarrollo y fortalecimiento de las mujeres hispanas como agentes morales, tiene que ayudarnos a entender que tenemos que ser sujetos de nuestra propia historia, que tenemos que ser nosotras quienes determinemos lo que significan nuestras vidas, cómo es que creamos significado a través de la manera en que vivimos, cómo es que somos agentes morales a pesar de la opresión que sufrimos. Este libro examina las conexiones que hay entre nuestra manera de entender "conciencia", cómo ésta funciona en nuestro quehacer moral, y el papel que la misma juega en nuestra praxis liberadora. Este análisis requiere que continuemos elaborando una teología mujerista: ¿cómo funciona como praxis liberadora? ¿qué papel juega en la lucha por sobrevivir de las latinas? ¿cuáles son sus propuestas principales?

Nuestro nombre

Nombrarse a sí mismo es uno de los actos más poderosos que hay. ¿Nos llamamos latinas o hispanas? Y quienes luchamos por la liberación, ¿nos

llamamos feministas latinas o feministas hispanas, o usamos otro nombre?
¿Llamamos a nuestra teología "feminista hispana" o la llamamos como
hicimos en el primer libro, teología de la liberación de las mujeres hispanas?
Porque un nombre es más que una identificación; un nombre provee el
marco conceptual, el punto de referencia, las estructuras mentales que se
usan para pensar, entender y relacionarnos con personas, ideas,
movimientos—es por eso que tenemos que preocuparnos de qué nombre
ponerle a nuestro quehacer teológico.

En cuanto a los términos "latinas" e "hispanas" hay que hacer notar que
entre nosotras casi nunca usamos ni el uno ni el otro. Mayormente usamos
el adjetivo que se refiere al país de donde procedemos o de donde vinieron
nuestras abuelitas. La única excepción son las méxico–americanas las cuales
usan este apelativo para indicar tanto su origen étnico como el hecho de
que son por nacimiento ciudadanas de los EE.UU.

A lo mejor encontramos difícil el decidir qué nombre usar no sólo por
la variedad de nuestros países de origen sino también porque sospechamos
que el dejarnos poner un nombre por la cultura dominante es cooperor,
en cierta forma, con los esfuerzos que se hacen constantemente para asimilar-
nos y controlarnos. También está el hecho de que no se nos puede definir
racialmente ya que entre nosotras hay personas de todas las razas. Tenemos
una sóla característica que todos compartimos: todos usamos o sabemos
usar el español. Pero no nos podemos llamar "españolas" ya que ese es el
apelativo que usan los nacidos en España.

En este libro vamos a turnar el uso de estos términos. En los capítulos
2, 4 y 6 usaremos "latinas"; en los capítulos 1, 3, 5 y 7 usaremos "hispanas".
No hago esto para evitar el escoger sino porque pienso que el decidirnos
por uno de estos términos es prematuro. Yo creo que sólo cuando nuestras
comunidades tengan poder podremos decidir cómo llamarnos. Ese
momento no ha llegado pero está más cerca de lo que la clase dominante
cree.

Y, ¿qué nombre le damos a la lucha de las latinas que combina la lucha
en contra del sexismo, del prejuicio étnico, y del clasismo? El llamarnos
"feministas hispanas" no ha resultado ya que muchas en nuestras comunidades consideran que las feministas de extracción europea no han
tomado en cuenta a las hispanas y no nos queremos identificar con ellas.
Sin embargo, las mujeres hispanas sí comprenden y están de acuerdo con
que mucho de nuestra opresión se debe al sexismo y por eso es que un grupo
de nosotras hemos empezado a usar la palabra *mujerista*.

Una mujerista es una mujer latina que lucha para liberarse no sólo ella,
individualmente, sino lo hace como miembro de una comunidad hispana.
Una mujerista crea conexiones entre hispanos y denuncia el sectarianismo
y las tácticas divisivas. Una mujerista sabe que su tarea consiste en

alimentar las esperanzas y expectativas de justicia y paz en su pueblo y que tiene que trabajar no para obtener la igualdad con la clase dominante sino para destruir las estructuras de dominación de la clase dominante. Las mujeristas hacemos una opción preferencial por nosotras mismas y por nuestras hermanas latinas, sabiendo que nuestra lucha por la liberación tiene que comenzar con un análisis profundo de cómo el sexismo, el prejuicio étnico y el clasismo se combinan y refuerzan entre sí para oprimirnos.

La teología mujerista y las divisiones de la teología tradicional

La teología mujerista siempre ha insistido en que hay una unidad intrínsica entre lo que tradicionalmente se ha llamado teología sistemática o dogmática y la teología moral o la ética. Explicaremos más ampliamente lo que queremos decir con ésto después, pero aquí es importante precisar lo siguiente: Al estudiar la historia del concepto *conciencia* hemos logrado entender cómo fue que la teología moral católica se degeneró en los siglos XVI, XVII y XVIII hasta llegar a convertirse meramente en una "ciencia de la culpabilidad y del pecado," preocupándose casi exclusivamente por darles una educación judicial a los sacerdotes. Hasta el Concilio Vaticano Segundo en este siglo la teología moral católica estuvo separada tanto de sus raíces especulativas como de la teologías dogmática y espiritual y fue ésta una de las causas principales de su degeneración. La teología mujerista no quiere caer en este mismo error y es por eso que en nuestro quehacer teológico entrelazamos la teología moral y la dogmática.

Otra razón por la cual no separamos la ética de la teología sistemática es porque la fuente de la teología mujerista es la experiencia cotidiana de las latinas y su tarea principal hasta el presente es el desarrollo de las mujeres hispanas como agentes morales. Ésto quiere decir que no seguimos los procedimientos tradicionales de la teología sino que estamos desarrollando nuestros propios métodos. Finalmente, en esta sociedad generalmente se piensa que las exigencias morales no deben depender de la religión ni que la ética debe depender de la teología. Ésto no es así en el mundo latino. A pesar de que vivimos en un país secularizado, la cultura hispana no es una cultura secular. Como explicaremos más adelante, la religión es parte integral de quienes somos y por lo tanto, lo que hacemos va mano a mano con nuestras creencias religiosas .

Otra distinción que la teología mujerista no acepta es la que usualmente se hace entre teología moral y ética. Nadie parece poder explicar claramente esta distinción, probablemente porque es imposible hacerla. En la teología mujerista nosotras usamos teología moral y ética en forma intercambiable.

Por último, para nosotras toda ética es ética social debido a la importancia que tiene la comunidad en nuestra cultura. Es por ésto que las mujeristas denunciamos la falsa dicotomía entre lo personal y lo político, dicotomía que a menudo se usa para manternernos orpimidas.

El inglés de esta cubana

Este libro en realidad es una traducción aunque fue escrito en inglés. Aunque insisto en que mi inglés sea correcto, no quiero "sonar" angla. Quiero que mi inglés me ayude a comunicar cómo se ve y entiende el mundo desde la perspectiva hispana. El idioma de los cubanos, no importa cual estemos hablando, está lleno de hipérboles y repeticiones que muchos consideran exageraciones. Lo que le parece hiperbólico a los no–hispano–parlantes para mí es un énfasis necesario; lo que parece repetición para quienes no son latinos para mí es una manera de entrelazar ideas y de incluir en todo momento en mis argumentos elementos que considero importantísimos.

Mi insistencia en "sonar" en el inglés escrito como yo misma y no como alguien para quien el inglés es su lengua materna es una manera de preservar mi identidad, de insistir que para contribuir a la tarea teológica las hispanas no tenemos que olvidar nuestra cultura, nuestro idioma. Es de suma importancia para mí que mi comunidad, las mujeres latinas, se sientan al leer este libro en inglés o en español, que ésto es parte de su mundo, parte de su lucha por la liberación.

CHAPTER 1

Hispanic Ethnicity and Social Locality in *Mujerista* Theology

THE COMMON CONCEPTION of ethnicity is that of a category or classification that includes among other traits race, language, country of origin of oneself or one's ancestors, and cultural practices once the person leaves the homeland. But I believe that ethnicity is a social construct and that the construction and maintenance of ethnicity is a vital process of Hispanic Women's struggle to survive. The ethnic identification of any given person is not necessarily a constant but a dynamic self-understanding and self-identification that can vary over time.[1] As a social construct, ethnicity for Hispanic Women is not a collection of "natural" traits such as language, race, country of origin, or gender. It may or may not include some or all of these "natural" traits, but it also includes such other elements as social, economic, and political reasons for being in the U.S.A., the way the dominant culture deals with us, our daily struggle to survive, and our vision of our future.[2]

In our articulation of *mujerista* theology we are using the term *social construct* in reference to ethnicity not as a conceptual framework but as an organizational tool, as a way of gathering the social forces that go into forming Hispanic Women in the U.S.A. We identify our ethnicity as a social construct *a posteriori,* that is, as a way of describing, of narrating who we are and how we live our daily lives. Ethnicity for *mujerista*

---

1. For amplification of this understanding of ethnicity see Mary C. Waters, *Ethnic Options— Choosing Identities in America* (Los Angeles: University of California Press, 1990). Also see Candace Nelson and Marta Tienda, "The Structuring of Hispanic Ethnicity: Historical and Contemporary Perspectives," in *Ethnicity and Race in the U.S.A. – Toward the Twenty–First Century,* ed. Richard D. Alba (London: Henley Routledge & Kegan Paul, 1985).

2. See Fernando Segovia, "Two Places and No Place on Which to Stand: Mixture and Otherness in Hispanic American Theology," *Listening* 27, no. 1 (Winter 1992): 27–33. Segovia uses the term "Hispanic American" precisely to include both ethnic as well as sociopolitical traits of our social location. I prefer including both traits under the single terms Hispanic or Latina/o.

theologians starts with given-ness, particularity, reality, the specificity of our lives. It is a tool used to speak about the multiple particularities that take into account the personal within the context of community, and of talking about our shared reality as Hispanic Women by bringing together the specific and the particular.

This is the understanding of ethnicity that *mujerista* theology uses. Because the lived-experience of Hispanic Women is the source of *mujerista* theology, our theological articulation must start with an analysis of our ethnicity, of who we are and how we understand ourselves. This first chapter, therefore, presents an exploration of what we consider are three of the main elements of Hispanic Women's ethnicity: *mestizaje*, survival, and our socio-economic reality. In chapter 2 we will deal with three other elements that are likewise intrinsic elements of our ethnic identity.

Identifying Hispanic Women

Time and again *mujerista* theology talks about the lived-experience of Hispanic Women. Who are these Hispanic Women? To whom does this theology refer and to whom is it important?

Officially, Hispanics are those who describe themselves as "Mexican American, Chicano, Mexican, Mexicano, Puerto Rican, Cuban, Central or South American, or other Spanish origin."[3] In this book, however, we will use Hispanic to refer only to the three most populous of these groups: Mexican-Americans, Puerto Ricans, and Cubans.

"Hispanics" in this work includes the vast numbers of Mexican-Americans whose home for many generations has been the southwestern part of this country. It is important to remember that this area was not always part of the U.S.A. Because of the Treaty of Guadalupe-Hidalgo in 1846, the border crossed the people who lived there, and not the other way around. Mexican-Americans, for the purpose of this work, also include Chicanos— that is, Mexican-Americans who are proud of their cultural heritage and the unique way they have adapted to the American society. Chicanos emphasize in their self-understanding the concept of *la raza*,[4] that is, a rejection of materialistic standards of individualistic self-achievement and an adoption of collective goals.[5] Under the rubric "Mexican-American" I am also including those born in Mexico, now living and working in the U.S.A. but still maintaining contact with and frequently visiting their native land.

---

3. Joan Moore and Harry Pachón, *Hispanics in the United States* (New Jersey: Prentice-Hall, 1985), 1.

4. More on this concept later in this chapter.

5. Moore and Pachón, 182. See also, Alma M. García, "The Development of Chicana Feminist Discourse, 1970–1980" *Gender and Society* 3, no. 2 (June 1989): 217–38.

"Hispanics" here also includes the more than two million Puerto Ricans living on the mainland of the U.S.A. Their country of origin was acquired by the U.S.A. from Spain in 1898 without Puerto Ricans having much to say about it. The Jones Act in 1917 gave Puerto Ricans U.S. citizenship and made them eligible for military draft. The new Puerto Rican constitution, drafted in 1947, which defines Puerto Rico as a free, associated state, has not changed this situation. Puerto Ricans "are still USA citizens, subject to military draft, but they do not pay income taxes and do not fully participate in federal government social service programs."[6] This means that Puerto Ricans can travel without any restrictions between the mainland and their island. The back and forth flow is enormous:

> reaching in one recent year more than 2 million people. . . . The flow of returning people is profoundly important. It means, first, that the Puerto Ricans offer the larger society not only a new and burgeoning minority but also a close relationship to a small and overcrowded Caribbean island with serious economic problems. Second, the nearby island gives Puerto Ricans themselves a sense of intactness, of closeness to an ancient home and reference group.[7]

The third group included in the term "Hispanics" in this work are the Cubans. There are about one million Cubans in the U.S.A., 60 percent of them living in the Miami area, about 20 percent in the New York-New Jersey area, and the rest mainly in California, Illinois, and Texas. Though most of these Cubans have been living in the U.S.A. for more than fifteen years and are not allowed by the Cuban government to return to their country, and although a high percentage of them have become U.S. citizens, this community as a whole continues to maintain close emotional ties with the island.[8] It is not surprising, therefore, that Cubans who have been relocated to other areas of the U.S.A. often return to Miami, the area which has become the center of the Cuban community in the U.S.A. not only because of the high percentage of Cubans living there but also because of its geographical proximity to Cuba. The dense concentration of Cubans in this area and the fact that they have been able to establish a high percentage of the same businesses and services which they owned and operated in Cuba, makes it possible for Cubans in Miami to move almost exclusively within Cuban circles without any need to speak English.[9] In many ways

6. Moore and Pachón, 31.

7. Ibid.

8. Though the term Cuban-American is beginning to be used mainly in political circles, it is not a term used by the community in most instances. Even Cubans born in the U.S.A. usually explain that they were born here of Cuban parents, and do not call themselves Cuban-Americans.

9. Close to one third of all businesses in Miami and 40 percent of the industry are Cuban owned. Twenty percent of the banks are controlled by Cubans: sixteen out of sixty-two bank presidents and two hundred fifty vice-presidents are Cubans. In the Miami area 75 percent

it is correct to say that the Miami-Dade County area has adapted itself to the Cubans, while they have not had to acculturate themselves to the U.S.A. [10]

Thus in this work "Hispanics" refers to people who call themselves Mexican-Americans or Chicanas, Puerto Ricans, and Cubans, and who are aware and critically conscious of their ethnicity and its role in their lives in this country. What about the rest of the Hispanic Women in this country? I do not wish to be exclusionary, but obviously I have had to set parameters to my research and my work. Though I do not attempt to subsume the rest of Hispanic Women under the three specific groups I deal with in this book, I do believe that much of what I say based on the experiences and understandings of Mexican-Americans or Chicanas, Puerto Ricans, and Cubans is also true about Hispanics from other countries in Latin America and the Caribbean.

When the term *Hispanic Women* is used, it is not to be understood as an attempt to mask differences, some of them important, among us. It is not my intention to represent Hispanic Women at large for that would require a massification that *mujerista* theology specifically rejects. Hispanic Women are too many and too different for any one person or any one group to speak for them. Hispanic Women are not a perfectly homogeneous group with no particularities or differences. For us, diversity is not a matter of different expressions of the same truth, but rather points to differences that touch the very core of who we are and what we believe. Our diversity is the source of our richness as a people and we, therefore, welcome it and celebrate it. Our diversity is at the core of our *mestizaje.*

Mestizaje—Embracing and Celebrating Diversity

In this book Hispanics or Hispanic Women also refers to the coming together here in the United States of these three groups with their cultural variants. This mingling necessarily brings about cultural modifications and innovations that, over a period of time, will no doubt become distinctive enough to be considered a new culture. The coming together of these three groups and other groups from Latin America and the Spanish speaking Caribbean adds a new dimension to the concept of *mestizaje,* to *la raza.* [11]

---

of the construction workforce is Cuban. Other Cuban strongholds are in the areas of textiles, food, cigars and trade with Latin America. See Nelson and Tienda, 59.

10. Moore and Pachón, 46.

11. Virgilio Elizondo makes extensive use of these two terms. See Virgilio Elizondo, *Galilean Journey—The Mexican American Promise* (Maryknoll, NY: Orbis Books, 1983), 7–18. For an overall exposition of the importance of *mestizaje* in the development of Hispanic theologies, see John P. Rossing, *"Mestizaje* and Marginality: A Hispanic American Theology," *Theology Today* XLV, no. 3 (October 1988): 293–304.

This *mestizaje*, this sense that we are actively contributing to the creation of a new race, *la raza cósmica*, the cosmic race, was originally formulated as a concept by the Mexican philosopher José Vasconcelos in the 1940s. For us Hispanic Women, the creation of a new race is a very real part of our daily lives. *Mestizaje* is grounded in the fact that we live in-between, at the intersection of our countries of origin and the U.S.A. In the U.S.A. we are mostly marginalized people relegated to the outskirts of society, not really fully belonging. Regarding our countries of origin we know that even if or when we do return, it is never really possible to go back. [12] Even for Puerto Rican Women, as well as for a certain segment of Mexican-American Women, many of whom live *con un pie en cada lado* (with a foot in each place)—the island and the mainland, or Mexico and the U.S.A.—their travels are never a going-back. "In history there is no returning, because all of history is transformation and novelty." [13]

And we also carry with us the mindset and reality of the *mestizaje* that exists in our countries of origin. It is a fusion of the different lineages and races out of which most of us in Latin America and the Spanish speaking Caribbean come. Nothing says it better than a popular saying, *un dicho*, from Venezuela: *Aquí todos somos café con leche; unos más café, otros más leche,* here we all are coffee and milk; some more coffee, others more milk.

It is important for non-Hispanics to understand that for us *mestizaje* is a reality which we have come to accept and of which many of us are proud. *Mestizaje* for us does not carry the negative connotations associated with miscegenation. It was and is a natural result of the coming together of different races. It is not the attempt of one race to make the other disappear—which seems to be the sense given to miscegenation by both African Americans and whites in this country. *Mujerista* theologians affirm *mestizaje* as the coming together of different races and cultures in a creative way that necessarily precludes the subordination of one to another; we affirm it as the going forward of humankind. [14] *Mestizaje* precludes the exclusion of some groups—Hispanics here in the U.S.A., for example—by other groups that control society. *Mestizaje* for us Hispanics is not only a matter of a mingling of races. As we shall see below, this understanding certainly

12. The poem by Lourdes Casals I have used as a preamble for this book expresses this idea which for those of us who live it is a very strong sentiment, a reality.

13. José Vasconcelos, *La Raza Cósmica,* 11th ed., Colección Austral (México: Espasa-Calpé Mexicana, 1948), 25.

14. I believe a positive understanding of *mestizaje,* though somewhat different from ours, will emerge out of the structures of the "commonwealth" of nations, politically and/or economically, that an increasing number of nations in different continents are adopting. However, at present the terrible ethnic wars in what was the U.S.S.R., in Eastern Europe, and in different parts of Africa and Asia, as well as the racism/ethnic prejudice of so-called hate groups in the U.S.A. and other parts of the world, certainly indicate that much needs to be overcome before a healthy sense of *mestizaje* can emerge the world over.

impacts and is defined by our religious beliefs and practices, our use of Spanish in an English speaking world, and our *proyecto histórico*, our historic project. But before exploring these elements of our ethnicity, it is necessary to understand our socio-economic reality.

Survival – Hispanic Women's Daily Bread

For Hispanic Women the questions of ultimate meaning that form the core of *mujerista* theology are basically questions of survival, which here means much more than barely living. Survival has to do with the struggle *to be* fully. To survive, one has to have "the power to decide about one's history and one's vocation or historical mission." [15]

Survival for Hispanic Women means a constant struggle against oppression. Our oppression results in an "anthropological poverty," which both includes and goes beyond material poverty. This anthropological poverty threatens to despoil us of our very being. "Being fully" or "not being" is what survival is all about. As Hispanic Women we are concerned with whatever can threaten or save us – our very being. For Hispanic Women, "being" designates existence in time and space; it means physical survival, and it means cultural survival, which depends to a large extent on self-determination and self-identity. [16] Survival starts with sustaining physical life, but it does not end there; being or not being also includes the social dimension of life. Hispanic Women need bread, but we also need to celebrate. Today we need a roof over our heads, but we also need to have possibilities for a better future for ourselves and our children – a future with some cultural continuity to our past and our present.

But for us survival is not something one assures just for oneself. Personal survival for Hispanic Women is integrally linked with the survival of the community and, in a special way, with the survival of the children of the community. The hopes, dreams, visions, and hard work of Hispanic Women are often for the sake of the children. But they are also for our own sake. We need to make our humanity as women and as Hispanics count in this society; we need to participate actively in defining the society in which we live, which is another way of saying that we need to struggle against the classism, ethnic prejudice, and sexism that threaten our very existence.

Our struggle for survival starts with an in-depth analysis of the reality of oppression that we suffer. This oppression has different modes that relate

15. Juan Carlos Scannone, "Teología cultural popular y discernimiento," in *Cultura popular y filosofía de la liberación* (Buenos Aires: Fernando García Cambeiro, 1975), 253–54.

16. The term "anthropological poverty" is found in "Doing Theology in a Divided World: Final Statement of the Sixth EATWOT Conference," in *Doing Theology in a Divided World*, ed. Virginia Fabella and Sergio Torres (Maryknoll, NY: Orbis Books, 1985), 185. Paul Tillich discussed "being" and "not being" in *Systematic Theology* (Chicago: Univ. of Chicago Press, 1951), 1, 44.

to one another: (1) "domination" due to racist/ethnic and sexist prejudices; (2) "subjugation," which has to do with the creation of oppressed subjects according to these prejudices; (3 & 4) "exploitation" and "repression" that are the result of societal institutions, economical mechanisms, and the state apparatuses.[17] In other words, our oppression has to do with the fact that we are women, that we are Hispanics, and that the majority of us are at the bottom of the economic ladder in the U.S.A. We understand that our gender, our ethnicity, and our economic status have been made into social categories that play a very important role in the domination, subjugation, exploitation, and repression that we suffer.[18]

An integrated analysis of the oppression we suffer is essential for two reasons. First, it is often difficult to determine whether we are being oppressed because of our gender, our ethnicity, or our economic status. For example, the way Hispanic Women who work as maids are treated is at the same time a matter of class, race/ethnic, and gender oppression. Second, we do not experience our oppression differently depending upon which of the modes of oppression is at work; neither do we experience the different modes independently of one another.[19] We do not suffer two or three different kinds of oppression, each stemming from different prejudices, each one at different moments or circumstances. Rather, the different modes of oppression are compounded into one multilayered burden which touches every aspect of our lives in an ongoing way.[20] None of these modes of oppression, therefore, comes before the other or is more intrinsic to our subordination. None of the prejudices at work in our oppression is paradigmatic, but together they support the structure of oppression at work in our lives. The links among them will be discovered only as we analyze each of them in depth.

The classification of people according to race/ethnicity is based on physical differences—skin color and other physical features—as well as on distinct languages, cultures, and social institutions. Racist thinking developed in Europe in the seventeenth and eighteenth centuries and became part of the Christian worldview.[21] During the nineteenth century racial/ethnic

17. Cornel West, "Marxist Theory and the Specificity of Afro-American Oppression," in *Marxism and the Interpretation of Culture,* ed. Carry Nelson and Lawrence Grossberg (Chicago: Univ. of Chicago Press, 1988), see particularly note 15.

18. Teresa L. Amott and Julie A. Matthaei, *Race, Gender & Work* (Boston: South End, 1991), 11.

19. Ibid, 13.

20. Rosemary Radford Ruether, "A Feminist Perspective," in *Doing Theology in a Divided World,* ed. Fabella and Torres, 70; see also Deborah K. King, "Multiple Jeopardy, Multiple Consciousness: The Context of a Black Feminist Ideology," in *Feminist Theory in Practice and Process,* ed. Micheline R. Malson, Jean F. O'Barr, Sarah Westphal-Wihl, and Mary Wyer (Chicago: Univ. of Chicago Press, 1989), 75–105.

21. Much of this thinking was based on the concept that Richard Lovejoy called "the Great Chain of Being." This was a plan and structure of the world in which there existed an infinite number of links arranged in "hierarchical order from the meagerest kind of existents, which

differences and inequalities were attributed directly to biology: human beings were divided into biologically distinct and unequal races with whites
at the top of the racial hierarchy "with the right and duty to dominate the
others."[22] These racist theories were and are used to justify social,
economic, and political practices which have made the nonwhite races *de
facto* unequal and have resulted in their subordination.

As Hispanics, it is very obvious to us that racial or ethnic domination
is intrinsically linked to economic domination. In our history, our
racial/ethnic differences have been used to displace us from land, to use us
as cheap labor, to exploit our countries for their prime resources, to insist
on the need for us to forgo our culture and values. It is important for us
to understand that though a small group of Hispanics are allowed social
mobility and rise above whites, all whites have some of us below them.
And the oppression we suffer as Hispanic Women has to do not only with
racial/ethnic and economic domination but also with sexism.

When we turn to the analysis of gender oppression, we quickly realize
that it cannot be understood apart from economic and racial/ethnic considerations. Gender differences across racial/ethnic and economic lines as
well as within Hispanic communities or among people of similar economic
status

> are based on, but are not the same thing as, biological differences between
> the sexes. Gender is rooted in societies' beliefs that the sexes are naturally
> distinct and opposed social beings. These beliefs are turned into self-fulfilling
> prophecies through sex-role socialization. . . . [23]

The kind of work assigned to men, different from that assigned to women,
is an intrinsic element of the social construct called gender and the differences
it creates. The differences in kinds of work have contributed greatly to considering the genders as complementary to each other—a complementarity
that almost always leads to inequality. Thus, for example, women have been
assigned work in the private or domestic sphere while men are assigned
work in the public sphere. But women's work in the domestic sphere is
unpaid and is considered as having little value. Men in the public world
are the ones who have the power, control the wealth, and make decisions
that affect the whole world. The work of women in the private, domestic

---

barely escape non-existence, through 'every possible' grade . . . to the highest possible kind
of creature, between which and the Absolute Being the disparity was assumed to be infinite."
Of course European whites were placed at the top of this hierarchy and the greater the physical
difference from them, the lower was the person in this chain of being. Richard Lovejoy, *The
Great Chain of Being* (Cambridge: Harvard Univ. Press, 1936), 59.

22. Amott and Matthaei, 17.

23. Ibid.

sphere, is seen as complementary, as necessary but determined by what the work and the workmen in the public sphere need. When women do venture into the public sphere, their work there is neither considered worth the same pay as men's work, nor does it relieve women of responsibilities in the domestic sphere. The situation is similar among Hispanic Women but not identical to what happens to Anglo women.

An analysis of gender oppression has to take into consideration the fact that sex-role socialization differs according to historical time and culture. This results in different conceptions of what is appropriate gender behavior and, therefore, in different experiences of gender oppression. This is precisely the reason why Hispanic Women resist the conception of sexism as defined by Anglo women. Of course there are similarities, but there are also differences created by different understandings of gender behavior and by the role played by racist/ethnic prejudice.

For example, forced sterilization of Hispanic Women in this country has repeatedly threatened our families and communities. [24] Maintaining our families is an intrinsic part of our struggle. Therefore, we are not willing to accept fully the Anglo feminist understanding of the family as the center of women's oppression.

An important example of the way the dominant group—men and women—mix ethnic prejudice and sexism is seen in the use of the word *machismo* by English speaking persons nowadays despite the fact that there is a perfectly comparable term, "male chauvinism," in the English language. Use of *machismo* implies that Hispanic men are more sexist than Anglo men. Using *machismo* absolves somewhat the sexism of Anglo men and sets Anglo men and Anglo culture above Hispanic men and Hispanic culture. Hispanic Women do not deny the sexism of our culture or of most Hispanic men. But it is not greater than the sexism of the U.S.A. society in general and of Anglo men in particular.

In the struggle against ethnic and racist prejudice it has to be recognized that the survival of Hispanic Women is directly related to the fate of Hispanic culture. Our culture is a social reality; it involves Hispanic Women's patterns of thoughts, feelings, and behaviors learned from the human group in which we have grown. Religious understandings and practices that have become part of the patterns of relationships and social structures that we use as a group to organize ourselves are key to what we learn. [25] Hispanic

24. See Rudolfo Acuña, *Occupied America: A History of Chicanos* (New York: Harper and Row, 1988), 395; María González, Victoria L. Barrera, Peter Guarnaccia, and Stephen L. Schensul, " 'La Operación': An Analysis of Sterilization in a Puerto Rican Community in Connecticut," in *Work, Family, and Health: Latina Women in Transition,* ed. Ruth E. Zambrana (Bronx, NY: Hispanic Research Center, Fordham Univ., 1982), 50.

25. See Paulo Agirrebaltzategi, *Configuración eclesial de las culturas* (Bilbao, España: Univ. de Deusto, 1976), 61–62.

culture has to do with our "symbolic system of meanings, values and norms,"[26] and Christianity plays an essential role in determining and sustaining this system. *Mujerista* theology, therefore, if it is indeed an articulation that has as its source the daily life of Hispanic Women, has to deal with Hispanic culture. But the relationship of *mujerista* theology to culture has another important aspect, that is to critique Hispanic Women's culture. Using our struggle for survival as its critical lens, *mujerista* theology evaluates culture from within. For example, *mujerista* theology embraces the Chicanas' critique of Hispanic culture and refuses to accept *machismo* simply because it is a cultural trait. Likewise, *mujerista* theology does not accept completely the operative understanding of family in the Hispanic culture for it limits us by defining us first and foremost as mothers, and because it refuses to accept families headed by lesbian or gay couples.[27]

How Hispanic Women's future will relate to Hispanic culture depends on whether or not the Hispanic culture here in the U.S.A. develops organically. If an organic development can take place, the distinguishing Hispanic cultural values and traits will not disappear but will be allowed to inform and guide the changes that take place as we come in contact with a different reality from the one we have known. This means that Hispanic values and traits would also play a role in society at large, influencing what is normative for all. But if, in order to survive, we have to deny our cultural roots, to become "Americanized," as the people in our communities say, then the development of the culture will be far from organic, and distortions—often directly related to the negative stereotypes imposed on us—will become increasingly common among Hispanics.

If values and traits are to survive, they have to be enfleshed, to be lived daily by Hispanics. Thus, if we do not know our language or cannot use it, if we are not able to interact with other Hispanics because of the isolation and individualism that often creeps into our way of life in the U.S.A., if we have to deny our own people instead of identifying with them and being loyal to them, if we are encouraged to consider ourselves as just another group of Americans instead of knowing and valuing the specificity of Hispanics, if the demands of society are such that we are not able to stay in generational proximity to our parents and extended family—if in order to survive and move ahead we have to give up all of this, then the Hispanic culture in the U.S.A. will be dead. Only the quaint and exotic aspects of our culture will survive, not having much meaning or value, mainly as a form of entertainment for the dominant culture. Already we are witnessing

26. Ibid., 364. See also Juan Luis Segundo, *The Liberation of Theology* (Maryknoll: Orbis Books, 1982), 185–86.
27. For a concise but important discussion of Hispanic Women's critique of our culture see García, "The Development of Chicana Feminist Discourse."

instrumentalization and commercialization of our culture. Hispanic music, food, typical dresses—that is what is known and accepted by the dominant culture. But what affirmation exists for our deep sense of community, our valuing of the elderly and the children, the religiosity of our culture, the importance of honor as an expression of the worth and value of every single person for us? Will such traits and values survive? Without them, will the Hispanic people in general, and Hispanic Women in particular, survive as Hispanics? Can we consider ourselves to have survived if we lose our culture?

The analysis of economic oppression starts with understanding "the important ways in which economic institutions and practices structure our lives, as well as the important role which the economy plays in creating and sustaining racial-ethnic, gender, and class conflicts."[28] Economic status and class are greatly impacted by gender and racist/ethnic exploitation. For example, access to ownership of the means of production and, concomitantly, to wealth, greatly depends in this country on being male and white. In the early history of the U.S.A. white males established their economic dominance, rationalizing their behavior by using the racist and sexist ideas prevalent in Europe at the time. Once they had done this, they "were able to perpetuate and institutionalize this dominance in the emerging capitalist system, particularly through the monopolization of managerial and other high-level jobs."[29]

Today's capitalist system, however, is quite different from the one that existed in the early history of the U.S.A. The backbone of the economic system has been the working class: those who sell their labor to produce goods that are sold for a profit which belongs to the owners of the wealth who control the means of production. It is to this working class that the majority of Hispanic Women belong. But the economic system has changed dramatically in the last few decades and now depends on highly mechanized and technically sophisticated industries, not on a large workforce. Given the fact that men are still considered by society as the ones who should work outside the home for a family wage, in a shrinking workforce, women and racial/ethnic minorities—and especially racial/ethnic women—are the last ones to be hired. There is no doubt that growing unemployment affects racial/ethnic women the most. This development in industry means that Hispanic Women, if they find work, will do so mainly in the service sector in which wages are significantly lower than in industry.

Furthermore, because of the diminishing need for industrial workers, Hispanic Women are part of a growing sector of society whose unemployment is not a passing situation, but a permanent one. Hispanic Women are part of a population surplus for which the economic system—and

28. Amott and Matthaei, 5.
29. Ibid., 24.

society—has no need, no use, and, therefore, society is not willing to invest money, time, or effort in satisfying our basic needs for food, health, housing, or education. The present system views us as a dangerous sector where prostitution, theft, drugs, and AIDS flourish. This leads to being excluded from, separated from, society at large. Indeed, many of us think that the neglect of society that is part of our daily lives is a strategy of the system to get rid of this population surplus which has no role to play in it.[30]

This multifaceted oppression frames Hispanic Women's everyday lives but does not define us. What is central to our self-understanding is not our suffering oppression but rather our struggle to overcome that oppression and to survive.[31] Our struggle is made all the more difficult by the dimness of our Hispanic communities' future. It is obvious that the steady immigration of very poor Hispanics into the U.S.A. will continue. This, coupled with the effects on the poor of cutbacks in federal programs during the Reagan-Bush era (1980–1992), is causing havoc in the Hispanic community. Let us take a closer look at some specifics of our economic oppression and how it intersects with sexism and racist/ethnic prejudice.

Socio-Economic Reality of Hispanic Women

A critical socio-economic analysis of the oppression of Hispanic Women is key to grounding *mujerista* theology in the life of Hispanic Women as it is actually lived. Without such analysis *mujerista* theology could not investigate the lived-experience of Hispanic Women effectively and hold it up for understanding and, when needed, critique. Ethics as an intrinsic part of *mujerista* theology must not be separated from life as it is actually lived by Hispanic Women or it will be irrelevant to our communities.[32] Also, dealing with our material condition and sociological reality will keep *mujerista* theologians from treating the experience of Hispanic Women abstractly, something we reject completely.[33] Thus, the socio-economic reality of Hispanic Women is more than a background one has to consider when doing theology, it is a key element of *mujerista* theology's method.[34]

---

30. Franz J. Hinkelammert, "La Crisis del socialismo y el tercer mundo," *Pasos* 30 (Julio-Agosto 1990): 1–6. See also Pablo Richard, "La Teología de la liberación en la nueva coyuntura," *Pasos* 34 (Marzo–Abril 1991): 1–8.

31. See below, chap. 6, where this theme is pursued further.

32. Bruce C. Birch and Larry L. Rasmussen, *Bible and Ethics in the Christian Life* (Minneapolis: Augsburg Fortress, 1989), 78–79. See also, Ada María Isasi-Díaz and Yolanda Tarango, *Hispanic Women: Prophetic Voice in the Church* (Minneapolis: Fortress Press, 1992), 77–79.

33. See below, chap. 6.

34. For the importance of the socio-economic reality of women in theology and ethics see Pamela K. Brubaker, "Rendering the Invisible Visible: Methodological Constraints on Economic Ethics in Relation to Women's Impoverishment" Ph.D. diss., Union Theological Seminary, New York, 1989.

According to information gathered by the U.S. Census Bureau, in 1972 11.9 percent of all U.S. persons were poor.[35] But the percentage of persons of Hispanic origin who were poor was twice that: 22.8 percent. In 1989 26.2 percent of Hispanics were poor compared with 12.8 percent of all U.S. persons;[36] in 1990 28.1 percent of all Hispanics were poor while only 12.1 percent of all non-Hispanics were poor.[37] By 1991 28.7 percent of all Hispanics were poor. It is important to notice that in 1978 the poverty rate of Hispanics was 2.5 times that of whites; by 1987, the poverty rate went up to 2.8 times that of whites.[38] Moreover, those most affected by this unbearable increase in poverty are the young and the elderly, groups usually the responsibility of women in our communities. In 1990 one in six persons living in poverty were Hispanics and about half of those were children under 18 years (47.7 percent).[39]

Poverty increasingly affects Hispanic youth in a special manner. About 38 percent of all Hispanics under the age of 18 in 1990 belonged to families living in poverty. For a Hispanic youth, the likelihood of living in poverty grew almost 50 percent between 1978 and 1987, while for a white youth that likelihood grew only 4 percent, from 11 percent to 15 percent. The high unemployment rate among Hispanic teenagers does not help their situation. In February 1992 30.3 percent of Hispanic youth between the ages of 16 and 19 were unemployed compared to 38.4 percent of African Americans, and 17.4 percent of whites.[40] Elderly Hispanics have not

35. U.S. Bureau of the Census, *Poverty in the United States: 1990*, P-60, no. 175. "The government includes a person or family among the poor if their income falls below an officially designated *poverty line* or *threshold*, which varies according to family size. In 1985 the poverty line for a family of four was $10,990; for a single person between the ages of 15 and 64, it was $5,590. Every year these thresholds are adjusted for inflation." The Center for Popular Economics, *A Field Guide to the U.S. Economy* (New York: Pantheon Books, 1987), sect. T.10. These thresholds are criticized by the poor and their advocates as unrealistic. What the government says it costs to have a roof over one's head and heat in the winter, enough food to eat, clothes to wear, and minimal medical attention, is inadequate for it does not take into consideration things like child care, time wasted in using government-sponsored programs, and lack of full-time jobs for women. The government's understanding also reduces living to barely living and thus creates a standard of living for the poor far below that of those who own property and have access to the benefits of being a citizen of one of the rich countries of the world.

36. U.S. Bureau of the Census, *Poverty*.

37. U.S. Bureau of the Census, Current Population Reports, Series P-20, no. 455, *The Hispanic Population in the United States: March, 1991* (Washington, D.C.: U.S. Government Printing Office, 1991), 8.

38. In this section we will use the word "white" instead of "Anglo" because "white" is the term used in the statistical studies we consulted to gather the information we present here.

39. *The Hispanic Population*, 8.

40. U.S. Department of Labor, Bureau of Labor Statistics. Data derived from the Current Population Survey, February, 1992. African American and white teen unemployment is seasonally adjusted, but Hispanic youth unemployment is not because of too small a sample; therefore, these figures are not strictly comparable.

fared much better. The relative number of Hispanics 65 and older who live in poverty decreased only from 23 percent to 22.5 percent between 1978 and 1990, while during the same period the white elderly poor population decreased from 12 percent to 10 percent.[41]

For Hispanic families, the median income in 1990 was about 71 percent that of white households. This means a Hispanic family earning the median income received about $8,900 less than a white family of median income. This represents an even worsening condition as Hispanic household incomes declined 3.4 percent between 1989 and 1990, while white households only declined by 2.6 percent.[42] While the so-called recovery of the 1980s pulled a small percentage of white families above the poverty line, the percentage of Hispanic families in poverty increased from 20.6 percent in 1980 to 23 percent in 1987,[43] and to 25 percent in 1990.[44] In 1990 9.5 percent of non-Hispanic families lived below the poverty level.[45]

Whether seen as a result or a cause, the increasing poverty of Hispanics is connected to the increase in the proportion of households headed by women. In 1970, 16.9 percent of all Hispanic families with children were headed by women, as opposed to only 10.8 percent of all American families. In 1981 the Hispanic figure had grown considerably, to 21.8 percent, compared with 18.8 percent of all American families with children under 18.[46] By 1991 23.8 percent of Hispanic families were headed by women with no husband present, and 9.1 percent of nonfamily households were headed by women compared to 10.8 percent headed by Hispanic males.[47] Of the families headed by Hispanic Women in 1991, 43.3 percent are Puerto Rican, 19.4 percent are Cuban, and 19.1 percent are of Mexican origin.[48]

Looked at from the perspective of children, these statistics mean that in 1980 only 72 percent of Hispanic children lived with both parents, compared with 84 percent of whites and 43 percent of African American children.[49] By 1988 only 66 percent of Hispanic children lived with

41. Bureau of the Census, *Poverty*.
42. U.S. Department of Commerce, Bureau of the Census, CB91-288, 26 September 1991.
43. "Recovery Fails Latinos," *Dollars and Sense* (November 1989): 19–20.
44. U.S. Bureau of the Census, *Poverty*.
45. *The Hispanic Population*, 18.
46. Moore and Pachón, 64.
47. *The Hispanic Population*, 16, 18. Family household is a household maintained by a family and is equal to the number of families, which is understood as people related by birth, marriage, or adoption and residing together. A householder refers to the person in whose name the housing unit is owned or rented. Nonfamily householder is a person maintaining a household while living alone or with nonrelatives. See 22–23 of same publication.
48. Ibid., 18–19.
49. *A Field Guide*, sect. 4.15.

both parents compared with 78 percent of whites and 41 percent of African American children.[50] Moreover, the number of Hispanic children is increasing. In 1985 66 percent of Hispanic families had children under 18, compared to 59 percent of African American and 49 percent of white families. Of Hispanic families, 22 percent had 3 or more children, compared to 17 percent of African American and 10 percent of white families.[51] In 1990 70.2 percent of Hispanic families had children under 18, compared to 67.8 percent of African American and 49.5 percent of white families.[52]

Another result of the severe economic limitations of Hispanic Women and the children who depend on them is the abysmal educational picture presented by Hispanic youth. For example, the overall high school completion rate for the general U.S.A. 18-to-24-year-old population remained relatively stable—81.2 percent in 1988 compared to 82.1 percent in 1986. But the Hispanic high school completion rate dropped to 55.2 percent in 1988 compared to 59.9 percent in 1986 and 61.2 percent in 1987. Hispanic Women continue to complete school at a substantially higher rate than Hispanic men.[53] There is also strong indication that the percentage of low income Hispanics who enrolled in college fell by 15 points, from 50.4 percent in 1976 to 35.3 percent in 1988. There has also been a drop in college enrollment among middle-income Hispanics. "In 1976, 53.4 percent of middle-income Hispanic high school graduates attended college, compared to 38.5 percent in 1987 and 46.4 percent in 1988."[54] While among low income Hispanic youth the drop in college participation occurred mainly among Hispanic males, among middle income Hispanics the decline for Hispanic men was only slightly higher than for Hispanic Women.[55]

This dismally negative picture of the education of Hispanic youth grows even more ominous when one considers that the job market in the future will show an increasing decline in low skilled jobs. Occupations of the future will require more education. For example, while at present 6 percent of current jobs require eight years or less of education, only 4 percent of new jobs will have such a low educational requirement.[56] There will be fewer jobs described as "helpers and laborers,

50. U.S. Department of Commerce, Bureau of the Census, SB-3-89.

51. *A Field Guide,* sect. 4.15.

52. U.S. Bureau of the Census, *Poverty.*

53. Deborah J. Carter and Reginald Wilson, *Eighth Annual Status Report on Minorities in Higher Education* (Washington, D.C.: American Council on Education, Publications Department, December, 1989), 1.

54. Ibid., 6.

55. Ibid, 5 and 6.

56. William B. Johnston, *Workforce 2000: Work and Workers for the 21st Century* (Indianapolis: Hudson Institute, 1987), Table 3-8.

hand workers, machine setters, transport workers, farmers, precision production, administrative, construction, and marketing and sales."[57] Jobs
which will exist in greater numbers are described as "technicians, teachers,
management, engineers, lawyers, natural scientists."[58]

The participation of Hispanic Women in the job market is less likely than
that of Anglo women or African American women. This is apparently due
to cultural prescriptions and imperatives, although these are often stretched
to the limit by the need for survival.[59] Only a third of Puerto Rican
Women are gainfully employed or even looking for work, though on the
mainland there are more Puerto Rican Women working outside the home
than in the island. Mexican-American Women since the 1970s are tending
to work more and more frequently outside the home but they still do so
less than Anglo women. Cuban Women, however, tend to work outside
the home more frequently than do Anglo women.[60] Comparisons among
Hispanic Women of different national roots seem to indicate that other
factors, such as education and the number of children coupled with cultural
expectations, play a significant role in determining whether Hispanic
Women work outside the home or not. Cuban Women, for example, are
more educated and have fewer children than other Hispanic Women.

Most of the Hispanic Women who do work outside the home do so in
marginal jobs, that is, jobs that have a combination of low wages, poor
working conditions, high turnover, and few or no fringe benefits, precisely
the kind of jobs of which there will be fewer and fewer in the future. Again,
the combination of better education and fewer children seems to help
Cuban Women obtain better jobs and higher income than most other
Hispanic Women.

Economic differences among Hispanic Women hold for the Hispanic
population at large. The 1990 median income for Cuban households stood
at $31,439 compared with $23,240 for Mexicans and $18,008 for Puerto
Ricans. This means that in 1990 37 percent of Puerto Rican families,
25 percent of Mexican American, and 13.8 percent of Cuban families lived
below the poverty line.[61]

The economic stratum of Hispanics is not the only factor, and in some
circumstances not the most important factor, that determines class status
among Hispanics. For example, the longer a family has been a member of
a given community, the higher is their class status. If a family has been among
the founders of a town, parish, or organization, the class status of its members

57. Ibid., Table 3–7.
58. Ibid.
59. Moore and Pachón, 103.
60. This is also true of Central and South American women. Ibid., 104.
61. *The Hispanic Population*, 18–19.

has little to do with their economic standing. Contributing factors to the class status of a person may also be the social position of her *comadres* and *compadres* (nonblood relatives who enter the family by being sponsors of the children at baptism) or *madrinas* and *padrinos* (sponsors of all sorts of different family enterprises). *Comadres, compadres, madrinas, padrinos,* they are all advocates for and protectors of the family, so their economic status within the community reflects on the family to which they become related. These factors, however, are mainly operative only within the Hispanic community and are not relevant in our dealings with society at large.

"Middle-class" Hispanic Women, like women in general in U.S.A. society, own hardly any property or investments. Most of us have only our labor power to sell, which strictly speaking makes us members of the working class. But, though the actual money that middle-class Hispanic Women have may be limited, we do profit from the privileges of the relatives and friends—both male and female—who belong to the dominant group and do control our lives to a greater extent than Hispanic Women in lower economic strata. [62] In other words, survival for middle-class Hispanic Women is a strong possibility. However, even for middle-class Hispanic Women, the possibility of survival is often threatened by the ethnic prejudice we suffer. We are keenly aware that maintenance of membership in the middle class often depends on our ability and willingness to conform to Anglo culture. We also realize that, like all other women, we are often "a man away from welfare"—that our economic status and privileges are, in great part, determined by whose daughters, sisters, and wives we are.

Though the struggle for physical survival is not a daily factor in the lives of middle-class Hispanic Women, survival is still our main preoccupation for, as we have already seen, survival for us is not only a matter of economics but is also cultural: "the cultural struggle is a struggle for life." [63] It has to do with questions of self-definition and self-determination. Survival for

62. I am making a distinction between women having privilege and women profiting from the privilege of their husbands and/or fathers. Also, this is intended to help us understand not only the diversity among Hispanic Women, but also the differences between Hispanic Women and women of the controlling race and ethnic origin.

63. Richard, "La Teología de la liberación," 5. For an explanation of the understanding of culture we use in *mujerista* theology, see Isasi-Díaz and Tarango, *Hispanic Women,* 71–73. Since writing *Hispanic Women* we have come to understand that our adaptation of one of Niebuhr's models regarding Christ and culture results in a symbiosis of culture and Christianity that does not resonate with the religious understanding and practices of Protestant, evangelical, and pentecostal Hispanic Women. However, we still understand *mujerista* theology to be cultural theology because it is a liberative praxis that happens within Hispanic culture and the religious understandings and practices of Hispanic Women are intrinsic to the definition of Hispanic culture.

middle-class Hispanic Women is related to the difficult task of living in a culture that is not our own; it comes down repeatedly to choosing between faithfulness to self or, at the risk of losing cultural values and identity, adopting the values and behavior of the dominant culture in order to maintain our status, to survive.

⊡ SÍNTESIS DEL CAPÍTULO 1: Etnicidad Hispana y Medio Social Local en la Teología *Mujerista*.

Para la teología *mujerista* la etnicidad no es una simple colección de características naturales como el idioma, la raza y país de origen, sino es un concepto construído socialmente el cual indica una auto-identificación dinámica. En este capítulo se analizan tres de los elementos de este concepto de etnicidad hispana: mestizaje, supervivencia, y realidad socio-económica.

Mestizaje en la Comunidad Hispana

En este libro nos hemos concentrado en los tres grupos de hispanas más numerosos en EE.UU.: méxico-americanas, puertorriqueñas y cubanas. "Mujeres hispanas" aquí se refiere a las mujeres de estos tres grupos que están concientes del papel que su etnicidad tiene en la manera en que se desenvuelven sus vidas en este país. El uso de "mujeres hispanas" en este libro no pretende esconder las muchas diferencias que existen entre nosotras. Al contrario, vemos la diversidad como un elemento positivo en nuestra cultura que hace resaltar la riqueza que existe en la misma. Es en esta diversidad que encontramos la semilla del mestizaje.

Cuando hablamos de mestizaje nos referimos a la confluencia en este país de tres variantes de la cultura hispana propias de méxico-americanas, puertorriqueñas y cubanas. Este mestizaje es un elemento que tenemos que añadir al concepto de "la raza cósmica" presentado inicialmente por el filósofo mexicano José Vasconcelos en la década de 1940. Este nuevo mestizaje que se está llevando a cabo en EE.UU. tiene que ver con el hecho de que nuestras comunidades se desenvuelven en un entre-aquí-y-allá. Este mestizaje tiene que ver con que vivimos con un pie en nuestros países o culturas originales y con el otro en la sociedad de EE.UU.

Mestizaje tiene que ver con la mezcla de razas y aunque existe prejuicio racial entre nosotras las hispanas, sabemos que la mayoría de nosotras somos, como indica un dicho venezolano, "café con leche: unas más café, otras más leche". La clase de mestizaje que la teología *mujerista* abraza es un mestizaje que no resulta en la opresión de una raza por otra. El mestizaje que abrazamos tiene que ver no sólo con mezcla de razas sino también con la mezcla de culturas africanas, amerindias, y la cultura española.

Supervivencia: Pan de Cada Día Para las Mujeres Hispanas

No nos referimos a un magro vivir cuando usamos la palabra "supervivencia". En la teología *mujerista* supervivencia tiene que ver con la lucha por ser plenamente, por poder decidir cuál ha de ser nuestra historia, nuestra misión, nuestra vocación. Sobrevivimos porque luchamos en contra de la opresión la cual tiene cuatro modalidades: dominación — basada en el racismo y los prejuicios étnicos del grupo dominante; subyugación — la cual nos convierte en seres oprimidos por dichos prejuicios; y explotación y represión — llevados a cabo a través de las instituciones y los mecanismos del estado, la economía, y la sociedad. La opresión que sufrimos nos lleva a una "pobreza antropológica" que amenaza nuestro propio ser no sólo a nivel material, sino también a nivel cultural y hasta a nivel ontológico. Sabemos que para poder luchar en forma efectiva en contra de tal opresión lo tenemos que hacer como comunidad, teniendo en cuenta que nadie se puede salvar a costa de nadie, ni en forma individual, dejando a las otras detrás.

Pero para que nuestra lucha sea efectiva tenemos que empezar por analizar en forma integral la situación en la que estamos, tomando en consideración los prejuicios étnicos, tanto como los sexistas y la explotación económica. No sufrimos diferentes prejuicios en diferentes momentos sino que experimentamos los diferentes prejuicios a la misma vez, como una opresión compleja, con muchas capas, que afecta todos los aspectos de nuestras vidas. Nos es obvio, por lo tanto, que el prejuicio racial o étnico está ligado a la dominación económica que sufrimos aquí tanto como a la explotación económica de nuestros países de origen. Y sabemos que nuestra opresión como mujeres no se puede separar de la opresiones étnica y económica que sufrimos.

La opresión que sufrimos las mujeres hispanas a causa del sexismo tiene mucho que ver con la división que existe entre el ámbito público y el privado. La socialización que recibimos asigna a los hombres el ámbito público en donde sus trabajos son mejor pagados. A las mujeres se nos asigna el ámbito privado en cual el trabajo no es remunerado o se recibe una remuneración muy baja. Cuando por diferentes razones salimos a trabajar en el sector público, el trabajo que conseguimos es casi siempre una extensión del que hacemos en la casa: costureras, enfermeras, maestras. Y aunque éstos son trabajos en el sector público, la paga es inferior a trabajos equivalentes realizados por los hombres.

Aunque existen similitudes, la manera en que somos socializadas varía de acuerdo a las diferentes culturas. Ésto quiere decir que el comportamiento que se espera de las mujeres y de los hombres en la cultura hispana es diferente al que se espera de nosotras en EE.UU. Es ésta una de las razones por la cual las mujeres hispanas tienen una orientación diferente a la de las mujeres anglas en nuestra lucha contra el sexismo.

La lucha de la mujer hispana en contra del racismo y el prejuicio étnico es una lucha por la supervivencia la cual está intrínsicamente ligada a la lucha por salvar la cultura hispana. La teología *mujerista* reconoce que la cultura tiene que ver con con la estructuración de relaciones, manera de pensar, los sentimientos y comportamientos del grupo humano en el cual nacemos y crecemos. Sabemos que la religión cristiana tiene un papel muy importante en nuestra cultura. Nuestra religión está intimamente ligada a nuestras vidas diaria y es por eso que la teología *mujerista* tiene como fuente la experiencia diaria de las mujeres hispanas. Pero la teología *mujerista* también tiene como una de sus funciones la crítica de la cultura hispana usando como lente la lucha por sobrevivir de la mujer hispana. Hay aspectos de nuestra cultura, como el machismo, el cual la teología *mujerista* denuncia.

La manera en que las mujeres hispanas nos relacionamos con nuestra cultura va a depender en gran parte de cómo nuestra cultura se desenvuelve y sobrevive en la sociedad de EE.UU. Desgraciadamente ya estamos experimentando la instrumentalización y comercialización de nuestra cultura: lo que se acepta y usa es lo que trae ganancia económica, como nuestras comidas típicas, nuestra música y bailes. Pero no existe una afirmación por parte de la cultura dominante de los valores de nuestra cultura.

El análisis económico de nuestra realidad tiene que tomar en cuenta las diferentes maneras en que la economía estructura nuestras vidas y mantiene el racismo o prejuicio étnico y el sexismo. Tenemos que comprender que el sistema capitalista de EE.UU. hoy día es muy diferente a como era cuando los otros grupos étnicos vinieron a este país antes de la Segunda Guerra Mundial e inmediatamente después de ella. En aquel entonces las industrias necesitaban muchos trabajadores y era posible mejorar económicamente a familias que trabajaban mucho y se sacrificaban. Pero hoy día el capitalismo depende de tecnología y maquinarias lo cual hace que se necesiten menos y menos trabajadores. Es por eso que existe tanto desempleo y cuando esto sucede los primeros que sufren son los grupos minoritarios — los hispanos entre ellos. Y entre los hispanos las que primero quedan desempleadas son las mujeres ya que se nos considera siempre como una fuerza laboral secundaria.

El resultado de todo esto es la opresión multifacética presente en la vida de las mujeres hispanas. Pero las mujeres hispanas no nos damos por vencidas. Al contrario, somos mujeres que luchamos en contra de la opresión y no nos doblegamos ante los prejuicios en contra nuestra que existen en la sociedad de los EE.UU. y en nuestra propia cultura.

Realidad Socio-Económica de la Mujer Hispana

La teología *mujerista* insiste en un análisis crítico de la realidad socio-económica de la mujer hispana ya que sin ello no se puede entender nuestra experiencia diaria, la cual es fuente de nuestra teología.

A continuación ofrecemos algunas estadísticas sobre nuestra realidad socio-económica en los EE.UU.

■ En 1972 era pobre al 11,9 por ciento de la población de los EE.UU. y el 22,8 por ciento de los hispanos. En 1989, 12,8 por ciento de la población era pobre y el 26,2 por ciento de los hispanos. En 1990, 12,1 por ciento de la población era pobre, y el 28,1 por ciento de los hispanos.

■ La mayoría de los pobres son niños y ancianos, quienes son mayormente la responsabilidad de la mujer hispana.

■ La pobreza afecta especialmente a la juventud hispana. En 1990, 38 por ciento de los hispanos de 18 años y menores vivían en familias pobres.

■ Entre 1978 y 1987 la posibilidad de que un joven o una joven hispanos fuera pobre creció un 50 por ciento, mientras que para un anglo o una angla creció sólo un 4 por ciento.

■ En febrero de 1992, 30 por ciento de la juventud hispana entre 16 y 19 años no tenía empleo, comparado con un 38,4 por ciento entre los afro-americanos y un 17,4 por ciento entre los anglos.

■ En 1990, 22,5 por ciento de los ancianos hispanas vivían en pobreza.

■ En 1991, 23,8 por ciento de las familias hispanas tenían a la cabeza sólo a una mujer. Ésto contribuye significativamente a la pobreza entre los hispanos.

■ Otro elemento que contribuye a la pobreza es la educación. En 1988, sólo 55,2 por ciento de la juventud hispana, entre 18 y 24 años, completaron secundaria (high-school), comparado con 81,2 por ciento de la juventud angla.

■ En 1976, 50,4 por ciento de hispanos o hispanas de clase económica baja se matricularon en college. En 1988, sólo se matriculó el 35,3 por ciento. En 1976, 53,4 por ciento hispanos o hispanas de clase media se matricularon en college. En 1988 la matrícula había bajado a 46,4 por ciento.

■ Ésto impacta negativamente el futuro de la juventud hispana ya que en el presente 6 por ciento de los trabajos en este país requieren ocho años o menos de educación. Pero el porcentaje de trabajos nuevos que necesitarán sólo ocho años de educación o menos va a ser el 4 por ciento.

■ Son menos las mujeres hispanas que las mujeres anglas o las afroamericanas que trabajan fuera del hogar. Ésto se debe en parte a factores culturales, en parte al número de hijos y en parte al nivel de educación académica.

■ Entre las mujeres hispanas, las diferencias económicas son las mismas que entre familias de diferentes grupos hispanos. En 1990 las familias cubanas tenian un promedio de ingresos anuales de $31.439; las familias méxico-americanas $23.240, y las puertorriqueñas $18.000. Esto quiere decir que el 37 por ciento de las familiar puertorriqueñas viven por debajo de lo que el gobierno considera pobreza, el 25 por ciento de las familias méxico–americanas, y el 13,8 de las familias cubanas.

Entre los hispanos, otros factores aparte de los económicos juegan un papel en la determinacion de clase social. Entre estos factores se encuentra el tiempo que la familia ha vivido en una localidad, si alguien en la familia es líder en alguna de las asociaciones o instituciones importantes para la comunidad y quiénes son los parientes carnales o políticos de uno.

Las mujeres hispanas de clase media, al igual que las mujeres anglas, raramente tienen capital o riquezas propias. Ser clase media en gran parte depende del capital de sus padres o esposos y por eso siempre corren el riesgo de quedarse pobres. Por ejemplo, el divorcio frecuentemente mueve a las mujeres a una clase económica más baja. Pero, la mayoría de las mujeres hispanas de clase media no tienen la preocupación de cómo sobrevivir físicamente. Sin embargo, sí son oprimidas por el prejuicio sexista y étnico por el que son oprimidas las mujeres hispanas de clase pobre, y todas nos tenemos que preocupar por nuestra supervivencia cultural.

CHAPTER 2

Popular Religiosity, Spanish, and *Proyecto Histórico* — Elements of Latinas' Ethnicity

WHEN THE PRESENT is limiting—oppressive—one looks to the future to find a reason for living. Historically, religion has been used to encourage the poor and the oppressed to postpone hopes and expectations to "the next world." But liberation theologies turn the focus of the hopes and expectations of the poor and the oppressed from "the next world" to this world. For this reason liberation theologies are feared and opposed by those interested in maintaining the status quo.

In this chapter we will explore the hopes and expectations of Latinas grounded in our reality and aimed at historical fruition. It is the contention of *mujerista* theology that the *proyecto histórico*, historical project, of Latinas is one of the key elements in constructing our reality. We will then analyze popular religiosity and the role it plays in Latinas' struggle for survival, and how the Spanish language functions as part of Latinas' self-understanding and ethnic identification.

Latinas' Preferred Future: Our *Proyecto Histórico*

Mujerista theology uses the term *proyecto histórico* to refer to our liberation and the historical specifics needed to attain it. Though the plan is not a blueprint, it is "a historical project defined enough to force options."[1] It is a plan that deals with the structures of our churches, as well as with social, political, and economic institutions of society. The articulation of Latinas' *proyecto histórico* presented here is not only an explanation but also a strategy: it aims to help shape Latinas' understandings in our day-to-day struggle to survive, and our identity as a community. This

---

1. José Míguez Bonino, *Doing Theology in a Revolutionary Situation* (Philadelphia: Fortress Press, 1975), 38–39. Chap. 3 of this book is perhaps the most detailed description of the meaning of *proyecto histórico* by a Latin American liberation theologian. *Mujerista* theology appropriates this term critically according to our lived-experience.

articulation springs from our lived-experience and is a prediction of "our hopes and dreams toward survival,"[2] of our *lucha*—struggle.

Latinas' *proyecto histórico.* is based on an understanding of salvation and liberation as two aspects of one process. This is grounded in the belief that there is but one human history that has at its very heart the history of salvation. By "history of salvation" we refer to what we believe are divine actions—creation, incarnation, redemption—as well as our human responses to them, whether positive or negative. For us Latinas, salvation refers to having a relationship with God, a relationship that does not exist if we do not love our neighbor. Our relationship with God affects all aspects of our lives, all human reality. As Latinas become increasingly aware of the injustices we suffer, we reject any concept of salvation that does not affect our present and future reality. For us, salvation occurs in history and is intrinsically connected to our liberation.[3]

For Latinas, liberation has to do with becoming agents of our own history, with having what one needs to live and to be able to strive towards human fulfillment. Liberation is the realization of our *proyecto histórico,* which we are always seeking to make a reality while accepting that its fullness will never be accomplished in history. Liberation is realized in concrete events which at the same time point to a more comprehensive and concrete realization.[4] For Latinas to talk about salvation, liberation, and the coming of the kin-dom of God are one and the same thing. Historical events are never clearly nor completely the fulfillment of the kin-dom of God, but they affect such fulfillment; they are "eschatological glimpses," part of the unfolding of the kin-dom which we do not make happen but which requires us to take responsibility for making justice a reality in our world.

The realization of the kin-dom of God—liberation—is related to our present reality. Our *proyecto histórico* is not divorced from the present but rather is rooted in it, giving meaning and value to our daily struggle for survival. The present reality of Latinas makes it clear that in order to accomplish what we are stuggling for, we need to understand fully which structures are oppressive, denounce them, and announce what it is that we are struggling for.[5] Our struggle for liberation has to start with an analysis of the root causes of our oppression. Such an analysis shows our

---

2. Audrey Lorde, "Poems Are Not Luxuries," *Chrysalis* 3 (1977): 8.

3. See Gustavo Gutiérrez, *A Theology of Liberation.* (Maryknoll: Orbis Books, 1988), xxxix, 83–91. See also Gustavo Gutiérrez, *The Truth Shall Make You Free* (Maryknoll: Orbis Books, 1990), 14–16, 116–21.

4. Gutiérrez, *Theology of Liberation,* 94.

5. Using Paulo Freire, Gutiérrez sees the relationship of what he calls "utopia" to historical reality as appearing under two aspects: denunciation and annunciation. See Gutiérrez, *Theology of Liberation,* 136–40.

oppression to be multifaceted—an intersection of ethnic prejudice or racism, sexism, and economic oppression—all of which are intrinsic elements of patriachal and hierarchical structures. Analysis of oppression must then lead to effective denunciation.

Denunciation as part of Latinas' *proyecto histórico* is a challenge to understand and deal with present reality in the name of the future. Such a challenge does not consist only in criticizing, reproaching, and attacking those who maintain the structures that oppress us. Denunciation also has to do with repudiating such structures—not aspiring to participate in them—and refusing to benefit from them.[6] Therefore, *mujerista* theology is not to be only a resource for social criticism from the perspective of Latinas but is also socio-critical at its point of departure.[7] This means that we insist on our preferred future from the very beginning and insist that our *proyecto histórico* grounds our theological task, which we understand to be a liberative praxis.

To denounce oppressive structures without having a sense of what we believe our future should be is irresponsible. For Latinas' denunciation of oppression to be effective, we must also announce, that is, proclaim what is not yet but what we are committed to bringing about. In this context, annunciation, like analysis and denunciation, is indeed a liberative praxis, an exercise that is intended to yield tangible results. Denunciation and annunciation have to contribute effectively to the creation of new structures that make possible the liberation of Latinas and of all humanity. To announce is an intrinsic part of our insistence on fullness of life against all odds and in spite of all obstacles. Such insistence is incarnated in the concrete daily struggle of Latinas, a struggle which makes tomorrow a possibility. Whether that tomorrow is for ourselves or for our children makes no difference to us. Our annunciation becomes reality in our struggle to find or create spaces for self-determination, a key factor in the struggle for liberation. The challenge to be agents of our own history is what pushes us on to do the analysis, denounce those who oppress us, and engage in building a future society with alternative values, no matter how foolish our efforts appear to those with power.[8]

Liberation is a single process that has three different aspects or levels[9]

6. This is why we avoid using the terms "minority" or "marginalized." These labels communicate the way the dominant group sees us and not the way we see ourselves; they imply that what we want is to participate in present structures that are oppressive. We see ourselves as a group that has a significant contribution to make precisely because we demand radical change of oppressive structures.

7. See "Larry Rasmussen," *Christianity and Crisis,* 22 October 1990.

8. For the effectiveness of this understanding of struggling to build a preferred future see Renny Golden, *The Hour of the Poor, The Hour of Women* (New York: Crossroad, 1991).

9. We have appropriated Gutiérrez's understanding of the three levels or aspects of the process of liberation. The specifics of each of these aspects arise from our lived-experience as Latinas.

which must not be confused or identified in any simplistic way. Each one maintains its specificity; each is distinct but affects the other; none is ever present without the others. None of those aspects exists in isolation from the others.[10] These three aspects of liberation also serve as points of entry for Latinas into the struggle for liberation because they are concrete aspects of our *proyecto histórico*. We refer to these different aspects of liberation as *libertad, comunidad de fe*, and *justicia*: freedom, faith community, and justice.

Libertad has to do with acting as agents of our own history. This aspect of liberation involves the process of conscientization, with how we understand ourselves personally in view of our preferred future. *Libertad* has to do with a self-fulfillment that renounces any and all self-promotion while recognizing that commitment to the struggle and involvement in it are indeed self-realizing. *Comunidad de fe* is the aspect of liberation that makes us face sin, both personal and social sin. *Comunidad de fe* is both our goal (rejecting sin) and the community that makes rejecting sin possible. *Justicia* here refers to the political, economic, and social structures we struggle to build that will make oppression of anyone impossible. *Justicia* has to do with the understandings that guide us, challenge us, and enable us to survive daily.

Since these three aspects of liberation are interconnected and happen simultaneously, it is difficult to speak about them separately. We do so to distinguish each from the other, to explain and understand how they interrelate without confusing them. The specifics we discuss as part of each of these three elements are not to be understood as relating only to a single element. Each of the specifics has implications for and relates to all three elements.[11]

The first element we will consider is that of *libertad*. In Latinas' struggle for survival we must take great care not to oppose structural change to personal liberation. What is "personal" for us Latinas is neither individual nor necessarily private. For us the term "individual" carries a pejorative meaning, a sense of egocentrism and selfishness that we believe to be inherently bad since it works against what is of great value to us, our communities. Our sense of community keeps us from arrogating a sense of privacy to all aspects of the personal. Therefore, for us, *libertad* involves

10. Gutiérrez refers to the "Chalcedonian Principle," and uses the Chalcedonian language regarding the two natures of the one person Jesus, in order to clarify the distinctiveness and intrinsic unity of the three aspects of liberation. In this, *mujerista* theology follows Gutiérrez quite closely. The distinctiveness of Latinas' struggle, however, will come in the "content" of each of the three aspects of the process of liberation. See Gutiérrez, *The Truth Shall Make You Free*, 120–24.

11. Following the venerable tradition refered to in Acts 1:26, we cast lots to decide the order in which we would deal with these three aspects of liberation! We know some will try to see in the order we use a certain priority of importance or relevance. That is indeed not our intention.

being aware of the role we play in our own oppression and in the struggle for liberation. It includes being conscious of the role we must play as agents of our own history. *Libertad* has to do with being self-determining, rejecting any and all forms of determinism, whether materialistic, economic, or psychological. [12] It has to do with recognizing that the internal aspiration for personal freedom is truly powerful, as both a motive and a goal of liberation. [13]

Libertad as an element of liberation for us Latinas happens, then, at the psychological and the social level. The two main obstacles to *libertad* among Latinas are apathy and fear. [14] As an oppressed group within the richest country in the world, Latinas view our liberation as such an immense task that a common response is apathy. We often think of our task as beyond accomplishment, and apathy appears as a protection against frustration. For those of us for whom the *proyecto histórico* becomes a motivational factor strong enough to enable us to shake off our apathy, our next struggle is with fear. Our fear is not mainly the fear of failing—fear of trying and not accomplishing what we set out to do—but rather the fear of being co-opted by the status quo. [15]

A central and powerful myth in the U.S.A. tells all those who come here, as well as everyone in the world, that, because this is the best of all societies, whether one accomplishes what one wants or not depends on the individual. It depends on whether one is ambitious enough, gets a good education (which the myth maintains is available to everyone), and is willing to work hard and sacrifice oneself. [16] This myth is promulgated constantly in the most pervasive way possible. It contributes significantly to the negative self-image of Latinas who cannot get ahead, not because we do not try hard, but because of socio-economic realities that militate against us in all areas

12. The only reason a *balsero,* a young man who escaped from Cuba in a makeshift raft, could give me for risking his life in such a way was the lack of *libertad* he experienced in Cuba. I assumed that for him, influenced by U.S.A. propaganda, *libertad* had to do with accessibility to consumer goods, with a better material life. But I was wrong. For him *libertad* had to do with self-determination, with wanting something different and being able to work towards making it a reality. Whether I agree or disagree with his assessment of the present Cuban situation, his understanding of *libertad* and his willingness to risk his life for it has helped me to understand what I and other Latinas mean by *libertad.*

13. Cf. Gutiérrez, *The Truth Shall Make You Free,* 132–34.

14. Since psychology is not my field of expertise, my attempt here is only to describe apathy and fear and to locate them in reference to the historical situation Latinas face.

15. This fear is compounded by the fact that seeing ourselves as different from the status quo is an intrinsic element of what it means for us to be Latina.

16. The best proof of this mindset is the name of the U.S.A. government program for Puerto Rico in the middle decades of this century: "Operation Bootstrap." The Puerto Ricans understood very clearly the American expression that was behind that title and they responded painfully and cleverly, "How do you expect us to lift ourselves by our bootstraps when we do not even have boots!"

of life. If a negative self-image is oppressive, the fact that this myth fills us with fear, often robbing us of even envisioning our *proyecto histórico*, is insidious.

In order to counteract apathy and fear, we have to continue to elaborate our vision of the future at the same time that we work to articulate the details of our *proyecto histórico*. Making our preferred future a reality needs much more than vague generalities. Latinas' *proyecto histórico* has to be specific enough for each of us to know how we are to participate in the struggle to make it a reality, and what our task will be when it becomes a reality. All Latinas must know what it is we are being asked to contribute. Our *proyecto histórico* must have concreteness and specificity. Only when we know the concrete details can we face our shortcomings and the tremendous obstacles that we find along the way. Knowing concrete details can also help us face and conquer the fear that an unknown future brings. We can mitigate our fear by insisting on particulars, by being precise, by concretizing our vision of the future. The more tangible our *proyecto histórico* becomes, the more realizable it will be, since once it moves from vision to implementable plan, we will be able to transfer to this task of building our preferred future all the skills we do have—those skills we use effectively to survive every day.

Our explanation of *comunidad de fe* as an element of liberation starts by recognizing that Latinas' relationship with the divine is a very intimate one. It is not only a matter of believing that God is with us in our daily struggle, but that we can and do relate to God the same way we relate to all our loved ones.[17] We argue with God, barter with God, get upset with God, are grateful and recompense God, use endearing terms for God. This intimate relationship with the divine is what is at the heart of our *comunidad de fe*. For Latinas, it makes no sense to say one believes in God if one does not relate to the divine on a daily basis.[18]

Because Latinas relate intimately to the divine, we know that sin hurts such a relationship. We know that sin, while personal, is not private, for it is something that affects our communities negatively. The reflections of grassroot Latinas about evil give a clear sense of their understanding of sin:

17. I use the word "God" here not to refer to one divine being but rather as a collective noun that embraces God, the saints, dead ones whom we love, manifestations of the Virgin (not always the same as manifestations of Mary, the mother of Jesus), Jesus (not very similar to the Jesus of the Gospels), Amerindian and African gods, and so forth.

18. To the accusation that this places us in the neo-orthodox ranks, we answer that Latinas have not been part of the "modern experiment"; that the kind of belief in the divine that for the enlightened, scientific mind signifies a lack of autonomous, critical, rational thought, is for us a concrete experience that we use as a key element in the struggle for liberation. See Christine Gudorf, "Liberation Theology's Use of Scripture—A Response to First World Critics," in *Interpretation—a Journal of Bible and Theology.* (January 1987): 12–13.

Sin is not a matter of disobedience but of not being for others. Not going to church is not a sin. But not to care for the children of the community—that is a sin, a crime! And the women take direct responsibility for what they do or do not do. Though they have a certain sense of predestination, they do not blame anyone but themselves for what goes wrong. On the other hand, God is given credit for the good that they do, the good that occurs in their lives.[19]

The analysis that our *proyecto histórico* demands can help us deepen our understanding of how sin affects those around us by helping us to understand "structural sin" and the role it plays in our oppression. We need to recognize that there are structures that have been set up to maintain the privilege of a few at the expense of the many and that those structures are sinful. Our analysis of oppressive structures will help us understand that sin is "according to the Bible the ultimate cause of poverty, injustice, and the oppression in which [we]...live."[20]

To understand the structural implications of sin, Latinas need to actualize our sense of *comunidades de fe* by setting up communities which are praxis-oriented, which bring together personal support and community action, and which have as a central organizing principle our religious understandings and practices as well as our needs.[21]

We have to accept, however, that most of the time we will not be able to depend on church structures and personnel to help us develop our communities. Once again we are going to have to depend on ourselves and, perhaps, we will be able to find help in the few national Latina organizations that claim to be committed to the struggle for liberation. Our *comunidades de fe* must also find ways of relating to community organizations. Where there are no Latina community organizations, the *comunidades de fe* need to fulfill that function. We must resist the temptation to let our *comunidades de fe* become "support groups" that separate our lives into realms: the personal from the communal, the spiritual from the struggle for justice.

Our *comunidades de fe* must also be ecumenical. We must embrace the grassroot ecumenism practiced by many Latinas who relate to more than one denomination because of their need to avail themselves of help no matter what its source. For others of us, our ecumenicism has to do with our belief

19. Ada María Isasi-Díaz and Yolanda Tarango, *Hispanic Women: Prophetic Voice in the Church* (Minneapolis: Fortress Press, 1992), 90.

20. Gutiérrez, *Theology of Liberation*, 24.

21. Though indeed we have much to learn from the Base Ecclesial Communities that are at the heart of the Latin American liberation struggle, our *comunidades de fe* have to develop their own characteristics based on our lived-experiences and needs. For a concise articulation of what Base Ecclesial Communities are and the role they play in Latin America, see Pablo Richard, "The Church of the Poor in the Decade of the 90s," *LADOC* XXI (Nov./Dec. 1990): 11–29

that the struggle for liberation—and not the fact that we belong to the same church—must be the common ground of our *comunidades de fe*. Our ecumenism must take into consideration and capitalize on our *religiosidad popular*, popular religiosity.

Finally, the *comunidades de fe* have to develop their own models of leadership, communal leadership that recognizes and uses effectively the gifts of Latinas. Characteristics emerging from our historical reality will make it possible for the *comunidades de fe* to contribute effectively to the building of our *proyecto histórico*.

The third element of liberation is *justicia*. Justice as a virtue does not refer only or mainly to attitudes but to a tangible way of acting and being; it involves not only personal conduct but also the way social institutions—the building blocks of societal structures—are organized, the way they operate, prioritize issues, and use resources. Justice is not only a matter of taking care of the basic needs of the members of society, nor is it a utilitarianism that insists on the greatest happiness for the majority of people.[22] Justice is not a matter of "to each according to one's needs," as Marxist principles proclaim.[23] For *mujerista* theologians justice is all of this and much more. Justice is a Christian requirement: one cannot call oneself a Christian and not struggle for justice.

Our understanding of justice is based on the lived-experience of Latinas, an experience that has as its core multifaceted oppression. In *mujerista* theology *justicia* is a matter of permitting and requiring each person to participate in the production of the goods needed to sustain and promote human life. It has to do with rights and with the participation of all Latinas in all areas of life. Justice is indeed understood as the "common good." But striving for the "common good" can never be done at the expense of anyone. The "common good" is to be judged by the rights and participation of the poorest in society; it never places the rights of individuals against or over the rights and participation in society of others, particularly of the poor. It understands "welfare" in a holistic way and not just as limited to the physical necessities of life. In *mujerista* theology *justicia* is concretely expressed by being in effective solidarity with and having a preferential option for Latinas.[24]

Effective solidarity with Latinas is not a matter of agreeing with, being supportive of, or being inspired by our cause. Solidarity starts with recognizing the commonality of responsibilities and interests that all of us have despite differences of race or ethnicity, class, sex, sexual preference, age. Solidarity has to do with recognizing and affirming, valuing and defending

22. See John Stuart Mill, *Utilitarianism* (New York: Bobbs-Merrill, 1957).
23. See also Acts 4:35.
24. For an excellent short analysis of six main justice theories see, Karen Lebacqz, *Six Theories of Justice* (Minneapolis: Augsburg, 1986).

a community of interests, feelings, purposes and actions with the poor and the oppressed. The two main, interdependent elements of solidarity are mutuality and praxis. Mutuality keeps solidarity from being a merely altruistic praxis by making clear that, if it is true that solidarity benefits the poor and the oppressed, it is also true that the salvation and liberation of the rich and the oppressors depend on it. Solidarity is truly praxis, because in order for a genuine community of interests, feelings, and purposes to exist between the oppressed and the oppressor, there must be a radical action on the part of the oppressors that leads to the undoing of oppression. Thus, for solidarity to be a praxis of mutuality, it has to struggle to be politically effective; it has to have as its objective radical structural change.[25]

Effective solidarity with Latinas demands a preferential option for the oppressed. This preferential option is not based on our moral superiority. It is based on the fact that Latinas' point of view,

> pierced by suffering and attracted by hope, allows them, in their struggles, to conceive another reality. Because the poor suffer the weight of alienation, they can conceive a different project of hope and provide dynamism to a new way of organizing human life *for all*.[26]

Solidarity with Latinas as oppressed people is a call to a fundamental moral option, an option that makes it possible and requires one to struggle for radical change of oppressive structures even when the specifics of what one is opting for are not known. As a matter of fact, only opting for a radical change of oppressive structures will allow the specifics of new societal structures to begin to appear.

The ability of Latinas to conceive "another reality," a different kind of social, political, and economic structure, is greatly hampered, as explained above, by the powerful U.S.A. myth regarding the possibility of success in this country for everyone. Poor and oppressed women in the shanty towns that surround Lima, Perú, for example, know very well that they will never be able to live — except as maids — in San Isidro, one of the rich neighborhoods in that city. Knowing that they cannot benefit from the present societal structures helps them to understand the need for radical change and to work for it. But it is not unusual to find Latinas living in the most oppressed conditions in the inner cities of the U.S.A. who think that if they work hard and sacrifice themselves, their children will benefit from the present order, and that they will eventually have the material goods and privileges this society claims to offer to all. I believe that this possibility, which becomes a reality

---

25. For a more comprehensive analysis of the meaning of solidarity see Ada María Isasi-Díaz, "Solidarity: Love of Neighbor in the 1980s," in *Lift Every Voice — Constructing Christian Theologies from the Underside*, ed. Susan Brooks Thistlethwaite and Mary Potter Engels (San Francisco: Harper and Row, 1990).

26. José Míguez Bonino, "Nuevas tendencias en teología," *Pasos* (1985): 22

for only the tiniest minority of Latinas and their children, hinders our ability to understand structural oppression. It keeps us from understanding that if we succeed in the present system, it will be because someone else takes our place at the bottom of the socio-economic-political ladder.

In order to overcome the temptation to leave behind oppression individually and at the expense of others, Latinas need to continue to set up strong community organizations. Such organizations are most important in constructing our own identity and strengthening our moral agency. Community organizations are fertile settings for supporting our liberative praxis. They provide spaces for us to gather our political will and power to help us question the present structures. Community organizations provide or help us to move into spaces that can bring together different political projects. These projects enable us to participate in the creation of a different kind of society—a participation that must be present if socio-economic transformation is to happen. Without community organizations that make it possible for us to analyze our reality and to explore alternatives, we will not be able to participate politically, socially, or economically at all levels of society; we will not be able to be agents of our own history, to make our *proyecto histórico* a reality.[27]

Our community organizing will be helped if those with privileges in this society are willing to stand in solidarity with us. To be in solidarity with Latinas is to use one's privileges to bring about radical change instead of spending time denying that one has privileges. For our part, Latinas must embrace the mutuality of solidarity; we have to be open to the positive role that those who become our friends by being in solidarity with us can play in our struggle for liberation. By culture and socialization Latinas are not separatists; we do not exclude others from our lives and from *la lucha,* nor do we struggle exclusively for ourselves. We extend this same sense of community to those who are in solidarity with us. They can enable us in our process of conscientization; they can help us see the deception behind the U.S.A. myth. They can assist us in getting rid of the oppressor within who at times makes us seek vengeance and disfigures our *proyecto histórico* when we seek to exchange places with present-day oppressors.[28]

At present the unfolding of our *proyecto histórico* requires that Latinas organize to bring about an economic democracy in the U.S.A. that would transform an economy controlled by a few to the economy of a participatory community. Concretely, we must insist on a national commitment to full employment, an adequate minimum wage, redistribution of wealth through

27. Fernando Romero, "Sentido práctico y flexibilidad popular," *Páginas* 111 (Octubre 1991): 43. See also, Arthur F. McGovern, *Liberation Theology and Its Critics* (Maryknoll: Orbis Books, 1990), 177–212.

28. For an amplification of this theme see Isasi-Díaz, "Solidarity," 37.

redistributive inheritance and wealth taxes, and comparable remuneration for comparable work regardless of sex, sexual preference, race, ethnicity, or age. Radical changes in the economics of the family that will encourage more "symmetrical marriages, allow a better balance between family and work for both men and women, and make parenting a less difficult and impoverishing act for single parents," the majority of whom are women, are a must.[29] We need a national health care plan with particular emphasis on preventive health care. Latinas call for a restructuring of the educational system so that our children and all those interested can study Latino culture and Spanish. We also call for a restructuring of the financing of public education so that its quality does not depend on the economics of those who live in the neighborhood served by a given school but is the responsibility of the whole community of that area, region, or state. Latinas must have access to political office to insure adequate representation of our community. Access to public means of communication including entertainment TV and movies is necessary so that the values of Latinas can begin to impact the culture of the nation at large.

Working for these changes in the U.S. system might not be considered radical enough. But we believe that these kinds of changes within the present system do strike at the

> essential arrangements in the class-power-ideology structure. To respond to these. . .[demands] would necessitate such a fundamental change in the ownership, and use of domestic and international wealth as to undercut the ruling class's position in American society and in the world, a development of revolutionary rather than reformist dimensions.[30]

These reforms demanded by Latinas significantly modify economic structures, gender, cultural relationships, and social and political institutions. Working for such changes also enhances our ability to build coalitions with other oppressed groups struggling for liberation. Thus we can have the numbers we need to be politically effective. Working for these changes strengthens our communities of struggle and makes our survival possible by enabling us to be self-defining and to strengthen our moral agency.[31]

Latinas' *proyecto histórico* is based on our lived-experience, which is mainly one of struggle against oppression. It has been argued that the subjectivity of lived-experience makes it impossible to consider it an adequate normative base. But the fact is that so-called adequate normative bases, such as different theories of justice, spring from the understandings of men, understandings

---

29. Teresa L. Amott and Julie A. Matthaei, *Race, Gender & Work* (Boston: South End, 1991), 346–48.

30. Michael Parenti, *Power and the Powerless* (New York: St. Martin's, 1978), 226.

31. Romero, "Sentido práctico," 45–47.

that are based on and are influenced by *their* experiences. The liberative praxis of Latinas, having as its source our lived-experience, is an adequate base for moral norms and values because it enables our moral agency and empowers us to understand and define ourselves – to comprehend what our human existence is all about and what its goal is. [32]

Popular Religiosity as an Element of *Mujerista* Theology [33]

The starting point for a study of the popular religiosity of Latinas is our struggle to survive. [34] Popular religiosity for us is a means of self-identification and our insistence on it is part of the struggle to exist with our own characteristics and peculiarities. Popular religiosity allows religion to remain central to our culture in spite of the neglect we suffer as a people from most organized religions in this country. [35]

It should not be surprising that Latinas, as persons who are "vitally engaged in historical realities with specific times and places," [36] and as persons who have to struggle for survival, are involved with and reflect on matters of ultimate concern. This reflection includes religious considerations that form "a system of symbols which acts to establish powerful, pervasive, and long-lasting moods and motivations... by formulating conceptions of a general order of existence and clothing these conceptions with such an aura of factuality that the moods and motivations seem uniquely realistic." [37]

Many of these powerful symbols arise from a certain kind of "official" Christian tradition. "Official" here refers to "those prescribed beliefs and norms of an institution promulgated and monitored by a group of religious specialists," [38] the clergy and, in particular, the hierarchy of the church. Without question Christianity is the religion of Latinas – Catholicism being the specific form of Christianity which about 80 percent claim and pass on to our children. But the Christianity to which we relate, our way of relating with the divine and expressing such connection, is not "official" Christianity, nor does it necessarily have the church – either Catholic or Protestant – as its main point of reference. The Christianity of Latinas is of a very specific variety because of its history in the countries of our ethnic roots.

---

32. Isasi-Díaz and Tarango, *Hispanic Women*, 77–80, 109–10; see below chap. 6

33. We set the basis for this section in chap. 3 of Isasi-Díaz and Tarango, *Hispanic Women*.

34. Though popular religiosity among Latinas is suffused with Catholic rituals and understandings, there begins to be a Protestant perspective regarding popular religiosity. See Tito Paredes, "Popular religiosity: A Protestant Perspective" *Missiology* XX, no. 2 (April 1992): 205–20; see also Juan Sepúlveda, "Pentecostalism as Popular Religiosity," *International Review of Mission* 78 (January 1989): 80–88.

35. Juan José Huitrado-Rizo, MCCJ, "Hispanic Popular Religiosity: The Expression of a People Coming to Life," *New Theology Review* 3, no. 4 (November 1990): 43–54.

36. Gutiérrez, *Theology of Liberation*, 13.

37. Clifford Geertz, *The Interpretation of Culture* (New York: Basic Books, 1973), 90.

38. Robert J. Schreiter, *Constructing Local Theologies* (Maryknoll: Orbis Books, 1985), 87–88.

Christianity came to Latin America at the time of the *conquista,* the conquest. It came not only, or even primarily, in the form of organized religion, but as an intrinsic part of the conquering culture. Theology was indeed "the main discourse in the ideological production of the sixteenth century."[39] This is why the *conquistadores,* the conquerors, planted crosses to symbolize their taking possession of the land, and named the territories and the natives in the same way as species and persons are named or renamed in the Bible – to indicate having authority over them.[40] The *conquista* was not just a political conquest, but a conquest in which even the religious world of the conquered suffered total devastation. Christianity was not only imposed on the natives but also played a very important role as moral justifier in the whole process of the *conquista.*

When the Spanish world and the world of the indigenous people of what was to become the Americas met, a process of acculturation was set in motion during which the culture of the conqueror was imposed unilaterally on the conquered people. Real enculturation –"the process of making personal the traditional culture of the society," that is, the society of the *conquistadores* – did not take place because education was not made available to the vast majority of the population. Instead, what resulted was a "culturization" of Christianity; Christianity became culture. It has become a cultural expression in a continent in which the Spanish and the indigenous cultures have come together to give birth to a new culture.[41]

The Christianity that became and is an intrinsic part of Latino culture is one that uses the Bible in a very limited way, emphasizing instead the traditions and customs of the Spanish church.[42] Therefore, the Bible, biblical truth, and revelation are not repudiated by Latinas but, for the majority of Latinas, they are not central, they are not considered very important, they do not play a prominent role in our lives. Most of us seldom read the Bible and know instead popularized versions of biblical stories – versions Latinas

---

39. Luis N. Rivera Pagán, *Evangelización y violencia – la conquista de América* (San Juan, Puerto Rico: Editorial Cemi, 1991), 1.

40. Ibid., 14–21. Rivera Pagán carefully explains how the discovery was accompanied by the juridical act of taking possession.

41. This definition of enculturation is found in Paulo Agirrebaltzategi, *Configuración eclesial de las culturas* (Bilbao, España: Universidad de Deusto, 1976), 82. The author explains the three terms acculturation, enculturation, and culturization on pp. 81–82. He indicates that what has become cultural expression is what is transcultural or transcendent. It also means the form in which culturally the Gospel message is realized in the Church. I use the term here in a narrower sense to mean simply that which has become a cultural expression.

42. Juan Luis Segundo, *The Liberation of Theology* (Maryknoll: Orbis Books, 1982), 185. Though it is true that an increasing number of Latinas are participating in denominations and churches that give great importance to the Bible, the majority of Latinas still relate to the Catholic church and do not use the Bible often. *Mujerista* theologians are concerned with the way the Bible is imposed on Latinas by some churches since it is done in a way that often threatens rather than enhances our moral agency.

create to make a point. One can consider these versions to be distortions, but for us they are "valid" interpretations, albeit imaginative ones, insofar as they contribute to the liberation of Latinas.[43]

The Christianity of Latinas also includes religious traditions brought to Latin America and the Caribbean by African slaves, and the Amerindian traditions bequeathed by the great Aztec, Maya, and Inca civilizations, as well as other Amerindian cultures, such as Taino, Siboney, Caribe, Araucano. The mingling of sixteenth-century Spanish Catholicism with religious understandings and beliefs of the African and Amerindian religions in these regions is what has given birth to Latino popular religiosity.[44]

Popular religiosity refers to the religious understandings and practices of the masses, in contrast to "official" Christianity or the Christianity of certain minorities that eschew popular religiosity. Popular religiosity is

> the set of experiences, beliefs and rituals which more-or-less peripherical [*sic*] human groups create, assume and develop (within concrete socio-cultural and historical contexts, and as an answer to these contexts) and which to a greater or lesser degree distance themselves from what is recognized by the Church and the society within which they are situated, striving through rituals, experiences and beliefs to find an access to God and salvation which they feel they cannot find in what Church and society have regulated as normative.[45]

Concretely we can say that the popular religiosity of Latinas has five general characteristics. First, it is a real religious subculture in the sense that it is a way of thinking and acting in their religious sphere not as individuals but as a group of persons. As a religious subculture, popular religiosity includes beliefs, attitudes, values, rituals, and so forth, that express the religiosity of Latinos. Second, insofar as rituals are concerned,

---

43. The same is often true of sermons we hear on Sundays. Imaginative interpretations are not considered "good theology" when Latinas do it, but it is all right when priests and/or pastors do it.

44. Sixto J. García and Orlando Espín are doing very exciting work on developing a Hispanic American theology using popular religiosity as its key element. In 1987 and 1988 they gave workshops at the Catholic Theological Society of America Conferences. Only synopses of the papers they presented there have been published. See Orlando Espín and Sixto García, "Hispanic-American Theology," *Catholic Theological Society of America Proceedings* 42 (1987): 114–19, and "The Sources of Hispanic Theology," *Catholic Theological Society of America Proceedings* 43 (1988): 122–25. In 1989 they gave a full presentation that has been published. See García and Espín, " 'Lilies of the Field'," *Catholic Theological Society of America Proceedings* 44 (1989): 70–90.

45. Espín and García, "Toward a Hispanic-American Theology," unpublished notes of workshop presented at *The Catholic Theological Society of America.* (1987): 6–7. All quotations from Espín and García's presentation at the CTSA conferences in 1987 and 1988 will be from unpublished notes the authors passed out which are much more complete than the published synopses.

central position is given to certain aspects of the Catholic tradition considered marginal, for example, "sacramentals."[46] Third, popular religiosity, as I have already begun to suggest, is syncretic for it invests Catholic
religious practices with meaning from other religious traditions. Fourth,
"official" religious practices are reinterpreted and given a different meaning. For example, Baptism and First Communion become rituals of
passage; the Mass becomes a public ceremony used to solemnize the most
important moments in the life of a person or a group of people. Fifth,
all these behaviors are transmitted as part of the Latino culture in contrast to being personal options.[47]

In *mujerista* theology we see popular religiosity as an essential part of
popular culture and, therefore, as a part of the identity of and central
to the lived-experience of the people. It is an essential part of our deepest
constitutive element.[48] In many ways popular religiosity is one of the
most creative and original parts of our heritage and our culture, being
a significant element in providing *fuerzas para la lucha*, strength for the
struggle. In this sense popular religiosity is valuable not only culturally
but also "in relation to its capacity for strengthening the political consciousness and mobilization of the people."[49]

Mujeristas take popular religiosity very seriously, then, finding it to be
an essential source of our theology because it is operative in the lives of
Latinas as a "system of values and ideas, and a complex of symbolic practices, discursive and non-discursive, enacted in ritual drama and materialized in visual images," relating us to the sacred, originated and maintained in a large measure by Latinas as poor and oppressed people.[50] But
this does not exempt popular religiosity from being examined through
the critical lens of the liberation of Latinas. As *mujerista* theologians
we recognize that the popular religiosity of Latinas has its failings and
ambiguities, as do other cultural forms of Catholicism and Christianity.[51]
Using a liberative lens, *mujerista* theology recognizes that popular

---

46. Sacramentals in the Roman Catholic tradition are things or actions—candles,
processions—used as reminders of God's effective presence in the world. The laity has access
to the use of sacramentals without having to depend on the priests.

47. Manuel M. Marzal, "La religiosidad popular en el Perú" in *Panorama de la teología
latinoamericana*, I, ed. Equipo Seladoc (Salamanca: Ediciones Sígueme, 1975), 28–29. These
are adaptations of elements presented by Marzal that I have translated in such a way as to
exclude the judgmental tone of his analysis, which I believe limits the value of popular
religiosity.

48. See Segundo Galilea, "The Theology of Liberation and the Place of 'Folk Religion,'"
in *What Is Religion: An Inquiry for Christian Theology.*, ed. Mircea Eliade and David W.
Tracy, *Concilium* 136 (Edinburgh: T. & T. Clark, 1980), 43.

49. Ibid, 44.

50. Michael R. Candelaria, *Popular Religion and Liberation* (Albany: State Univ. of New
York Press, 1990), 13.

51. Ibid., 43.

religiosity has elements that legitimize the oppression of Latinas. However, this does not lead us to minimize or dismiss it.

The evangelizing role that popular religiosity has had and continues to have among Latinas and within the Latino community is instrumental in the struggle for liberation because it is a major force in preserving the Latino community. "The historical neglect to which Latinos have been submitted in this country, by Church and society, added to the constant pressure to become 'anglicized,' would have long ago done away with Catholicism among Latinos and with Latino culture in general."[52] Instead, Latino Christianity and culture are alive today thanks to the evangelizing role of popular religiosity through which Latinas transmit the religious, cultural, and social values of our people. Moreover, it has provided common ground for the great variety of Latinos who live in the U.S.A., thus binding the different Latino communities together.[53]

For Latinas, popular religiosity also has another important role: it allows us to experience the sacred in our everyday lives. In many ways it makes it possible for us to live out religiosity as an intrinsic element of who we are and all that we do; it makes it possible to integrate the sacred and the secular. It is through the practices of popular religiosity that Latinas are aware of the sacred in the private as well as the public, in the personal as well as the social.[54]

"Official" churches, instead of seeing popular religiosity as a positive element,[55] either denounce it and work actively against it, or look for ways of purifying it, of "baptizing" it into Christianity—accepting only those elements that can be Christianized.[56] In *mujerista* theology we will not dismiss "the normative, graced, and even universal dimensions of the 'salvific' manifestations of non-Christian religions."[57] As *mujerista* theologians we are suspicious of an imperialistic approach that refuses to recognize and accept as true, good, and life-giving any and all religious understandings

---

52. Espín and García, "Sources of Hispanic Theology," unpublished notes of workshop presented at the Catholic Theological Society of America (1988): 4.

53. García and Espín, 'Lilies of the Field,' 72.

54. María Pilar Aquino, *Nuestro Clamor por La Vida* (San Jose, Costa Rica: Editorial D.E.I., 1992), 218–22.

55. See Isasi-Díaz and Tarango, *Hispanic Women*, 67, where we indicate that popular religiosity could offer needed correctives to some of the religious understandings of "official" Christianity.

56. Ibid., 14–26. See also II Consulta Ecuménica de Pastoral Indígena, *Aporte de los pueblos indígenas de América Latina a la teología cristiana* (Quito, Ecuador, 1986). Espín and García, "Toward a Hispanic," 4. Jaime R. Vidal, "Popular Religion among the Hispanics in the General Area of the Archdiocese of Newark," in *Presencia Nueva* (Newark: Office of Research and Planning, Archdiocese of Newark 1988), 250–54.

57. Espín and García, "Toward a Hispanic-American Theology," 17. On this point Espín and García contradict themselves. In spite of the assertion they make here, they make only one reference to Amerindian and African religions and not in a very positive light. They place the Amerindian and African religious elements operative in popular religiosity in what they call a "second constellation" with which they seem to deal only insofar as it goes hand in hand with the "first constellation," which they call "popular catholicism." See pp. 4–6.

and practices that do not directly relate to a magisterial understanding and interpretation of the gospel, that do not have Christ as center, model, and norm.[58] We take exception to such refusal because it does violence to a valid understanding of Jesus as portrayed in Scripture: Jesus clearly indicated that his mission was not to point to himself, but rather to point the way to God.

This imperialistic attitude on the part of "official" churches, particularly vis-à-vis the Amerindian and African strands in popular religiosity, is anti-cultural, and in this case, anti-Latino. To insist on imposing the divinity of Jesus as the only true and relevant expression of the divine on people who because of cultural factors either believe differently or for whom such claim is irrelevant, shows a lack of respect for a people whose religion includes other claims, and whose religion is central to their culture.[59] Is this imperialistic attitude not one of the main reasons for the lack of pastoral care and inclusion of Latinos in the life of the church in the U.S.A.?

Latinas' Christianity is indeed a mixture, a fusion of different religious strands. In this regard it follows in the footsteps of "official" Christianity. For example, Christmas is celebrated at the time of the year when the Feast of the Unconquered Sun took place at Rome in the late third and early fourth centuries;[60] pagan buildings such as the Pantheon were turned into churches; civil offices and the garbs of different periods and cultures have become religious offices and liturgical garb; Greek philosophical concepts of substance are used by Catholics to talk about the Eucharist. Once this syncretism became official, however, it has been used as an orthodox norm which has excluded and continues to exclude other syncretisms.

But such an exclusion does not obliterate syncretism from the Latinas' *religiosidad popular,* popular religiosity. Is Our Lady of Guadalupe the Mother of Jesus, or is she Tonantzin, the Aztec goddess, Mother of the Gods on whose pilgrimage site, the hill of Tepeyac, Our Lady of Guadalupe appeared?[61] In their hearts, and often quite openly, Latinas with Caribbean roots who pray to St. Barbara are identifying her, directly or indirectly, with Chango, the Yoruban God of Thunder. The hierarchy's decision to declare the story of St. Barbara a legend and the improbability that such a person ever existed is irrelevant to them.

58. Tom F. Driver, *Christ in a Changing World* (New York: Crossroad, 1981), 32-81.

59. See Isasi-Díaz and Tarango, *Hispanic Women,* 13–55.

60. John F. Baldovin, S.J., "The Liturgical Year: Calendar for a Just Community," in *Liturgy and Spirituality in Context,* ed. Eleanor Bernstein, C.S.J. (Collegeville: The Liturgical Press, 1990), 104.

61. Compare the difference in interpretation and explanation of Guadalupe between Elizondo and Lafaye. See Virgilio Elizondo, *La morenita* (Liguori, MO: Liguori Publications, 1981), and J. Lafaye, *Quetzalcoatl et Guadalupe* (Paris: Gallimard, 1974).

The history of Christianity shows that orthodox objections to syncretism have less to do with the purity of faith, and more with who has the right to determine what is to be considered normative and official. For the articulation of religious understandings, beliefs, and practices to be an act of liberation, it has to be an act of self-determination, not an attempt to comply with what the "official" church says, with what it considers to be orthodox. This is why *mujerista* theology does not shrink from claiming that the fusion of Christian, Amerindian, and African religious strands operative in the lives of Latinas may be good and life-giving.

Popular religiosity as a subculture pervades the lives of Latinas. Perhaps because of the precariousness of our lives, perhaps because our variety of Christianity is an intrinsic part of our culture, and because we are keenly aware of our culture since it is different from the dominant one, religion, religious thinking and practices, provide for us the moods and motivations operative in our day-to-day life. Questions of ultimate meaning, understandings of the divine and of ourselves and of our relationship to the divine are not matters for religion experts only. No, they are matters which preoccupy, touch, and affect everyone. "*Si Dios quiere,*" God willing, is not an empty phrase for us. The belief that the divine cares about us and participates in our lives is something very real for us, something constantly taken into consideration. There is no doubt for us that what we are able to accomplish is due to much hard work; but it is also a fact that God has had something to do with it, and due credit is given to the divine by fulfilling promises at any physical or monetary cost.[62]

The day-to-day acknowledgment of the role the divine plays in our lives as well as a firm belief in the ongoing revelation of God in the midst of and through the community of faith is what leads us to claim the lived-experience of Latinas as the source of *mujerista* theology. This belief continues the long tradition very much present in the Hebrew Scriptures that God's revelation happens in and through the history of Israel's people. Salvation history is not something different from what actually happened to the Jewish people. Salvation history *is* precisely what happened to them; it has to do with how they interpreted what happened to

---

62. One of my earliest memories has to do with fulfilling a promise my father had made to Our Lady of Charity, the title under which Mary is patroness of Cuba. During World War II my father tried to produce glucose from yucca starch. As a chemical engineer he knew that this could be done, but the process is an industrial secret and he had to start from scratch. To be sure he would succeed, he promised Our Lady of Charity a visit to her sanctuary by the whole family if she would help him, enlighten him in his research. He was able to get glucose from yucca starch, something needed and, therefore, profitable during the war. It was not until a few years later that he was able to keep the promise. We traveled over twelve hours by car and then walked up the hill on the top of which the sanctuary sits. Thus we all honored the divine intervention in the life of my family. I was about seven years old at that time.

them, with the role that God played in their struggles and accomplishments. Our claiming Latinas' lived-experience as the source of our theology is firmly rooted in this biblical understanding of the revelation of God. Knowing that as Latinas we have indeed been created in the image and likeness of God, trusting that our struggle to be faithful to our understandings of the divine make us worthy members of the Christian community of faith, we believe that God's revelation happens in the day-to-day living of Latinas.

Spanish: "The Language of the Angels"[63]

The Spanish language functions for Latinas not only as a means of communication but as a means of identification. Spanish has become "the incarnation and symbol" of our whole culture, making us feel that here in the U.S.A. we are one people, no matter what our country of origin is. The Spanish language identifies us by distinguishing us from the rest of society. It gives us a specificity that we need to be a certain kind of people within a culture not our own.[64]

White Americans are willing to accept Latinos who are "white enough" as one of them when we become sufficiently middle-class and sufficiently "Anglicized." Many African Americans are also ready to claim black Latinos. But Latinas in general consider ourselves neither white nor black:[65]

> ...for Hispanics the prime identifier is not color, but language, and so the Hispanic, whether black or white, tends to think that those who speak Spanish are 'his [*sic*] people' no matter what their color, while those who

---

63. This is exactly what my grandmother always said!

64. A few years ago I arrived at the very southern tip of Manhattan for a 7 PM meeting. I could not find the building where we were to meet, so I decided to park my car and find someone who could help me. Since there are no homes in that area, at that hour of the evening it is not unusual to see not a single soul. Finally I saw a man who was emptying trash cans in the back entrance of one of the huge office buildings. I approached him a little apprehensively and asked him for directions. Apologetically, he started in a very broken English to tell me he did not understand me. I stopped him by repeating the question in Spanish. His eyes lit up, he squared his shoulders, and told me he did not know where that building was. He then looked into my eyes and said, *"Venga aca, usted es cubana?"* (Listen here, are you Cuban?) When I told him I was, he became all the more helpful. Talking to me as you do to an old friend, he let me know that the doorman around the corner was also Cuban and that he surely knew the answer to my question. Without thinking much, because he spoke Spanish and was a Cuban, I put aside all the cautions I should have been taking and asked him if he thought my car was safe there. *"No hay problema, no hay problema"* (No problem, no problem). I smiled broadly, thanked him, and went to get directions from the Cuban doorman, whom I was sure would help me because I was his *compatriota* (compatriot), and he did!

65. I am not claiming that there is not racism in our culture, and certainly in our countries of origin, skin color, though dealt with in a different way from the way it is operative in the U.S.A., plays a role in societal stratification.

speak English (whether black or white) are 'the others'. For Hispanics the 'Anglo' is not the Anglo-Saxon, but the Anglophone.[66]

The Spanish language for us Latinos here in the U.S.A. has become "the bearer of identity and values."[67] Our attachment to it is such that even those Latinos born and raised in the U.S.A. who understand a little Spanish and can speak only a few words insist on saying that they do know Spanish. Since the importance of Spanish for Latinas is not so much to be able to communicate but to be able to identify each other, grammatical and pronunciation correctness is totally secondary. For us Spanish is indeed a social construct and, therefore, we do not use Spanish to exclude from our communities those who know little Spanish or use it improperly.[68]

In a market study done in 1981 for the SIN National Spanish Television Network, 90 percent of Latinos claimed they knew at least enough Spanish to get by. Only 1 percent of Latinos said they knew only English. Twenty-three percent said they knew only Spanish, 20 percent said they knew Spanish and enough English to get by, 47 percent consider themselves bilingual, and 9 percent know English and enough Spanish to get by. Based on data gathered by the 1980 census and considering that any undercounting probably happened among undocumented Latinos who speak mostly Spanish, one can conclude that only in 10 percent of Latino homes is Spanish not used.[69]

The numbers of those who speak Spanish and use it at home go hand in hand with our sense of national allegiance: 88 percent consider themselves Latinos, 46 percent claiming they are Latino first, American second, and 42 percent saying that they are equally Latino and American. They also are in line with the 89 percent that either agree or strongly agree with the statement, "we should pass on to our children a sense of belonging to our religious and national tradition."[70]

The study also presented an open-ended question asking for the aspect of Latino culture and traditions that we feel is most important to preserve. Eighty one percent mentioned the Spanish language as the most important — 83 percent of Puerto Ricans, 77 percent of Mexicans, and 95 percent of Cubans.[71]

66. Vidal, "Popular Religion among the Hispanics," 257.

67. Ibid.

68. See Eldin Villafañe, "The Socio-Cultural Matrix of Intergenerational Dynamics: An Agenda for the 90s," *Apuntes* Year 12, no.1 (Spring 1992): 13–20.

69. Justo González, *The Theological Education of Hispanics* (New York: The Fund for Theological Education, 1988), 12. Notice that there is a difference between "knowing" Spanish (the question investigated by the SIN National Spanish Television Network), and "using" Spanish in the home (the focus of the 1980 U.S.A. Census study used by González).

70. *Spanish USA — A Study of the Hispanic Market in the United States*, by Yankelovich, Skelly & White, Inc. (New York: Yankelovich, Skelly & White, 1981), 7, 16.

71. The same table in this study gives a quick handle on what Latinos consider the most valuable elements of our culture which we wish to preserve. Here they are in descending

Yet maintaining usage of and fluidity in Spanish is no easy task for Latinas. In the U.S.A. the governing principle in this regard continues to be "one population—one language...[and it] has assumed overtones of moral, social, and psychological normalcy."[72] The recent successful attempts in several parts of the U.S.A. where Latinos are numerous to pass a law declaring English *the* official language make this obvious. At the same time this insistence on having an English-as-official-language law indicates that Spanish is used widely in certain states in the U.S.A. Laws will not stop Latinas from using Spanish, because it is a social construct that has enormous importance in maintaining our identity, and we will do everything in our power to continue to speak it and teach it to our children. We are aware that as an oppressed group we are not able to preserve the use of Spanish because we are "limited in being able to establish and control institutions of language monitoring, language ideologization [*sic*] and, most particularly, language use via the establishment and control of significant political and economic bases of...[our] own."[73] It is our hope, however, that the constant flow of new Spanish speaking people into the U.S.A. plus the frequent return to their country of origin of Latinos will help us preserve Spanish.

Latino Ethnicity: Social Construct

In these two first chapters I have analyzed the main elements of Latino ethnicity. Our ties with Latin America and the Spanish speaking Caribbean, *mestizaje*, our multilayered oppression and struggle for survival, popular religiosity, the insistence on speaking *español*, Spanish, and our *proyecto histórico*—all of these are pieces that together constitute and shape Latinas' ethnicity. It is the intersection and interplay of all of these elements that give us our pecularities and distinctiveness as Latina Women. In other words, the shared cultural norms, values, identities, and behaviors that form the core of our ethnicity are linked to these six elements we have explored.

At the same time we know that these cultural norms, values, identities, and behaviors are irreversibly impacted by the prejudice and discrimination to which we are subjected in this society.[74] This means that the oppression we suffer as Latinas has become an integral part of our ethnicity—of Latino ethnicity—and, therefore, it impacts every aspect of our lives as does our daily struggle to survive.

---

order of importance: care of and respect for elders, music, religion, family/commitment to family, art/literature, food and beverages, love for life/know how to enjoy life, happy people, holidays/celebrations.

72. Joshua A. Fishman, "Language Maintenance," in *Harvard Encyclopedia of Ethnic Groups*, ed. Stephan Thernstrom (Cambridge, MA: The Belknap Press of Harvard Univ. Press, 1980), 631.

73. Ibid., 636.

74. Nelson and Tienda, "The Structuring of Hispanic Ethnicity: Historical and Contemporary Perspectives," in *Ethnicity and Race in the U.S.A.—Toward the Twenty-First Century*, ed. Richard D. Alba (London: Henley Routledge & Kegan Paul, 1985), 53.

◪ SÍNTESIS DEL CAPÍTULO 2: Religiosidad Popular, Hispana y Proyecto Histórico: Elementos de la Etnicidad de las Latinas.

En este capítulo examinamos las esperanzas y expectativas de las latinas las cuales están arraigadas en nuestra realidad cotidiana y esperamos den frutos en este mundo. Lo que llamamos nuestro proyecto histórico es la realidad que nos esforzamos por construir y elemento vital en la construcción social de nuestra identidad latina. Otros dos elementos importantes de nuestra identidad y realidad latina que analizaremos en este capítulo son la religiosidad popular y el uso del español.

El proyecto histórico

El proyecto histórico de las mujeres latinas es nuestra liberación y lo que específicamente necesitamos hacer para lograrlo. Aunque este proyecto histórico no es un plan detallado, sí es un proyecto lo suficientemente concreto como para forzar a las personas a escoger, a declararse en favor o en contra. Lo que decimos aquí sobre nuestro proyecto histórico no es sólo una explicación sino también una estrategia que tiene como fin ayudar a moldear nuestra lucha cotidiana por sobrevivir al igual que nuestra identidad como comunidad. Lo que aquí decimos del proyecto histórico de las mujeres latinas está basado en nuestra experiencia y es la meta que nos esforzamos por alcanzar.

El proyecto histórico se basa en un entendimiento de la salvación y la liberación como dos aspectos de un mismo proceso histórico. La historia de la salvación se refiere al actuar de Dios—creación, encarnación, redención—tanto como a la repuesta humana a este actuar de Dios. Para nosotras las latinas la salvación tiene que ver con nuestra relación con Dios la cual no existe si no amamos a nuestro prójimo. Nuestra relación con Dios afecta todo los aspectos de nuestras vidas. Para nosotras el proceso salvífico se da en la historia y está intimamente relacionado con nuestra liberación.

Liberación para las latinas significa ser sujetos de nuestra historia y tener lo que necesitamos para vivir y poder realizarnos plenamente como seres humanos. Para las latinas la llegada del reino de Dios, la salvación y la liberación son una misma cosa. Nosotras creemos que nuestra labor en favor de la justicia y la paz es indispensable para la realización plena del reino de Dios.

La llegada del reino de Dios está relacionada con nuestra realidad diaria la cual requiere que denunciemos la injustica a la vez que anunciamos el futuro por el que luchamos. La denuncia como parte de nuestro proyecto histórico nos llama a analizar profundamente las estructuras que nos oprimen y a criticar y censurar a quienes mantienen estas estructuras y se benefician con ellas. Pero la denuncia también tiene que llevarnos a repudiar estas estructuras opresivas, no a que aspiremos a participar en ellas, a beneficiarnos con ellas. Esta insistencia en la denuncia hace que uno de los elementos del punto de partida de la teología mujerista sea la crítica social.

Denunciar sin anunciar el futuro que queremos y necesitamos es irresponsable. Es más, para la que denuncia sea efectiva tiene que ir acompañada del anuncio de la meta por la que luchamos. El anunciar en medio de la opresión ya es una manera efectiva de luchar por nuestra liberación.

El proceso de liberación tiene tres apectos o niveles los cuales no se deben confundir. Cada aspecto mantiene su especificidad, cada uno es distinto del otro pero afecta a los demás, ninguno está presente sin que lo estén los otros. Estos tres aspectos del proceso de liberación son elementos del proyecto histórico. Las latinas nombramos estos tres niveles o aspectos del proceso de liberación "libertad," "comunidad de fe" y "justicia."

"Libertad" aquí se refiere a nuestra lucha por ser sujetos históricos. En esta lucha las latinas tenemos que tener cuidado y no creer que los cambios estructurales y la liberación personal se pueden separar. Lo "personal" para nosotras no excluye a otros ni es necesariamente privado. Este sentido de "libertad" nos ayuda a las latinas a comprender el papel que nosotras mismas jugamos en nuestra propia opresión a la vez que nos llama a luchar para poder ser nosotras las que determinemos quiénes somos y qué hacemos.

La "libertad" como aspecto del proceso de liberación se desarrolla a nivel sicológico tanto como social. Los dos obstáculos principales para que las latinas logremos "libertad" son la apatía y el miedo. Al sabernos un grupo oprimido dentro del país más rico del mundo, las latinas sentimos que la lucha es tan ardua y dura que nos descorazonamos y nos volvemos apáticas. Nuestra meta—nuestra liberación—nos parece tan lejana que la apatía surge como protección en contra de la frustración.

Aquellas de nosotras que logramos no sentirnos frustradas y apáticas tenemos que luchar en contra del miedo: miedo a fracasar, no tanto al no lograr lo que queremos, sino miedo a que vamos a aceptar el *status quo* y de que acabaremos dedicándonos a ver cómo nos podemos beneficiar con las estructuras opresivas de la sociedad.

Para poder contrarrestar la apatía y el miedo, las mujeres latinas tenemos que continuar elaborando nuestra visión del futuro a la vez que vamos articulando los detalles de cómo lograr lo que queremos. Necesitamos ser bien concretas para saber cómo es que cada una puede participar en convertir nuestra visión en realidad.

"Comunidad de fe" como aspecto del proceso liberador de las latinas tiene como eje central nuestra íntima relación con lo divino. Esta relación se basa no sólo en nuestra creencia en que Dios está con nosotros en nuestro caminar cotidiano sino también en que nosotras nos relacionamos con Dios de la misma manera que nos relacionamos con nuestros seres queridos.

Discutimos con Dios, peleamos con Dios, nos contrariamos con Dios, le estamos agradecidas a Dios, adulamos a Dios, hasta recompensamos a Dios. Sabemos que el pecado daña esta íntima relación con Dios a la vez que afecta negativamente a nuestras comunidades. Para nosotras el pecado no es tanto un desobedecer como un no ocuparnos de los demás, un no ser responsables por los demás por quienes somos y por lo qué hacemos.

El análisis de la realidad opresiva que sufrimos nos puede ayudar a entender mejor que el pecado tiene siempre un elemento social porque afecta a otros. Y entendemos que el pecado social es el pecado encarnado en estructuras que explotan y oprimen, y que tenemos que luchar en contra de dichas estructuras.

Las latinas tenemos que actualizar nuestro sentido comunitario trabajando en grupos y organizaciones que tengan una orientación práctica y que se ocupen de apoyarnos a nivel personal tanto como de organizar proyectos comunitarios. Es importante que no perdamos el tiempo en organizaciones y grupos cuyo enfoque sea lo espiritual o la acción en favor de la justicia, o lo personal o lo comunitario. Tenemos que aceptar el hecho de que aunque nuestras creencias religiosas son la mayor parte de las veces la motivación principal para nuestro trabajo comunitario, desgraciadamente no podemos contar mucho con la ayuda de las iglesias. Por el contrario vamos a tener, de nuevo, que depender de nosotras mismas y a lo mejor, de las pocas organizaciones nacionales de latinas que dicen estar comprometidas con la lucha por la liberación.

Nuestras "comunidades de fe" tienen que ser ecuménicas. Tenemos que abrazar el sentido ecuménico de las latinas de la base que se relacionan con diferentes iglesias sin experimentar contradicciones al hacerlo. La base del ecumenismo tiene que ser la lucha por la liberación y no la uniformidad de creencia. Nuestro ecumenismo tiene que tomar en consideración la religiosidad popular que muchas compartimos a pesar de pertenecer a diferentes iglesias.

Por último, nuestras "comunidades de fe" tienen que desarrollar su propio estilo de liderazgo. Necesitamos lideres comunitarios que reconozcan y utilicen los dones de las latinas, líderes que posibiliten y capaciten en vez de convertirse con gran facilidad y rapidez vertiginosa en caciques.

El tercer aspecto de la lucha por la liberación es la "justicia." La justicia es una virtud que tiene que ver principalmente con la manera en que actuamos y la manera como las instituciones sociales están organizadas, las prioridades que tienen y la forma en que usan sus recursos. La "justicia" como aspecto de la lucha por la liberación tiene que ver con mucho más que con proveer a las necesidades básicas de todos los miembros de la sociedad. La verdadera "justicia" no es utilitaria insistiendo en la felicidad de sólo la mayoría de la gente; la verdadera "justicia" no es sólo cuestión de "a cada uno de acuerdo con sus necesidades", como dice el dictamen marxista.

En la teología mujerista la "justicia" se entiende como requisito del cristianismo; para nosotras la "justicia" le permite a cada persona y requiere de cada una el participar en decidir qué es lo que necesita la comunidad para mantener y promover la vida al igual que en la producción de esos bienes; la "justicia" tiene que ver con el derecho de las latinas a participar plenamente en todos los aspectos de la sociedad, incluyendo las iglesias. La "justicia" es la lucha por el bien común. El bien común no se puede lograr a costa de nadie ni puede poner los derechos individuales de las personas por encima de la participación de todos—en especial de los pobres— en la sociedad. El éxito del bien común se debe juzgar de acuerdo a los derechos que en él tienen los más oprimidos. El bien común tiene que ver no sólo con las necesidades físicas sino también con lo que le permite a las personas expandir sus horizontes: la educación, la música, el arte.

La "justicia" en la que la teología mujerista insiste, requiere una opción preferencial por las latinas que encuentre expresión en una solidaridad efectiva con nosotras. Dicha solidaridad requiere que quienes se benefician de las estructuras presentes usen sus privilegios para lograr los cambios que se necesitan para que florezca la "justicia." Aquellas que se hacen solidarias con la causa de las latinas nos pueden ayudar a no caer en la tentación de creer que sí se puede lograr la "justica" dentro de las presentes estructuras; quienes se hacen solidarios con nuestra causa nos pueden ayudar a deshacernos del "opresor internalizado" que a veces nos hace ser vengativas desfigurando nuestro proyecto histórico.

La religiosidad popular como elemento de la teología mujerista

El punto de partida para el estudio de la religiosidad popular de las latinas es nuestra lucha cotidiana por sobrevivir. Para nosotras la religiosidad popular es parte de nuestra auto–identificación; nuestra insistencia en valorar la religiosidad popular es parte de la lucha por mantener nuestras propias características y peculiaridades. Es gracias a la religiosidad popular que la religión continúa siendo elemento central de la cultura latina a pesar del descuido de nuestras comunidades por las iglesias en este país.

El cristianismo que es, sin dudas, la religión de la vasta mayoría de las latinas, no es el cristianismo "oficial" ni tiene necesariamente a las instituciones eclesiásticas como punto central de referencia. Nuestro cristianismo se basa en la religión que trajeron los conquistadores españoles a América Latina, un cristianismo que fue parte del violento proceso de la conquista y que ayudó a aniquilar el mundo y la cosmología de los nativos. El cristianismo que se convirtió en parte integral de la cultura latina usaba la Biblia en forma muy limitada haciendo, por el contrario, énfasis en las tradiciones y costumbres de la iglesia española. El cristianismo de las latinas hoy en día incluye también las tradiciones religiosas de los esclavos africanos al igual que las de las culturas amerindias. Es precisamente de la mezcla del cristianismo español del siglo XVI, las religiones africanas de los esclavos y las creencias y prácticas religiosas de las culturas amerindias que surge la religiosidad popular latina.

Por religiosidad popular entendemos las experiencias, creencias y ritos que grupos marginalizados crean, asumen y desarrollan como respuesta a situaciones socio-culturales específicas, y que se distancian de las instituciones eclesiásticas y los grupos dominantes de la sociedad tratando de encontrar acceso a Dios y a la salvación lo cual no creen que puedan lograr a través de las iglesias "oficiales" y de la sociedad.

La religiosidad popular de las latinas tiene cinco características. 1) Es una subcultura religiosa ya que es una manera de pensar y actuar no de algunos individuos sino de todo un grupo de personas. 2) Los ritos que se usan se basan mayormente en tradiciones católicas, tales como los sacramentales, que la iglesia "oficial" considera secundarias. 3) La religiosidad popular es sincrética ya que le da a prácticas religiosas católicas significados que vienen de otras religiones. 4) Hay prácticas "oficiales" que se reinterpretan dándoles otros significados. 5) Todas estas conductas se transmiten como parte de la cultura latina.

La teología mujerista considera que la religiosidad popular es uno de los elementos más creativos y originales de nuestra cultura y de nuestra herencia y que es uno de los elementos que más nos anima en la lucha por la liberación. La religiosidad popular es una fuente importante de la teología mujerista porque es un sistema de valores e ideas y de prácticas simbólicas representadas por medio de ritos y materializados en imágenes visuales que relaciona a las latinas con lo divino y que se origina en gran parte debido a nuestra marginalización. Pero el que no sea oficial no quita el que la religiosidad popular se deba de mirar a través del lente de la liberación. Como teólogas mujeristas reconocemos que la religiosidad popular tiene sus fallas y ambigüedades al igual que la tienen otras formas culturales del catolicismo y el cristianismo. Reconocemos que algunos de los elementos de la religiosidad popular son opresivos para las latinas. Pero por otro lado reconocemos el papel evangelizador que ha jugado la religiosidad popular y el rol tan importante que tiene en preservar nuestra cultura.

Otro papel importante de la religiosidad popular para las latinas es que nos ayuda a experimentar lo sagrado en lo cotidiano, en lo ordinario y corriente de nuestras vidas. Es la religiosidad popular lo que hace posible la no–desacralización de nuestra cultura. Son las prácticas de la religiosidad popular las que nos permiten a las latinas estar conscientes de lo sagrado en todos los aspectos de nuestras vidas: tanto en lo público como en lo privado, tanto en el orden personal como en el social.

Sin embargo, las iglesias "oficiales" en vez de considerar la religiosidad popular como algo positivo o la denuncian y trabajan activamente en contra de ella o buscan maneras de purificarla, de "bautizarla", aceptando sólo esos elementos que se pueden reconciliar con el cristianismo "oficial". Pero no importa cuánto han tratado, las iglesias "oficiales" no han podido hacer que el pueblo latino en general y en particular las mujeres latinas dejen de recurrir a Santa Bárbara—identificada con Changó, dios yoruba del trueno y el relámpago en la lucha diaria; o que sea en Guadalupe—identificada con la diosa azteca Tonantzín, en quien piensan cuando piensan en la divinidad.

El español: el idioma de los ángeles

El español funciona para las latinas no sólo como medio de comunicación sino también como medio de identificación. El idioma español se ha convertido en este país en símbolo de nuestra cultura, haciendo posible que sintamos que somos un solo pueblo aquí en los EE.UU. El español nos identifica y nos distingue del resto de la sociedad. Nos da la especificidad que necesitamos para sobrevivir como grupo dentro de una cultura que no es la nuestra. Los que hablan o saben usar el español son los nuestros; los que no lo hacen son "los otros". El español es portador de nuestra identidad y de nuestros valores. Y es por eso que lo importante no es tanto que nos podamos comunicar en español como que lo reclamemos como parte de nuestra identidad.

Es precisamente por ésto que hay tanta oposición al uso del español en esta sociedad. La clase dominante entiende que el uso del español es elemento importantísimo en la construcción social de nuestra identidad latina. Sabemos que nos es muy difícil mantener el español ya que no podemos influenciar las decisiones sobre el uso del español ni la ideología lingüística de este país, ni tenemos los medios económicos y políticos para insistir en el uso de nuestro idioma en el ámbito público. Pero confiamos en que la constante llegada a los EE.UU. de nuevos inmigrantes hispano–parlantes y nuestras frecuentes visitas a nuestros países de origen nos ayude en la lucha por preservar el español.

La etnicidad latina como construcción social

En estos dos primeros capítulos hemos analizado seis elementos principales de nuestra etnicidad latina: nuestros lazos con América Latina y el Caribe, el mestizaje, nuestra opresión y la lucha por sobrevivir, la religiosidad popular, el español y nuestro proyecto histórico. Es la interacción entre estos elementos lo que constituye y le da forma a la identidad latina aquí en los EE.UU. En otras palabras, estos elementos están relacionados con las normas culturales, los valores, las identidades y las formas de comportamiento que son el corazón de nuestra etnicidad. Pero también sabemos el impacto negativo que tienen el prejuicio y la discriminación a que estamos sometidos en esta sociedad sobre nuestra etnicidad. Ésto quiere decir que la opresión que sufrimos por ser latinas es parte integral de la etnicidad latina y, por lo tanto, es algo que impacta todos los aspectos de nuestras vidas. Nuestra esperanza está en que también impacte nuestras vidas nuestra lucha cotidiana por la liberación.

CHAPTER 3

Mujerista Theology's Methods: Understandings and Procedure

BEGINNING AN ARTICULATION of *mujerista* theology and ethics with an explanation of Hispanic Women's ethnicity indicates the significance of our everyday world, how we understand and describe our bodily and material existence as Hispanic Women for this enterprise. That social locality is central to *mujerista* theology is consistent with our insistence on the lived-experience of Hispanic Women as the source of our theology, which calls for a theological method that not only explicitly identifies such experience but also presents it as unmediated as possible. Likewise important is the commitment of *mujerista* theology to provide – to be – a platform for the voices of Hispanic Women. Such requirement and commitment have led to an exploration of the social sciences to find understandings and methods that will not objectify us and our experience, that will not ultimately discard it, but rather will enable us to gather our lived-experience, to explore it and present it to others with integrity.

This chapter presents a mosaic of *mujerista* theology's methods, a mosaic that will be seen in its totality only if one first notices and studies the pieces. First, we present an overview of the main sociological considerations that ground our method. A brief exposition of ethnomethodology – a critique of professional social sciences that focuses on the particularities of the persons being investigated – follows. Then comes an analysis of the role of *mujerista* theologians as researchers. Two qualitative research methods (ethnography and meta-ethnography) used to gather the voices and lived-experiences of Hispanic Women are then explained.

The chapter ends by arguing that *mujerista* theologians must present in our writings particular voices from the communities in which our theology is rooted. Otherwise we will run the risk either of objectifying grassroot Hispanic Women by talking about "them" and for "them," or we will speak exclusively for and by ourselves instead of providing a forum for the theological voice of our communities. Only if *mujerista* theology is a theological discourse that serves as a platform for oppressed Hispanic Women's voices can it claim to be a liberative praxis.

Sociological Methods and Theories

Precisely because of the absence of Hispanic Women's voices from theological discourses, our lives, our understandings, and meanings are what *mujerista* theology seeks to bring to light. But as important as bringing them to light is the way in which this is done. Often we have seen the experiences of other marginalized groups, including Hispanics, molded to fit into the accepted formats of theological discourse. We believe this has led to distortions that have resulted in new ways of silencing these groups, such as using their experiences as examples to illumine answers to questions determined by those who control the systems, while never allowing the marginalized groups to pose the questions. To avoid this, when considering what method to use in elaborating *mujerista* theology, we have kept in mind two things. First, the moral agency of Hispanic Women has to be the determining factor in our methodological considerations. Therefore, second, though we understand the elaboration itself of *mujerista* theology to be a liberative praxis, *mujerista* theology as a discourse cannot be considered more important than Hispanic Women's development as agents of our own lives and of our own history.

In struggling to maintain Hispanic Women as agents and subjects, instead of making them into objects, *mujerista* theologians discovered that we needed the voices of Hispanic Women themselves to be present in the theological discourse. These voices do not claim to be representative. Neither are they to be understood as examples of a worldview or perspective. We believe that the voices of particular Hispanic Women have validity in themselves and that without claiming to be representative they point to the reality of all Hispanic Women because they make our reality more understandable. Instead of attempting to present a universal voice, our attempt has been to point to the universal by being as specific as possible. Just as radical immanence is a different way of understanding what up to now has been called transcendence, so, too, the more specific and particular the voices we present in *mujerista* theology, the more they encompass the reality of all Hispanic Women.

But we realized this was not enough when we saw that no matter how faithfully we present specific Hispanic Women's voices, there are always numerous mediations that tend to muffle them. We also had, first of all, to investigate and understand—an ongoing process that we do not think will ever end—who we are, how we understand ourselves and elaborate meaning for ourselves. Understanding our Hispanic-ness, our ethnicity, as a social construct and identifying the key elements in it has helped us to grasp better our world and the situation of oppression in which Hispanic Women live. The second element has to do with the dialogic relationship those of us conducting the research and doing the writing of *mujerista* theology have established with the Hispanic Women whose voices we include in our discourse. Furthermore, a very important role here also is the role our religious understandings and practices play in *mujerista* theology.

Third, we have worked with the women whose voices we include so that the process of gathering the voices helps them to understand better their daily struggle to survive. Our attempt has been not to turn them into "types" but to see them as they see themselves, as persons who seek to know the meaning of their lives out of their daily struggles.[1] One of our goals has been to enable the development of their moral agency not by analyzing their religious understandings and practices but rather by seeing how they construct those understandings and practices.

Our methods have had as their objective to help these women come to know themselves, to know what they think about questions of ultimate meaning, and how these questions are used in Hispanic Women's everyday struggle to survive in the midst of great oppression. One of our objectives has been to hold up our everyday religious practices and to value them. Grounding our methods has been the firm conviction that our task is not to present already fixed representations, "pretheorized reality."[2] On the contrary, our insistence on presenting the voices of Hispanic Women has been to destabilize the balance of power and knowledge that exists between Hispanics and the dominant groups in the U.S.A., and between Hispanic Women and women of the dominant groups in the U.S.A. Such destabilizing will make possible—at the same time that it is partially caused by—the critical consciousness and practice of Hispanic Women.[3]

Gathering and presenting their voices allows Hispanic Women to be subjects of their own history, to see and present themselves as moral agents with a critical consciousness. It also makes it possible for them to understand and to present to others "powerful and insightful commentaries on the social order" that are embedded in their self-disclosing discourse. What they have shared in their narratives they understand as relating not just to themselves. They understand who they are and what they go through as something that goes beyond them, as something that has to do with the Hispanic community at large and with the whole of society.

1. Ruth Behar, "Rage and Redemption: Reading the Life Story of a Mexican Marketing Woman," *Feminist Studies* 16, no. 2 (Summer 1990): 229.
2. Ibid., 230.
3. Ibid., 231.

As we gather and present the voices of grassroot Hispanic Women, *mujerista* theologians have come to understand more clearly that the conceptual frameworks and epistemological presuppositions of the world of theology cannot hold the meaning of our daily lives and our concerns, knowledge, and understandings of the divine without distorting them. The old wineskins cannot hold new wine, but if by chance they do, the new wine will turn into vinegar!

Ethnomethodology

Ethnomethodology is a critique of professional social sciences initially proposed by Harvard social psychologist Harold Garfinkel. His primary criticism is that in professional sociology there is no "actor," but rather an ideal type, a dummy. Ethnomethodologists argue that it is difficult to find in sociological studies a real person with a biography and a history. The person to whom the studies keep referring is the creation of the social scientist, and therefore the self-understanding and everyday life of that person are absent from consideration. Ethnomethodology, on the other hand, is a theory of everyday life.

The basic presuppositions of ethnomethodology provide a pointed explanation of this "new" method that wants to be available for everyone to use in any discipline. The first presupposition is that people have and use "practical rationality," that is, people accomplish everyday life. Second, everyday life is reflexive, that is, it is contextual and self-descriptive, not explanatory. Reflexivity in this context refers to people's everyday creation of life and their holding each other accountable for appropriate participation in it. Reflexivity here has to do with the definition of the situation at hand, with its integrity in itself. The third presupposition is that social interaction can be indexed, it can be documented. These last two presuppositions are undergirded by an understanding of language — gestures, expressions, symbols, deportment — which create the social world.

Because of the centrality of description to ethnomethodology, the test of whether or not what one has observed corresponds to the self-understanding of the person being described is critical. In the case of the written accounts of *mujerista* theology, the test will be whether or not Hispanic Women can say, "Yes, this is my life, this is what I understand, this is what I mean."[4]

Ethnography

Mujerista theology recognizes and makes explicit the culture of the community out of which it arises, the Hispanic culture. It is appropriate,

---

4. See Harold Garfinkel, *Studies in Ethnomethodology* (Cambridge, England: Polity Press, 1984), 1–115. See also, Thomas Dale Watts, "Ethnomethodology: A Consideration of Theory and Research," *Cornell Journal of Social Relations* 9, 1 (Spring 1973): 99–115.

therefore, for those of us doing *mujerista* theology to avail ourselves of the techniques and principles of qualitative research which is concerned with coming to know by "watching people in their own territory and interacting with them in their own language, on their own terms."[5] Furthermore, because qualitative research "involves sustained interaction with the people being studied,"[6] it is a highly appropriate technique for *mujerista* theologians, who should be an integral part of the community out of which the theology they are formulating arises. Qualitative research is " 'grounded' in the everyday lives of people,"[7] and looks for explanations of "social or cultural events based upon the perspectives and experiences of the people."[8]

Of the different methods used in qualitative research, ethnography is one particularly well suited to doing *mujerista* theology. It is used by social sciences to describe and classify cultures by dealing with the distinctive characteristics and customs of those cultures. Ethnography is a way of conducting research that has as its foundation "the complex relationship between the researcher and his [*sic*] informants."[9] Ethnographical principles call for participation of the informants, of those who are being studied, in developing the method used. Ethnography calls for as little mediation as possible in describing and making known the culture in question.

Using ethnographic principles, *mujerista* theology presents the understandings and opinions of Hispanic Women, as much as possible, in their own words. To do this we conduct ethnographic interviews. These interviews are much more a conversation, a dialogue, than the standard survey form of questions and answers. In contrast to other kinds of interviews, ethnographical interviews have as their goal "to learn from people, to be taught by them,"[10] instead of just gathering information about them. This learning from the people occurs in the dialogic process that takes place between the researcher and the informants. Ethnographic interviews also make it possible to hear many voices instead of only the voices of the leaders of the community. They provide an opportunity for different members of the community to reflect on their experiences, to grasp better what they believe and how those beliefs impact their everyday lives. The interviews, therefore, are part of a liberative praxis; they are a consciousness raising

5. Jerome Kirk and Marc L. Miller, *Reliability and Validity in Qualitative Research*, Qualitative Research Methods 1 (Beverly Hills, Calif.: Sage Publications, 1988), 9.

6. Ibid., 12.

7. George W. Noblit and R. Dwight Hare, *Meta-Ethnography: Synthesizing Qualitative Studies*, Qualitative Research Methods 11 (Beverly Hills, Calif.: Sage Publications, 1988), 12.

8. Ibid.

9. James P. Spradley, *You Owe Yourself a Drunk—An Ethnography of Urban Nomads* (Boston: Little, Brown and Company, 1970), 7.

10. James P. Spradley, *The Ethnographic Interview* (New York: Holt, Rinehart and Winston, 1979), 4.

experience for Hispanic Women not only because it gives them an opportunity for reflection but also because they are often a vehicle for Hispanic Women to develop their own voices. Without this voice-of-one's-own, Hispanic Women are not able to be agents of our own history. [11]

In doing *mujerista* theology I have conducted ethnographic interviews in two different settings. One is what the women who participated called "retreats," that is, reflection done in community during a weekend. The information gathered during these weekends has proved to be extremely rich. The women sparked and challenged each other to become more and more reflective and explicit about their experiences and understandings. These weekends have included celebrations as well as the development of strategies for dealing with problematic circumstances at home, in the workplace, or in the community at large. [12] I prefer this way of conducting ethnographic studies.

When this process has not been possible because of lack of money or time, the interviews have been conducted individually in the homes of the Hispanic Women or wherever they have chosen. In these one-on-one interviews, as in group interviews, I have freely mixed techniques used for focused interviews, free story interviews, case studies, and life histories. Because I have an ongoing relationship with most of the Hispanic Women whose voices are heard in the studies I have done, they themselves have provided me with extensive information about their life histories and their process of socialization. The fact that I have worked with them, that we have engaged in praxis together, has helped me to comprehend better their religious understandings, and to see how those understandings motivate them and are rooted in their actions.

Given the great variety among Hispanic Women, I had to make sure that the group of Hispanic Women chosen for this study were generally representative of the total population. [13] Therefore, I have included in the sampling not only Hispanic Women I know and have worked with, but also Hispanic Women from communities in areas of the United States where I have been only marginally involved. I have interviewed Hispanic Women

11. Ethnographic interviews are only one of the tools used by *mujerista* theology. Observation, studies of traditional religious understandings and beliefs, studies in comparative religions—all of these are also tools used by *mujerista* theology.

12. I am referring here to the research done for this book and the one we did for the book Ada María Isasi-Díaz and Yolanda Tarango, *Hispanic Women: Prophetic Voice in the Church* (Minnesota: Fortress, 1992).

13. I never ask the Latinas I interview if they are Roman Catholic. However, that is my own faith tradition and the church in which I have worked in different ways for many years. Also, most of the women I have worked with in articulating a *mujerista* theology are Roman Catholic. On the other hand, most of my work in the decade of the 1980s was in ecumenical settings. This allowed me to come in contact with and learn from Hispanic Women who belong to Protestant denominations and also to Pentecostal churches.

with Mexican-American, Puerto Rican, and Cuban roots. Those I have worked with in articulating a *mujerista* theology come from different socio-economic strata and different degrees of formal schooling. They vary in age from the early 30s to the late 60s. Some are deeply involved in the church at the local, regional, and even national level. For others, the church is something, at best, marginal to their lives.

In order to ensure diversity in the sampling, I asked Hispanics working in different parts of the country, Hispanic Women with whom I do not have much in common or whose praxis is very different from mine, to choose persons from their communities for interviews. I have also gathered information from Hispanic Women whose point of view differs from mine and, indeed, I have incorporated that information if it is not an isolated opinion or experience and if it contributes to the struggle for liberation.

Beyond the gathering of information through interviews, ethnographers need to include in their cultural research social, economic, and political elements. Knowing about these different elements of culture helps the researcher understand what she is seeing and hearing;[14] they help her develop a critical awareness of the everyday reality of those whose culture is being studied.

Meta-Ethnography

Mujerista theology is shaped by the experience of a great variety of Hispanic Women with historical roots in different countries and in different socio-economic contexts. In order to bring together multiple ethnographic accounts, I use the basic understandings and techniques of meta-ethnography.[15] The meta-ethnography I use does not attempt to aggregate the information gathered in interviews but rather to interpret it. First I present the different accounts as they were actually voiced by Hispanic Women. I then attempt to bring together the single accounts by pointing out some of their commonalities and differences. This results in what meta-ethnography calls "knowledge synthesis," a synthesis which is both inductive and interpretative.[16]

This knowledge synthesis (or interpretative synthesis) uses an *emic* approach that is holistic and considers alternatives.[17] As used in *mujerista*

14. I have used the basic understanding of ethnography presented by Spradley and adapted it according to the values I hold as a *mujerista* theologian. See Spradley, *The Ethnographic Interview*, 3–16.

15. Though basically following the understandings and techniques explained in the works quoted in this section, I have also adapted meta-ethnography according to values I hold as a *mujerista* theologian.

16. Noblit and Hare, *Meta-Ethnography*, 16.

17. An emic approach is one that deals with various elements of a culture as they are related to each other rather than describing them in reference to a general classification decided in advance, outside the culture. The "emic" approach can best be understood in reference to

theology, an emic approach is one that does not judge the religious understandings and practices of Hispanic Women, nor does it try to make them fit into traditional theological frameworks or those articulated by others. *Mujerista* theology, then, is not only concerned with theological answers but, more importantly, asks theological questions from the perspective of Hispanic Women. This emic approach is holistic because it takes into consideration the cultural context of Hispanic Women. In other words, it does not present their religious understandings as something apart from their day-to-day living. In fact, in many ways, *mujerista* theology is an accomplishment of everyday life.

Finally, *mujerista* theology takes into consideration alternative interpretations of the understandings and experiences of Hispanic Women. There is no desire on the part of *mujerista* theology to present a single voice. On the contrary, we recognize that differences are part of the specific identity of each person. We consider differences to be a reality which enriches our theology, helping to keep it vital and viable.

What is the process used in meta-ethnography to arrive at knowledge synthesis? After the information is gathered from different persons over a certain period of time, the accounts of that information are read repeatedly, and commonalities and differences noted. Key ideas and understandings begin to emerge. The next step in the process is that of "translating the accounts into one another":

> Translations are especially unique syntheses, because they protect the particular, respect holism, and enable comparison. An adequate translation maintains the central metaphors and/or concepts of each account *in their relation to other key metaphors or concepts* in that account. It also compares both the metaphors or concepts and their interactions in one account with the metaphors or concepts and their interactions in the other accounts. [18]

In an attempt to avoid reductionism as much as possible, meta-ethnography, instead of combining accounts, uses analogies. For example, meta-ethnography does not posit that "Olivia and Lupe say the same thing or mean the same thing when they say..." Instead, meta-ethnography brings together what the two women say by indicating that "Olivia's experience seems to be similar to Lupe's except that..." Olivia's experience is not incorporated into Lupe's or vice versa but one is understood in comparison to the other. The differences between their experiences are not

---

the "etic" approach which is a generalized approach working to fit the different elements of a culture into general categories claiming to apply to all cultures. See *Oxford English Dictionary*, 2d ed., s.v. "emic" and "etic."

18. Noblit and Hare, *Meta-Ethnography*, 28–29. To avoid confusion, I will use quotation marks around the word "translation" when it refers to the process just identified.

erased but read together; the similarities they suggest create the themes which *mujerista* theology must take into consideration.

The purpose in doing "translations" for *mujerista* theology is to discover the themes that are important to the women, the ones about which they feel the strongest, which move them, which motivate them. In *mujerista* theology we refer to these themes as generative words.[19] They emerge from the world of Hispanic Women and express the situations they have to grapple with as well as their understanding of themselves in those situations. These generative words or themes are not only those "with existential meaning, and, therefore, with greatest emotional content, but they also are typical of the people."[20]

Because of the goal of *mujerista* theology and the value it places on community, the process of "translating" differs somewhat from the process used in other meta-ethnographies. The latter place both the similarities and differences found in the various individual accounts into an interpretative order which results in what is called a "lines-of-argument synthesis"[21] which has as its goal to interpret what each one of the persons involved is saying. In *mujerista* theology, however, the main interest and ultimate goal is a liberative praxis of Hispanic Women that uses interpretation but does not stop there. Another difference is that the interpretation used in arriving at generative themes in *mujerista* theology is not drawn from what one person says but rather from the lived-experience which makes up the daily life of Hispanic Women as a community.

From the very beginning, the mental constructs and experience of the person conducting the ethnographic investigation and the meta-ethnographic analysis play a significant role in the process. But at the point when the writer explains, from her own perspective, of course, similarities and differences, she becomes, in a very special way, a key element in the process. At this point the materials gathered are "translated" into the experiences and understandings of the writer and, one hopes, a reverse process also takes place. This is another reason why writers of Hispanic theologies should be immersed in their communities.

Mujerista Professional Theologians as Insiders

Mujerista professional theologians do theology from within our own communities.[22] Therefore, the understanding of researcher as insider is most

19. This is the name given to them by Freire. See Paulo Freire, *La educación como práctica de la libertad* (Madrid: Siglo Veintiuno de España Editores, S.A., 1976), 108–13.

20. Ibid., 109.

21. Ibid., 62–64.

22. Professional theologian is one of the kinds of Hispanic Women Theologians that *mujerista* theology recognizes, takes into consideration, enables, and welcomes. *Mujerista* theology also welcomes the grassroot Hispanic woman theologian, who does theology in the simple

appropriate for us. There are three important points to consider in this regard. First, the role of insider corresponds with the understanding that the doing of *mujerista* theology is a liberative praxis—a praxis that contributes to the liberation of *mujerista* professional theologians as well as to their community. In other words, as insiders, *mujerista* professional theologians also profit from their doing of theology.

Second, one of the characteristics of ethnographic methodology is the dialogic relationship between the researcher and those being researched. Dialogue is a horizontal relationship between equals which involves communication and intercommunication. Dialogue refers to a "relation of 'empathy' between two 'poles' who are engaged in a joint search,"[23] a joint effort to understand and articulate meaning. The professional theologian-researcher is one pole; the community being researched is the other. The joint search is a valuable strategy in our struggle for liberation as Hispanic Women. When the professional theologian is not herself part of the community—that is, when she has no vested interest in the liberation of those involved because her liberation is not connected to the liberation of others in the group—the dialogue becomes dishonest, the group being researched is objectified, and theology itself becomes a tool of oppression.[24]

Also, as insiders *mujerista* professional theologians are able to establish this dialogic relationship much more readily than an outsider could. Very often the research is made possible or enhanced by long-term relationships between the *mujerista* professional theologian and the community, or the research itself becomes the beginning of an ongoing relationship.[25] This has made it possible for me not only to listen intensely but also to share my own insights openly while conducting interviews.

But I have had to accept the fact that I am both an insider and an outsider in the community of Hispanic Women. I have struggled to distinguish what I hold in common with the respondents (because I am woman and Hispanic) from what is different, that is, class, age, role, degree of formal education, and so forth.[26] It is important to recognize that identities are

---

sharing of what happens in day-to-day life, who is gifted in analyzing and expressing the beliefs which ground her religious practices. A third "kind" of *mujerista* theologian includes those Hispanic Women who have some training in religious studies: catechists, pastoral workers, and ordained Hispanic Women in Protestant churches.

23. Paulo Freire, *Cultural Action for Freedom* (Cambridge: Harvard Educational Review, 1970), 45.

24. Ibid., 52.

25. This has happened to me repeatedly with the women I interviewed. I knew most of them before and I have continued to be their friend. Two of those whom I met for the first time during the research for the book have kept in contact with me, and we too have become friends.

26. Elizabeth Jameson, "Introduction," in *Insider/Outsider Relationships with Informants*, Working Paper No. 13 (University of Arizona: Southwest Institute for Research on Women, 1982): 3.

always complex and multifaceted, and, therefore, no researcher is ever totally an insider.

The third consideration has to do with factoring in the experience and understanding of a professional theologian-researcher who is more an insider than an outsider. Initially I tried to listen to everyone but myself. I soon realized that it would be impossible to stay away from my own experience. I realized that whether I wanted to or not, my voice would play a role and that I needed to listen to it instead of allowing it to operate surreptitiously. I came to understand that I had to pay attention to my own voice, to observe carefully and reflect methodically on my own experience as a Hispanic Woman working for many years with my own people. The challenge for me has been and will always be not to allow my experience and my understandings to become a sifter for the experiences and understandings of others. Two things have helped me avoid this. First of all, as an insider and because of the dynamics of liberative praxis, I accept seriously my responsibility to take back to the community, in a way that is meaningful to it and in a way that can be used as a tool for liberation, the understandings gained from the community.[27] If the community fails to recognize itself in the *mujerista* theology that I present, then it is obvious that I have manipulated and changed the voices of Hispanic Women instead of providing a platform for them. Second, I am eager to have the informants assess my work. I take their critique very seriously and I am committed to changing whatever they identify as not coming from them or as misrepresenting them.[28]

What can be done when the professional theologian is less an insider than an outsider? The less the professional theologian is an insider the more she must be immersed in and stand in solidarity with the community. In other words, she must allow herself to be deeply engaged by the community so that she can, as much as possible, come to understand the community from within. The difference between her context and that of the community will not disappear, but at least she may be better able to grasp the perspectives, understandings, and experiences of the community. This will lessen the likelihood of equivocation and will steer the writer away from erroneous understandings and explanations of the commonalities and differences among Hispanic Women.[29]

27. Elizabeth Jameson, "May and Me," in *Insider/Outsider Relationships with Informants*, Working Paper No. 13 (University of Arizona: Southwest Institute for Research on Women, 1982): 11.

28. Linda Light and Nancy Kleiber, "Interactive Research in a Feminist Setting: The Vancouver Women's Health Collective," in *Anthropologists at Home in North America* (Cambridge: Cambridge Univ. Press, 1981), 167–84. The authors report that the informants they dealt with demanded that they share their research notes!

29. Ada María Isasi-Díaz, "Solidarity: Love of Neighbor in the 1980s," in *Lift Every Voice: Constructing Christian Theologies from the Underside*, ed. Susan Brooks Thistlethwaite and Mary Potter Engel (San Francisco: Harper and Row, 1990), 31–40.

Why We Use Ethnography and Meta-Ethnography
in *Mujerista* Theology

Ethnography and meta-ethnography provide understandings and tech-niques that make it possible to discover, organize, present, and interpret the source of *mujerista* theology: the lived-experience of Hispanic Women. The reasons for using ethnography and meta-ethnography, then, are to be found in the reasons we have for placing this lived-experience at the center of our theological task.

Though the expression "lived-experience" might seem tautological to some, in the context of *mujerista* theology it refers not only to what has happened—what a person has endured or made happen—but to that ex-perience upon which she reflects in order to understand its significance and to value it accordingly.[30] Because of the centrality of religion in the day-to-day life of Hispanic Women, our understandings about the divine and about questions of ultimate meaning play a very important role in the process of giving significance to and valuing our experience. It is impera-tive for us, therefore, to comprehend better how religious understandings and practices impact our lives. In order to do this, we need to start from what we know—ourselves, our everyday surroundings and experiences.

In society the dominant understandings and practices that are considered as having important religious significance, the ones that carry weight and impact societal norms, arise from the experience of the dominant culture, class, race, and gender. Whether or not those people actually invest themselves in these understandings and practices, they abide by the under-standings, consciously or unconsciously. These are elements of the struc-tures that keep them in power. By using our lived-experience as the source of theology, Hispanic Women start from a place outside those structures, outside the traditional theology which is controlled by the dominant group. This gives us an opportunity to be self-defining, to give fresh answers, and, what is most important, to ask new questions.

For us who do *mujerista* theology it is essential to look at the questions being asked in theology.[31] Our task, in general, is not that of answering centuries-old questions from a different perspective without looking at the

---

30. Following Gramsci, I believe that action has a reflective quality. This assertion is very important for Hispanics because U.S.A. society tends to disregard our intellectual ability due to a certain lack of formal education. Following Gramsci I claim that Hispanic Women are organic thinkers and that *mujerista* theology, which is based on "the principles and problems raised by...their practical activity," is organic theology. See Antonio Gramsci *Prison Notebook*, ed. and trans. Quintin Hoare and Geoffrey Nowell Smith (New York: International Publishers, 1975), 6, 330.

31. As Rosaldo said, "What is needed...is not so much data as questions." M. Z. Rosaldo, "The Use and Abuse of Anthropology: Reflections on Feminism and Cross-Cultural Under-standing," *Signs* 5 (Spring 1980): 390.

questions themselves. Our task is not to use grassroot Hispanic Women's answers to old questions. This results in so-called "new" answers, which are most often nothing but reinterpretations of old answers, old answers with different words and different emphases, but basically within the parameters of the old answers. We consciously seek to avoid manipulating what grassroot Hispanic Women say to fit the parameters established by traditional questions and "old" answers.

For example, some Hispanic theologians give great importance to Scripture. Their goal is to present Jesus in such a way that the common folk can relate to him. Undoubtedly, the experience of Hispanics also plays a part in the hermeneutical work of these theologians. But in their work, the fact that the great majority of Hispanics relate very little to Jesus is never confronted. Instead, it is glossed over. This results, therefore, in a "new" emphasis on Jesus but never in new questions about Jesus or about how Jesus has been used by theologians and those with power in the churches to oppress and marginalize Hispanic Women.[32]

Mujerista theology, on the other hand, using the lived-experience of Hispanic Women as its main source, pushes out the old parameters and insists on new questions. In the case of Jesus, for example, we ask Why is it that the majority of Hispanic Women do not relate to Jesus? What does this mean about their understanding of the divine and the presence of the divine in their lives? *Mujerista* theology, then, often becomes a subversive act by enabling Hispanic Women to be suspicious of what we have not participated in defining.

A third reason for insisting on the lived-experience of Hispanic Women as a source for *mujerista* theology concerns our struggle for liberation and our sanity. As people who live submerged within a culture which is not ours, we often question our ability to comprehend "reality." In a very real way, as Hispanic Women, we have to "go out of our minds" in order to survive physically.[33] You can often hear Hispanic Women, especially older women, respond to "that's the way things are done here," with the phrase, *en qué cabeza cabe eso?*, in what kind of head does that fit? The reality that impacts our daily lives is often incomprehensible to us. What we say does not count; our cultural customs—dance, food, dress—are divorced from us and are commercialized; our values hardly count in society; our language is considered a threat, and millions have voted to have Spanish declared "not an official language"; our social reality is ignored.

---

32. See Virgilio Elizondo, *Galilean Journey: The Mexican-American Promise* (Maryknoll, NY: Orbis Books, 1983).

33. The first person I ever heard give this expression the interpretation I present here was Barbara Zanotti, who together with me and four other women participated in a dialogue with United States Bishops on the issue of the ordination of women in the Roman Catholic Church at the beginning of the 1980s.

As a people we continue to slip into poverty and to suffer from the social ills prevalent in the culture of poverty.

By using our lived-experience as the source of *mujerista* theology, we are trying to validate our world, our reality, our values. We are trying to reverse the schizophrenia that attacks our lives by insisting that who we are and what we do is revelatory of the divine. The lived-experience of Hispanic Women constitutes our common and shared reality. The "common sense" of Hispanic Women is not wrong. We can trust it to inform and guide our day-to-day life. *Mujerista* theology wants to affirm the worldview of Hispanic Women, shaped as it is by our lived-experience. For it is precisely in our worldview, in our paradigm of social reality, that we find "the categories and concepts through and by which we construct and understand the world,"[34] and understanding and constructing our world is a liberative praxis.

Finally, what much of the above implies is that the centrality of the lived-experience of Hispanic Women in *mujerista* theology is based on what liberation theologies call the epistemological privilege of the poor and the oppressed. This privilege is not based on the moral or intellectual superiority of the oppressed; it does not mean that Hispanic Women personally are better or more innocent or more intelligent or purer in our motivations. No, this epistemological privilege is based on the possibility the oppressed have

> to see and to understand what the rich and the powerful cannot see nor understand. It is not that their sight is perfect, it is the place where they are which makes the difference. Power and richness have a distortionary effect—they freeze our view of reality. The point of view of the poor, on the other hand, pierced by suffering and attracted by hope, allows them, in their struggles, to conceive another reality. Because the poor suffer the weight of alienation, they can conceive a different project of hope and provide dynamism to a new way of organizing human life *for all*.[35]

The lived-experience of Hispanic Women, therefore, brings a new dynamism to theology. It is our lived-experience which allows us to conceive another theological reality, a new theological reality, a liberative praxis, which we call *mujerista* theology.

The Ethnographic Interview

Because we understand *mujerista* theology to be an integral part of the process of the liberation of Hispanic Women, the first consideration in

---

34. Liz Stanley and Sue Wise, *Breaking Out: Feminist Consciousness and Feminist Research* (London: Routledge & Kegan Paul, 1983), 154. Also, Janet Silman "In Search of a Libertive Methodology," unpublished paper, May 7, 1988.

35. José Míguez Bonino, "Nuevas Tendencias en Teología," in *Pasos* 9 (1987): 22.

designing interviews conducted specifically for this study, was to use the kind of questions that allow people to reflect on their experience and to articulate it in their own words.[36] The main purpose of the interviews was to provide Hispanic Women with an opportunity to reflect on themselves as decision makers, to enable them to enhance their moral agency. The questions were designed to illumine their process of decision making, to investigate how they exercise their moral agency thus creating meaning in and through their lives. The same core, grand tour questions around the issue of moral decision making were asked of each of the interviewees. When at times one of the questions that had been planned did not elicit a response, I put that question aside and formulated another one or relied on one of the other prepared questions to elicit the information I hoped to gather. Supplementary structural and attributional questions helped in the interaction and clarified the meaning of the core questions or explored different topics brought up in the Hispanic Women's answers.

The first few questions sought to elicit general information about the self-understanding of the person being interviewed.[37] The important thing initially was to elicit enough information to indicate the areas which would need to be explored as the interview continued. I asked no questions about the general background of the person except in two instances (when those being interviewed had not participated in the previous research project I had conducted). With women whom I knew earlier, I did ask questions to update the information I had and I did call back some of the interviewees to ask for further details.

The next set of questions was conceived as "warm-up" questions and consisted of third person or hypothetical questions. These allowed the person being interviewed to voice her values, disvalues, criteria for decision making, and so forth. It also gave her an example of the kind of situation in her own life that the third set of questions would ask her to identify. Close to the time of the interview, several of the Hispanic Women interviewed, however, had been faced with very important decisions in their lives so the "warm-up" questions were not necessary at the beginning. They were used later in the interview to clarify issues brought up in the conversations.

The third set of questions formed the core of the research. These questions

36. These interviews together with the information gathered when we did the research for *Hispanic Women,* plus my own experience as a Latina, plus my observation of other Hispanic Women during many years, provide the information about Latinas' experience that is the source of this study.

37. With the women I did not know very well, I asked two questions used by Gilligan, "How would you describe yourself to yourself?" "If you had to describe the person you are in a way that you yourself would know it was you, what would you say?" Carol Gilligan, *In a Different Voice* (Cambridge: Harvard Univ. Press, 1982), 33. Gilligan does not present in toto the protocol she used in her research. Her questions are scattered throughout the text.

were designed to elicit values operative within the lives of Hispanic Women and in their decision making process. I asked them to describe two very important decisions they have had to make in their lives. Asking for more than one important decision making situation made it possible for me to begin to discern patterns instead of criteria and processes used only in an unusually serious situation.

In most cases, it was only toward the end of each interview that I used words such as *moral* and *immoral.* By then I felt I could risk using words that are not part of the women's daily vocabulary but are the regular ones used by "church people." The confidence we had established, as well as what I had already learned about the person I was interviewing, helped me ascertain whether she was giving me "catechism" answers or whether she was answering out of reflection on her own experience.[38]

The interviews were intense, lasting one to two hours (not a lengthy interview considering the concept of time in the Hispanic culture). The relative brevity of the interview was possible because, as I have indicated before, most of those interviewed had participated in a previous weekend long research project. Of course the success of this kind of in-depth interview depends to a large extent on the "rapport, mutuality of trust, and sense of reciprocity"[39] that is established between interviewer and interviewee. Since I have known the majority of the interviewees for a long time and all of them had previously shared at length with me, trust already existed between me and the Hispanic Women.

In order for interviews to yield valuable information there are four elements that must be taken into consideration: commitment, meaning, fluidity, and assimilation.[40] Commitment to the interaction determines the quality of what the interviewee shares. All along, the interviewee determines, consciously or unconsciously, how much to share, how candid to be in view of what impression she wants to make. For example, one of the interviewees asked me to send her the questions ahead of time so she could prepare "good answers." She was indeed committed to the interview but was too preoccupied with the impression she would make. When I came over to her house for the interview, she criticized her input in the previous process and told me she hoped she could do better this time. Her critique of herself, her willingness to see me for the interview during a holiday, her desire to "have the answers ready," and the fact that she

38. After the first couple of interviews I realized there was no point in asking the women whether they considered the decisions they had taken to be moral or immoral, good or bad. What I did mostly was to ask them "What comes to your mind when you hear the words moral or immoral?"

39. John B. Williamson, David A. Karp, and John R. Dalphin, *The Research Craft* (Boston & Toronto: Little, Brown and Company, 1977), 165.

40. Ibid., 168–75.

considered it a privilege that I wanted her to participate in this second project, all show her commitment to the interaction. Her concern also shows that participation in this project enhances her self-esteem. This is consistent with how she had felt when she participated in the last project. She insisted I use her real name when publishing the materials to which she had contributed.

The second element to be taken into consideration is meaning: "the ability of each party to understand the true intent of the other's actions and statements."[41] In intensive interviewing—the kind of interviewing done for this study—it is always possible to obtain clarification of what the interviewee is saying. Different ways of phrasing the questions, customizing them according to the clarification one needs from each of the interviewees, cannot, however, interfere with "equivalence of meaning." The questions asked should "have the same meaning to each interviewee, even though [they] may have to be phrased differently from interview to interview to achieve the goal."[42] The second set of questions in the interview was important in establishing equivalence of meaning. These questions helped the interviewees understand the meaning of the central set of questions in the interview, that is, the third set.

During the interview the conversation must be fluid. To achieve this, the interviewer has to adapt content and course of the conversation to meet both her need and the needs of the interviewee. The more the interview is in the mode of normal discourse, the more at ease the interviewee will be and the more she will be able to open up and respond according to her experience without being concerned about what the interviewer wants to hear.

The fourth element that has to be taken into consideration is assimilation. Since I personally interviewed the Hispanic Women whose voices are presented here, I had the opportunity "to assimilate or digest the results of one interview before undertaking another."[43] This made it possible for me to modify and mold my expectations of the interviews according to the information I was gathering from the different women. The interviewees themselves, one by one, helped me find the best possible way of describing and bringing together what I heard from them.

Intensive interviewing is an appropriate technique to use in doing *mujerista* theology because it provides an opportunity for the interviewees to articulate their lived-experience, to tell their own story in a way that makes them understand what being agents of their own history is all about. Whereas structured questionnaires tend to mold answers, intensive

41. Ibid., 168.
42. Ibid., 171.
43. Ibid., 173–74.

interviews allow for free flowing answers which are not unduly directed or shaped by the questions. Given that meta-ethnography is not a quantitative analytical tool, the limitations of intensive interviewing are not detrimental to the results needed for doing *mujerista* theology.

⌘ SÍNTESIS DEL CAPÍTULO 3: Métodos de la Teología *Mujerista:* Presupuestos Básicos y Procedimientos.

En los dos primeros capítulos de este libro hemos explicado cómo se sitúan socialmente las mujeres hispanas en los EE.UU., y cuáles son los elementos claves de lo que es ser mujer hispana en este país. Este enfoque refuerza nuestra insistencia en que la fuente de la teología mujerista es la experiencia vivida por las hispanas y de que nuestra teología tiene que ser un foro para sus voces. Esta manera de pensar nos ha llevado a explorar las ciencias sociales con el fin de encontrar métodos que no objetiven a las hispanas, a nuestra experiencia y nuestra realidad. Este capítulo presenta un mosaico de los métodos de la teología mujerista, un mosaico que sólo se puede apreciar si primero se estudian sus diferentes elementos.

Métodos y teorías sociológicas

Los métodos que hemos escogido para presentar las voces de las hispanas son aquellos que nos ayudan a no distorcionarlas en el empeño de que quepan en esquemas pre–establecidos. Lo más importante para nosotras ha sido el escoger métodos que amplíen la agencia moral de las hispanas y que no impidan, por lo tanto, el que la teología mujerista sea en sí una praxis liberadora. Fue ésto lo que nos llevó a descubrir que en nuestro discurso teológico teníamos que incluir las voces de las mujeres hispanas. Estas voces no se presentan como representativas ni como ejemplos de un punto de vista general de todas las hispanas. Creemos que las voces de estas hispanas tienen validez en sí y no necesitan ser representativas para señalar la realidad de las mujeres hispanas. En vez de presentar una voz universal hemos tratado de señalar lo universal siendo muy particulares y específicas. La teología mujerista argumenta que las voces de mujeres hispanas específicas encierran en sí la realidad de todas las hispanas.

El segundo punto a considerar es el diálogo que se establece entre las investigadoras y escritoras de la teología mujerista y las mujeres hispanas cuyas voces incluímos en nuestro discurso teológico. Tercero, al recopilar las voces de estas hispanas hemos tratado de ayudarlas a que entiendan mejor su lucha cotidiana por sobrevivir. Hemos tratado de no convertirlas en "tipos" sino de verlas como ellas se ven a sí mismas: como personas que reflexionan sobre sus luchas diarias para poder entender el significado de sus vidas. Para ayudarlas a desarrollar su auto–comprensión y auto–determinación lo que hemos hecho es tratar de entender cómo ellas entienden y construyen el significado de sus prácticas religiosas en vez de simplemente analizar esas prácticas. En esto nos ha ayudado el que nuestro fin no es encasillar el pensar religioso de las hispanas en teorías ya existentes. Al contrario: presentamos el entendimiento de estas hispanas para desestabilizar el balance que existe entre poder y conocimiento, entre los hispanos y el grupo dominante en esta sociedad, entre las mujeres hispanas y las mujeres del grupo dominante. Es por ésto que las voces que presentamos no sólo son una revelación personal y comunitaria de estas hispanas sino que también funcionan como comentario perspicaz y poderoso del presente orden social.

El proceso de recolectar y presentar las voces de las mujeres hispanas ha llevado a las teólogas mujeristas a comprender que las categorías conceptuales y las presuposiciones epistemológicas del mundo teológico tradicional ni abarcan el significado de las vidas de las mujeres hispanas ni sirven para explicar sin distorcionar nuestras preocupaciones al igual que lo que sabemos y entendemos de lo divino. Las viejas botas de vino no pueden usarse para vino nuevo, y si se usan ¡lo más probable es que estropeen el vino!

Etnometodología

La etnometodología critica a las ciencias sociales por que presentan usualmente no a un "actor" sino a una idealización tipológica, a un "muñeco". Esta crítica insiste en que es difícil encontrar en estudios sociológicos a personas reales con su propia historia y biografía. Las personas a quienes los estudios usualmente se refieren son la creación de los científicos sociales. En las consideraciones de estos científicos no están presente la realidad cotidiana de dichas personas ni la forma en que se entienden a sí mismas. La etnometodología, al contrario, es precisamente una teoría sobre la vida cotidiana.

Las presuposiciones básicas de la etnometodología son las siguientes: Primero, las personas tenemos y usamos una "racionalidad práctica" y es por eso que logramos vivir cada día. Segundo, la vida diaria es reflexiva, es contextual y descriptiva, no explicatoria. Lo reflexivo aquí se refiere al hecho de que la gente día a día crea la vida, el mundo y hace que los demás participen en él en forma responsable. Reflexivo también se refiere a cómo se define la situación presente y la integridad de esa situación en sí misma. Tercero, la interacción social se puede documentar.

Etnografía

En la teología mujerista usamos métodos cualitativos de investigación los cuales observan a la gente en su propio ambiente, interactúan con ellas en su propio idioma y de acuerdo a sus costumbres. Esta es una técnica muy apropiada para las teólogas mujeristas ya que consiste en una interacción prolongada con la gente que se está investigando y nosotras, las teólogas–investigadoras, somos parte integrante de ella. La investigación cualitativa, al igual que la teología mujerista se centra en la vida cotidiana de la gente y busca saber cuáles son las explicaciones que la misma gente tiene de eventos culturales y sociales.

Entre los diferentes métodos de investigación cualitativa el que más usa la teología mujerista es la etnografía. Las ciencias sociales usan la etnografía para describir y clasificar culturas, sus características peculiares y su costumbres. La etnografía depende en gran parte de la relación que se establece entre las investigadoras y las informadoras. Los informadores se supone que deben participar en el desarrollo de los métodos que son usados para el estudio de su cultura. La etnografía requiere la menor mediación posible entre lo que es y lo que se presenta en el estudio. Es por eso que la teología mujerista cita directamente y en forma extensiva las palabras de las mujeres hispanas.

Las entrevistas etnográficas que tenemos con las mujeres son más que preguntas y repuestas, más que una conversación, más que un diálogo. Nuestro fin no es el aprender acerca de las mujeres hispanas sino aprender de ellas, es dejar que ellas nos enseñen. Nuestro fin no es aprender sólo de las líderes de la comunidad sino el aprender de muchas mujeres hispanas.

Para que las entrevistas provean información valiosa tienen que considerarse cuatro elementos: Primero, tiene que haber compromiso por parte de todas por hacer posible, facilitar y alimentar la interacción estando dispuestas a compartir abiertamente, no tratando de decir lo que creemos que las demás quieren que digamos. Segundo, hay que saber entender lo que se dice y lo que se oye y hay que tratar de que todas las que participan entiendan igual las preguntas aunque para eso haya que repetirlas de diferentes maneras. Tercero, la entrevista tiene que ser una conversación fluída para que todas se sientan a gusto y puedan participar plenamente. Si se mantiene estrictamente el formato de pregunta–respuesta puede ser que las informadoras se sientan interrogadas y no participen en el proceso a gusto. Cuarto, la investigadora tiene que asimilar bien la información de una entrevista antes de pasar a la próxima. Esto permite ir entendiendo y clarificando tanto el proceso como lo que se va aprendiendo. Ésto lleva a que al final de las entrevistas se pueda hacer la síntesis de conocimiento sin muchos problemas.

Las mujeres hispanas con las que hemos dialogado han sido escogidas de la mayor variedad posible de trasfondos socio–económicos, de diferentes edades y con maneras muy diferentes de relacionarse con las iglesias. He incluído a propósito a mujeres hispanas que sabía que pensaban diferente a mí, siempre y cuando haya considerado que tenían un sentido de la lucha por la liberación.

Meta-etnografía

En la teología mujerista usamos la meta–etnografía para entrelazar la información que se recoge de las diferentes mujeres hispanas. La meta–etnografía es un método interpretativo. Primero es imprescindible presentar las voces de cada hispana; después se entrelazan señalando lo que tienen en común al igual que las diferencias. Ésto es lo que la meta-etnografía llama "síntesis de conocimiento," una síntesis que es inductiva e interpretativa, integral, considera alternativas, y es holística, relacionando diferentes elementos entre sí en vez de referirlos a una clasificación general impuesta desde afuera. Usamos una metodología holística porque no queremos encasillar el pensamiento religioso de las mujeres hispanas en los esquemas tradicionales de la teología y porque ésto nos permite darle más importancia a las preguntas que surgen de lo que dicen las hispanas. Finalmente, la síntesis del conocimiento al entrelazar las diferentes voces no las reduce a una sola voz sino que permite que se distinga la identidad de cada voz, la particularidad y especificidad de cada hispana.

La síntesis del concimiento se logra al leer repetidamente lo que han dicho las hispanas hasta que se empieza a ver y entender cuáles son los temas centrales. Entonces se ve lo que cada cual dice sobre esos temas sin reducirlo a una sola voz. Es por eso que en vez de combinar las voces se usan las analogías. Por ejemplo, no decimos "Olivia y Lupe dicen que. . . ." En vez decimos, "La que dice Olivia es similar a lo que dice Lupe excepto que, . . ." Las diferencias entre ellas no se borran sino que se leen juntas; y las similitudes nos llevan a los temas generadores a los cuales ya nos hemos referido. Es durante este proceso que las investigadoras–teólogas tenemos que tener mayor cuidado para no influenciar indebidamente el material recopilado. Es aquí donde se puede apreciar mejor la importancia de que la investigadora sea parte de la comunidad que se está investigando.

Las teólogas mujeristas como participantes-observadoras

Las teólogas mujeristas hacemos teología desde adentro, como miembros de la comunidad de mujeres hispanas somos participantes en todos los diferentes momentos del quehacer teológico mujerista. Este quehacer teológico es liberador para las investigadoras y escritoras tanto como para las mujeres hispanas que hablan a través de este texto. Nuestra liberación está intimamente relacionada con la liberación de todas las mujeres hispanas. El dialogar que es parte del método etnográfico de la teología mujerista se facilita grandemente porque las teólogas mujeristas somos parte de la comunidad que investigamos.

Pero además de participante también soy observadora: la estrechez de mis lazos con las mujeres que entrevisto es suavizada por el hecho de también ser observadora. Yo he tratado constantemente de notar y entender las diferencias que hay entre mi realidad y la de las mujeres entrevistadas. Compartimos mucho pero también hay diferencias considerables entre nosotras. Y el hecho de ser investigadora es una diferencia muy importante que no puedo ignorar. Inicialmente esta diferencia me llevó a tratar de no escucharme a mí misma. Pero pronto me dí cuenta de que era imposible no ser yo parte del proceso. Fue entonces que decidí que era importante prestarme atención a mí misma, escucharme y reflexionar metodicamente sobre lo que pienso. Para tener controles externos que me ayudasen a no excluír aquellas voces que no están de acuerdo conmigo me he comprometido a discutir lo que escribo con mujeres hispanas y ver si ellas se encuentran reflejadas en lo que he escrito. También he tratado de darle a leer a las informadoras el texto escrito y estoy dispuesta a cambiar lo que crean que no representa adecuadamente lo que ellas han dicho o han querido decir.

¿Y si la teóloga es más observadora que participante por no ser miembro de la comunidad? En ese caso sólo una verdadera solidaridad le hará posible a la teóloga comprender adecuadamente la comunidad de mujeres hispanas. La solidaridad tiene que ser tal, que a pesar de no ser una mujer hispana, la liberación de la teóloga esté entrelazada con la de las mujeres hispanas.

Razones para el uso de la etnografía y la meta-etnografía

La etnografía y la meta-etnografía se usan en la teología mujerista porque proveen conceptos y técnicas que hacen posible descubrir, organizar, presentar e interpretar la experiencia cotidiana de las mujeres hispanas— fuente de este quehacer teológico. La experiencia cotidiana de las hispanas es fuente de nuestra teología, entre otras razones por la importancia que tiene la religión para nosotras. Es imprescindible para nosotras entender mejor cómo la religión impacta nuestras vidas. En segundo lugar, la experiencia cotidiana de las hispanas no se valora en esta sociedad, no impacta lo que es normativo. Al usarla como fuente de nuestra teología no dejamos que la experiencia del grupo dominante sea lo que controle la teología mujerista. El uso de la experiencia de las hispanas como fuente nos lleva a preocuparnos no de proveer nuestras respuestas a preguntas tradicionales ya que ese tipo de respuestas son mayormente reinterpretaciones de respuestas tradicionales que tienen "sabor" hispano sino un verdadero contenido mujerista. Nuestro propósito es ampliar los horizontes conceptuales y de la praxis insistiendo en nuestras propias preguntas. Es por eso que la teología mujerista es subversiva, animando a las mujeres hispanas a sospechar de lo que no hemos participado en definir.

Una tercera razón por la cual insistir en la experiencia cotidiana de las mujeres hispanas como fuente de la teología mujerista tiene que ver con nuestra liberación y nuestra salud mental. Como personas que vivimos dentro de una cultura ajena, a veces nos preguntamos si entendemos lo que está pasando, lo que estamos viviendo. En una forma muy real como hispanas tenemos que dejar a un lado lo que es nuestra realidad—tenemos que volvernos locas—para sobrevivir en circunstancias tan opresivas. A menudo escuchamos a hispanas, especialmente a mujeres mayores, responder a la frase, "así es como se hace eso aquí," con la expresión, "¿en qué cabeza cabe eso?" La realidad que impacta nuestra vida diaria a menudo nos es incomprensible. El uso de nuestra experiencia cotidiana como fuente de la teología mujerista es un tratar de valorizarnos a nosotras mismas; el insistir en que la revelación de Dios continúa a través de nuestra experiencia cotidiana es un antídoto contra la esquizofrenia que nos ataca de todas partes. La experiencia cotidiana de las mujeres hispanas es fuente de la teología mujerista porque es nuestra realidad común. Lo que pensamos, nuestro sentido común, no está equivocado; podemos confiar en que nuestro sentido común nos puede informar y guiar día a día. La teología mujerista quiere afirmar la perspectiva e ideología de las mujeres hispanas ya que ahí se encuentran las categorías y los conceptos que usamos para construir y entender nuestro mundo—praxis liberadora por excelencia.

Mucho de ésto que acabamos de decir se basa en lo que otros teólogos de la liberación han llamado el privilegio hermenéutico de los oprimidos. El privilegio hermenéutico de las mujeres hispanas no se basa en una superioridad intelectual o moral; no creemos que somos mejores o más inocentes o más inteligentes o que nuestros motivos son más puros. Nuestro privilegio hermenéutico se basa en el hecho de que porque el orden presente no nos beneficia, podemos concebir una realidad diferente que los que tienen privilegios en la sociedad presente no son capaces de imaginarse. Debido a la alienación que sufrimos en la sociedad de los EE.UU. el proyecto histórico de las mujeres hispanas puede proveer el dinamismo que se necesita para organizar esta sociedad en tal forma que no haya ni opresores ni oprimidos.

CHAPTER 4

In Their Own Words: Latinas as Moral Agents

THE FIRST AND main reason for interviewing Latinas for this study was to enhance the moral agency of Latinas by helping those I spoke with to reflect on how they deal with their everyday world and by helping them to grasp how they are self-defining as they struggle to survive and to be liberated. Given the influence of Catholicism in Latino culture, it is not surprising that one of the key elements Latinas use to talk about their ability and efforts to be self-defining is that of "conscience." Also, I had long ago noticed how the institutional churches often use "conscience," knowingly or unknowingly, as an instrument of control and domination. And then there is the fact, which I will discuss in the next chapter, that helping Latinas become conscious of their oppression is a necessary beginning in the process of liberation. These are the reasons I structured my conversation with Latinas for this project around "conscience."

Presenting the voices of nine Latinas in this chapter makes their lived-experience available for other Latinas as we struggle to be agents of our own history. To be self-determining one has to speak for oneself—a second reason why *mujerista* theology provides a platform for the voices of Latinas instead of telling about their lived-experience.

There are four other reasons why the voices of Latinas are presented in *mujerista* theology as unmediated as possible. First, there is the richness of the understandings and experiences Latinas have shared and been willing to entrust to me. It is impossible for any author to say better, more eloquently, more simply, or with greater pathos what they say. Second, the materials presented here and in other texts of *mujerista* theology fill a vacuum. One reason why the theological world at large has paid little attention to Latinas' religious experiences and practices is that they have not been available. We had had little opportunity to speak and much less to be heard. Third, there is a need to listen to Latinas to understand how and why religion is a central vivifying element of Latino culture. The voices we present here help one to see how the religious dimension in their lives constitutes a "revolutionary urge," the desire to continue to struggle for survival, for liberation, and the strength to do it.[1]

Finally, *mujerista* theology wishes to respect variations among Latinas' religious moods, motivations, and practices, and such variations can best be appreciated by listening to what the women themselves have to say. Although their own words are used, I do not claim that the material presented in this chapter is raw data. Even with a concern not to shape what the women say according to my own thought patterns and words, I realize that there is always some filtering in the process of selection and in the ordering of its presentation. Besides, some adaptation of what the interviewees have said occurs when it is transposed from oral to written form, and, in several cases, when it is translated from Spanish, "Spanglish,"[2] or *Mexicano*[3] into English. The only corrective to the bias of the interviewer that can be introduced here is to recall once again the presuppositions and goals that undergird and help to form *mujerista* theology.

The second part of this chapter begins to formulate what meta-ethnography calls "knowledge synthesis." Knowledge synthesis points out commonalities and differences; it provides generative themes, central elements in the enablement of the moral agency of Latinas;[4] it protects *mujerista* theology from schemas imposed from the outside on the reality — that is, practical, everyday living (survival) — of Latinas. In short, knowledge synthesis is part of the method that *mujerista* theologians use to gather the the lived-experience of Latinas as the source of our theology.

The purpose of this knowledge synthesis is not to establish norms and values — though they may be deduced quite easily — but to elucidate the self-understanding of Latinas in order to contribute to the enhancement of their moral agency. The purpose of this knowledge synthesis is not to create categories, illumine issues, or answer classical theological questions, but to enable Latinas to grasp better their daily lives so they can more effectively

---

1. Alysius Pieris, "Place of Non-Christian Religions," in *Irruption of the Third World*, ed. Virginia Fabella and Sergio Torres (Maryknoll: Orbis Books, 1983), 134.

2. Spanglish is the result of constant switching between English and Spanish. Spanglish also has "new" words resulting from mixing parts of Spanish words with parts of English words. For example, the Spanish ending added to the root of verbs of the first conjugation to form the present participle is *ando*. Latinos, especially those of us coming from the Caribbean, will take a verb, for example, "to rain," and add the Spanish verb ending. The result is "rainando." Finally, Spanglish uses a lot of transliteration instead of translation.

3. *Mexicano* is what Mexican-Americans who have little formal education call the Spanish they speak. *Mexicano* is indeed Spanish with a heavy dose of colloquialisms, mistakes in grammar and pronunciation, and a fair amount of transliteration.

4. See the last section in this chapter for an explanation of generative themes.

struggle for survival and liberation. The purpose of knowledge synthesis is not to examine what the women say to the point where the analysis and not the lived-experience of Latinas becomes central to the theological enterprise, but to allow the voices of Latinas to be heard because they have the right to be heard. The purpose of knowledge synthesis is not to instrumentalize—objectify—the lived-experience of Latinas, but to recognize the right Latinas have to express how they view and understand their reality. The purpose of knowledge synthesis is not to translate Latinas' reality into a theological discourse that claims to be scientific, but to present the voices of Latinas as a central element in a hermeneutics of suspicion about the role of religion and theology in our lives.

Who Are These Latinas?

INEZ is a Puerto Rican born in the U.S.A. and taken to Puerto Rico when she was a little girl.[5] Raised there in a rural setting by her grandparents, Inez finished high school in the early 1970s, entered the convent, and was sent to Venezuela to do her novitiate. There she spent three difficult and painful years and, in the end, was not allowed to take religious vows by the superiors of the congregation she had entered. After that she moved to the U.S.A., which she calls "the cold country."

Inez is an extremely articulate person, deeply committed to working with grassroot women—a classification she ascribes to herself. Most of her involvement is related to Puerto Rican Women's participation in the Roman Catholic Church. Inez worked for many years in a job that combines both advocacy and service. When her responsibilities there became more managerial and she was less involved with the people, she left. At present she is working for a large hospital in the public relations office. Her ambition is to find a job in the field of public communication and this is why she recently completed a Master's in Communication. Inez lives by herself in an apartment in the South Bronx, an area of New York City heavily populated by Latinos. Her father, with whom she had lived since her mother died over 12 years ago, died this last year.

Inez likes herself and has a very healthy self-understanding. A happy and gregarious person, Inez prefers to talk in Spanish whenever possible. This preference reflects not only the fact that her Spanish is very good while her English is somewhat limited, but also that she sees speaking Spanish as a means of preserving her Puerto Rican roots, a means of self-identification for Puerto Ricans. For her, to speak Spanish is a political action. She rarely speaks English or Spanglish. Inez is an *independentista*— never giving up hope that one day Puerto Rico will be independent.

5. Some of the names used for the women are not their real names, as most of them requested.

ADELA is a single mother of two, a boy and a girl about to become teenagers. She was married in Mexico when she was very young, but the marriage did not last. Until very recently she lived in one of the border cities of Texas. Listening to her story, one has to marvel at her resiliency. On different occasions she attempted to find a job in the U.S.A., and each time she suffered great injustices. Once when she worked as a maid, the woman she worked for drove her back across the border, and as Adela got out of the car, paid her only one third of what she owed her. At that time, Adela found that all her belongings, which she had stored in someone's house during her U.S.A. stay, had disappeared.

One of the times she crossed the border into the U.S.A., Adela found some stability, mostly because she lived with a man who fathered her two children. But that relationship did not last long and Adela was again on her own. She has raised her two children by herself—a task made all the more difficult since her son has a learning disability as a result of childhood encephalitis.[6] For several years Adela also "mothered" a girl who was no relation to her. Adela's own mother, who lives in Mexico, had taken the girl in, and one of the times Adela went to visit, the girl came back with her. This young woman is now married to one of Adela's brothers and is living in Mexico.

When I first met Adela about five years ago, she had no legal documents, but now she has her U.S.A. residency papers. At the time she was the cook in a parish rectory, a steady job which she did not mind except for the fact that one of the priests dealt with her always as if she were a "nonentity," to quote Adela.

When I tried to contact Adela to interview her for this project, I could not find her. I spoke with key people in the Latino community of the city where she lived, all to no avail. She seemed to have disappeared, and people thought she might have either moved to the West Coast or gone back to Mexico. One day I received a note from her, giving me her new address. Someone who knew I was looking for her had seen her and given her my address. We were able to talk on the phone and I flew out to interview her.

She seemed to be doing well and felt in control of her life. She had a job as a day caretaker for older folks and was going to school at night to learn English. She had her son in a school for children with learning disabilities and her daughter was doing well in school. She told me about her plans to move to another state in a couple of years and start a small business, a bakery perhaps. Four months after I interviewed her she called me. She had fallen, and though now she had recuperated fully, the agency

6. See Ada María Isasi-Díaz and Yolanda Tarango, *Hispanic Women: Prophetic Voice in the Church* (Minneapolis: Fortress, 1992), 24.

for which she was working was giving her only part-time work. She called to ask me if I could arrange for her to move in with some people I knew because her landlord was evicting her for back rent. She was concerned, but not desperate. Adela is the kind of person who never seems to get in a panic. She is a hard worker and trusts herself to be able to move ahead. My friends have visited her and are in the process of helping her obtain some government aid for her rent.

MARTA was born and raised in Cuba. Married in Cuba, she has a married son and is a grandmother. She also has a daughter in her twenties who has recently married. In the early sixties Marta came to the United States as part of the large exodus of Cubans who left the island because of the Castro regime. She has been a single woman for the last eight years. Her sister, also a single woman, has lived with her for the last fifteen years. They both brought up the children and share equally now in maintaining the household.

After managing a highly profitable import-export business for several years, Marta has established her own business. She is a hardworking woman, highly motivated. She belongs to the so-called upper middle class: she lives in an elegant condominium, owns a boat, and vacations away from the city where she lives.

Marta speaks a mixture of English and Spanish—a sentence might begin in English and finish in Spanish or vice versa. Marta is extremely articulate and likes to express what she thinks, to grapple with it, and to be sure that she is communicating adequately what she believes. Marta went to an American school in Cuba, but has not pursued her studies further.

LUPE is a Mexican-American who has lived all her life in the Southwest. The oldest of a large family, she helped her parents raise her younger brothers and sisters and helped the family out financially. She finished her college education when she was older, is now married, and has no children. Lupe is a business woman in a large corporation and in her job she can relate directly to grassroot people—something she chooses to do as much as possible. Her job has brought her high visibility, and, being very civic minded, she has become involved in many community activities and is also very active in the church.

Lupe made it very clear when I started the interview that she has grown much since participating in the weekend retreat that provided data for *Hispanic Women: Prophetic Voice in the Church*. She often refers to that weekend as a very important event in her life. Lupe gives much thought to what she does, to what she should do, and the reasons for both. So it was not hard for her to respond to the questions I posed. Lupe speaks mostly in English, using Spanish only for emphasis.

MARÍA was born in Puerto Rico but was brought to the U.S.A. when she was very small. She was the youngest of eleven children, and her mother gave her to an aunt to bring up. María married and had twelve children; three died when they were young.

María has been involved in church affairs and in politics in her neighborhood for many years. She has been a district leader and also has been elected to the school board. Though she now lives by herself—her husband died of cancer—she is very close to her children and travels to different cities in the U.S.A. where they now live. A few months before our conversation, she was mugged in the elevator of her building and no longer felt safe. Some of her children urged her to move to a different city from the one María has insisted on living in since coming from Puerto Rico. María finally agreed to move but only with the proviso that she would have her own place to live. The situation in the new city did not work out for María and she is now back to the place she has lived most of her life.

María speaks both English and Spanish and used both languages for this interview. She is very precise and expresses herself with great ease.

OLIVIA is a Texas born Mexican-American who moved with her young family to the Midwest almost thirty years ago. They drove for three days in an old station wagon with only $80 in their pockets, and three very small children—two sons and a daughter. Olivia has been married for more than thirty years and now has several grandchildren. At present she works in a bakery just a few blocks from her house and is working on getting her G.E.D. in order to become a teacher's aide.

Olivia was very enthusiastic about participating in this study. She said repeatedly she was honored to be chosen. She has a boundless enthusiasm when speaking about religion and is single-minded about her relationship with God. As the interview progressed it became obvious that her religious convictions run very deep.

Our interview took place in her kitchen on Mother's Day. Later I had lunch with her family, a bountiful meal which I was honored to share. Though Olivia can understand Spanish, she asked me to put the questions to her in English. Though she said she would answer in "Mexicano," the fact is that she spoke almost exclusively in English.

MARGARITA is a Cuban who has lived in New York City for many years. She came here forty years ago, invited by her aunt. She married a man born of Cuban parents in Tampa, but they did not stay together for long. She had twins; her son is now a father of six children; her daughter is single and lives with Margarita.

Margarita is a deeply religious person. When she was growing up she wanted to be a nun, but she says that she never found a way of following that calling because she was poor and black. After she moved to the U.S.A., she followed her second preference and became a licensed practical nurse.

She has worked the night shift in one of the city hospitals for the last nineteen years. She has recently retired but is going to do volunteer work at the hospital so as not to get bored. Her plans are to work with senior citizens as much as possible.

Margarita speaks both Spanish and English with great ease. The interview was conducted in Spanish.

JULIETA is the poorest of the women interviewed for this study.[7] She is a Mexican who lives in Los Angeles. As a matter of fact, I got in touch with her through a shelter for women with which I have had some contact for several years. She is thirty-four years old and has been in the U.S.A. for twelve years. Julieta's mother had twenty-one children, of whom only half survived. Julieta has six, the oldest one eighteen years old and the youngest five. One of her children died of broncho-pneumonia. Julieta goes back to Mexico once in a while to see her mother. The first time she came over she paid the "coyote," the man who guided them across the border, $400. After that she learned the way and now crosses on her own.

Julieta's mother is a religious person who took time to teach her children about God. Julieta says that for her, God is the greatest thing that exists. In her problem-ridden life Julieta has always gone to church to "ask God" whenever she has a problem. "And I feel that it helps me. Maybe it is the faith that I have, because I believe much in God, and if I have great pressures, I go into a church, and I come out more at peace." Her mother taught her the little bit she knew and Julieta learned the regular prayers and made her First Holy Communion. Julieta's faith may be considered simple but it is not unreflective.

The day I interviewed Julieta at the women's shelter, she told me that to get enough money to eat the previous day she and her husband had sold some merchandise on the sidewalk. Her husband has an old, dilapidated truck, which is of great value to them. One of the ways they get money is by driving around and picking up discarded mattresses from the sidewalks. They can sell each for about $5 or $6. She tries to find work as a maid, but having a little one to take care of does not make that easy. She does not have her immigration papers and, therefore, cannot work in a factory without running the risk of being picked up by the *migra* (the Immigration and Naturalization Service).[8]

7. Neither Julieta nor Caridad participated in the weekend reflections that we did to collect material for the book *Hispanic Women*. I am introducing them here at greater length than the others in order to provide information about them that is available about the others in the book *Hispanic Women*. I include Julieta's understandings and perspectives because I believe that being on welfare gives her insights and understandings that are important for this study given the socio-economic reality of the majority of Latinas.

8. She did not avail herself of the opportunity to get her immigration papers during the recent "amnesty programs" because she was told that if she did, they would cut off her welfare check. This kind of disinformation and misinformation about this program and many others is rampant in the community.

When I interviewed her, her husband was also out of work so they were surviving on welfare. She feels bad that she had to lie about her husband not living with her in order to get welfare but if not, "we would starve to death." At the end of the interview I gave her, "as a sign of gratefulness for helping me," $20. But she did not want to accept it. She told me that she was not going to accept money for talking about religion. I explained to her that I was hoping eventually to publish this study and that I would make a profit then, that this little bit of money was my way of sharing something of that profit with those who helped me. It took a while but she finally accepted the money.[9]

CARIDAD was born and raised in Cuba.[10] She lived in the countryside and her family was very poor. They lived about ten kilometers from the nearest small town and they did not go to church. She does remember her mother invoking Our Lady of Charity—the title under which Mary is venerated in Cuba—and she remembers that there was a picture of the Guardian Angel on the wall above their bed. She was baptized in the Catholic Church when she was born but that was the extent of her religious upbringing, though she did marry in the church *"en este país,"* in this country.[11] Caridad and her husband go to church but do not receive communion. So her boy started to ask them why. Since this is a second marriage for both of them, they decided to look into having their previous marriages annulled so they could get married in the church.

Caridad has found religious instruction to be very good for her. "I begin to feel full of something that I know was not in me before." She goes to church now, but not because she has strong beliefs, "those beliefs are strong when they are inculcated in you in your home," she says. She goes because "something has to exist, I have to have some beliefs, because I cannot just drift. And after my son was born, I do not want things to be for him the way they were for me. I do not blame my mother, but I want my son to receive the sacraments, to have some faith inculcated in him. My husband is different. I do not know if there is a connection between religiousness and class. He comes from a family that had means, so he went to Catholic school, and so forth."

Caridad is extremely honest with herself. She realizes that she goes through certain religious mechanics like making the Sign of the Cross, but

9. I decided to interview Julieta when I thought I could not get in touch with Adela. Personally I was moved by her story and by Julieta as a person in a very special way.
10. I include Caridad's understandings and perspectives because, having had no religious upbringing, her input provides different and important insights for this study.
11. This way of referring to the U.S.A. by Cubans and other Latinos indicates the "space" that we place between ourselves and this country even if we are U.S. citizens. At present she is trying to find time to go to religious instruction so she can then receive First Communion and Confirmation.

that she does not really believe. She wants to, she wants God to be revealed to her, but she says she really does not have faith: "I am cold inside."

Caridad came to the U.S.A. in 1969 and is now forty years old. Everything about her is energetic and said or done with great determination. She understands very little English and speaks Spanish at great speed!

Initial Explorations of Latinas' Decision-Making Process
The material that follows is but a small part of what these Latinas shared during the interviews. The order in which the material is presented does not necessarily follow the order of conversation. I have included only the back-and-forth of dialogue when I sense that my response or further questions on a specific point may have influenced the course of the conversation.

QUESTION
What should a mother do who has no money to feed her child?

INEZ   "Well, she has to look for a way to provide for the child. I think that to want to do it means to be able to do it, and if she really wants to feed her child, she is going to find a way to buy food. Maybe she has to be a maid or beg in the streets. As they said in the Middle Ages, the end justifies the means, so if I have a son and I love that son, I am going to do what seems impossible, to look for food for that son. To beg, do what seems impossible. If she is really interested she could do something not so—well, I would not call it low; something so desperate as to beg. I think that if she looks she will find something [a job]."

How can she go to work with a child?

"She can take the child with her."

As a maid they are not going to let her take her child.

"I think that if she looks. . . What else can I suggest? If she looks she can find something."

And if she finds no other way, should she steal?

"I think that if she uses all other means and cannot find anything, well, if you have to steal for your son, steal. But it has to be as a drastic measure. I think that what is essential is not to allow the child to die of hunger. I do not know. For some people it is an option to give him up for adoption, give him to someone else."

Who is going to want the children of the poor?

"No one. So I think that the mother of the child should always stay with him. I think she must do even the impossible until she finds something."

MARTA   "I think that the survival of a son justifies everything except killing another person. Everything, stealing, everything to save his life. In very difficult times, in the worst of times—well, imagine, very few people find themselves in this kind of situation in the western world. But in a place where there is famine, one has to make all kinds of decisions. But you can understand that if a person has a son who is starving to death, to steal some apples from an orchard, for me that is *pecatta minuta* (a small sin)."[12]

LUPE   "For me—very quickly I say—you need something, you go get it. The most important thing is to keep that baby. Give him food. We can get into a long discussion of the places where the people can get . . ."

What about the poor guy who owns the store from which the woman takes what she needs for her child. What about him? He is going to be out of money?

"I can only think of a mother and a child. It is not the normal thing that a mother has to see her children starve. A mother will do anything for her child, things she would not have done before. Like the cannibals that have eaten each other. . . You can do a lot of things. And I think that when there is a great immediate necessity that has to do with a life. . . To me it is just not any big moral problem. If that is the only way out. . . You can always say, there is always a place where she can go to get food so she does not have to steal. I am considering the question thinking that there is no other way for her to get food. No matter what value

12. It is indicative how much Roman Catholicism is/was a part of Marta's life that she here uses the Latin expression, not the Spanish!

anything else has, it is overshadowed by the necessity of the mother to see that the child is fed. She'll have to take the consequences if she is caught. It is hard."

MARÍA   "I think I would even steal, if I had to do it. You have to feed that *criatura,* infant, at all costs.[13] I would beg, I would supplicate, and if it comes to the point where I cannot get food any other way, I would steal. I lived with my children *una época bien fuerte,* very difficult times, *bien fuerte, bien fuerte.*[14] When I was raising them and the situation was really bad . . . I remember my husband and I selling newspapers at night. We would wait for the newspaper truck and buy the newspapers at two cents and sell them at five cents, and that helped us a lot. And I remember going to bed hungry so my children could have enough to eat because in the house there was not enough for everyone to eat. So I think that a mother goes to any extreme when she sees that her child is hungry. God has given us that thing so beautiful, to have the right to be mothers. But at the same time God has given us a really hard job not only of carrying the child for nine months, and bringing it into the world, but also the responsibility goes on because the work contract of a mother never finishes. It is for all eternity. And I am surprised at times when I see how mothers, with great ease, wash their hands of their children and, if the children have problems, let them have them! But I believe that the one that has real maternal instinct, the job of being a mother goes on, that job never ends. On the contrary, I believe that it multiplies because when they get married, the question is whether you get to love the daughter's husband or not; because, be it as it may, he is already part of your family, so then he also becomes your concern. Then the grandchildren arrive, and your responsibility keeps stretching."

OLIVIA   "First of all I would tell her to get to the Lord in prayer."

After she prays she still has to feed her baby.

"Does she have any relatives?"

13. The use of the word *criatura* in Spanish is very different from the one in English. We use it to refer to a defenseless child, an innocent child.
14. The literal translation of this phrase is, "a very strong epoque, very strong, very strong."

No.

"I would go for help to a neighbor, with a friend."

Do you think she should steal or let the baby die?

"No, she should not let the baby die. She has to do whatever she has to do and pay the consequences afterwards. If there is absolutely no other, I mean no other way, she has to do what she has to do to feed the baby. A life is much more important than the consequences she is going to have to pay if she has to go to jail or something . . . I would do it, sure, I would not let the child die."

MARGARITA   "I do not think stealing would be good. The children would not die of hunger because there is always a neighbor who gives one a helping hand. I do not think it is possible for there to be no other way, because I struggled, I struggled with my children and I never had to steal. Because there is always a good soul who gives you something. I do not think that stealing is good because one does it once and then one becomes used to doing it and, without realizing it, one commits other crimes. And besides, it is bad example for the children. One becomes used to doing it, it was easy to take something, so I do it the next time around, I continue to do it and give my children bad example."

QUESTION
Faced with having to choose which of your two baby children you have to surrender to be killed when only one is allowed to live, what would you do?[15]

INEZ   "I think I would tell him, 'There is no way that I can decide.' Look, I remember something very similar, that really happened. In the early 1970s many of my cousins were in the Vietnam War—I remember especially all the work we had

15. This is what I remember the movie *Sophie's Choice* to be about. Most of the time I shared more details from the movie with the women, how this was the choice a woman had to make when arriving at a concentration camp. I insisted on the fact that there was no way she could get around deciding. I also shared with them the outcome, how she gave up her daughter to be killed and never really knew if her son survived, and how she really became crazy even if she did survive the concentration camp. See Allan Pakula, dir., *Sophie's Choice* with Meryl Streep (Hollywood: Universal Pictures, 1982).

to do around Christmas time to cook *pasteles* for them.[16] There was this lady whom I heard talking to my aunt. The lady had two sons, and both were drafted. And her friends kept saying to her, 'That is wrong, they are not supposed to take both of your sons. You have to write a letter to the Red Cross, or whoever, and tell them that you want one of your sons home, because you do not want both of them to be in danger of being killed.' But the lady insisted she did not have the heart to do anything like that. 'If I, for example, ask them to send Rafael back, the other one, Daniel, is going to feel inferior and is going to say I love Rafael more. And if I ask for Daniel, Rafael is going to think I love Daniel more. So I place all of this in God's hands and let God decide. I cannot decide.' The same with this example you give me, I cannot decide."

Then they are going to kill both of them.

"But what am I going to decide? It would be a very difficult decision. I do not have children but I would like to have a daughter. I could say, 'Well, I'll keep the girl.' But I will always have it on my conscience that I gave up my son. Another person might say, 'I am going to keep the son so the name of the family can be carried on.' But I think that in moments like that you do not think about anything like that. I think that under such intense pain one cannot decide. That is what I would tell the man, 'I cannot decide.' I would beg the man not to kill them, that they are all I have, that they are my children, that I *los adoro*, adore them, with all my heart. That if they have to kill someone in the family, well, I believe I would give my life for my children. I think it is very difficult for me or for any other woman."

He is not going to settle for anything but for you to decide between one of your children.

"I really could not decide. I have never been in a situation like that. I would beg the man not to kill them. Neither one

---

16. One of the typical dishes of Puerto Rico, *pasteles* are made of grated plantains, yautía, and pieces of meat or chicken. All of this is wrapped in plantain leaves and boiled until solid. It is a dish requiring much work and that is why it is prepared only for special occasions.

or the other; and they are not even one year old. I would decide that if they are going to kill one, let them kill all three of us and that is that."

Do you think that human beings are capable of making such a decision?

"I do think that human beings can make such a decision. My conscience would tell me, I cannot give you to kill either of them. It would be difficult, very difficult to decide."

Do you think God would punish if you decided one way or the other?

"I do not think of God, I do not think of being punished...none of that. I think that I in particular, for me it would be something that would always stay in my conscience. No, God . . . I don't bring God into this."

ADELA   "I tell you the truth, if I had a pill or something [to commit suicide], I would share it with my children. Having to keep only one child or dying, I would prefer to die with my two children. I would do that. It would be impossible to decide. How can one live without a child? No, no. This is like the story in the Bible when the women were arguing and saying, 'No, no, I am the real mother.' And the real one said, 'Do not divide the child.' My children know this story because I show them the Bible I have in my house. And they say, 'She was right, mami, to let her child go with the other women so nothing happens to the baby.' Oh no, if they asked me to decide . . ."

MARTA   "Between one child and the other, *concho* [expletive], twins! Well I can imagine what must go through a mother's mind to be able to make such a decision. Only God knows what would go through my mind if I was in that situation. Imagine I have two children. What would I decide? I don't have the foggiest idea. I think that one has to be really in that situation, all kinds of things would go through one's mind. If one of the two has children, right now maybe I would decide for my son who has a child than for my daughter who is single. When they were small, I simply cannot imagine. I imagine that if one is sickly and the other one has a better chance of survival . . . Imagine, in a concentration camp when people have to make this kind of decision, only God knows how they would evaluate the situation. I imagine that it must be devastating for a parent to make such a decision. Thanks be to God, many people are not placed in that situation. I think that at that moment the person would evaluate a whole bunch of things: who is more needed, who has a better chance to survive, who . . . I don't know, I don't know what type of evaluations would be needed."

MARÍA   "What a thing for a mother to face! If I had to choose . . . Was there no other alternative? I would have to choose? [Long pause] Well, I would consider two points. If the son lives, he can carry on the family line, the family name will be preserved. If the girl lives, she would have a greater opportunity of expanding the family, of having more children, of carrying on. But it is too difficult a decision, too difficult."

OLIVIA   "That is a very bad decision to make because you do not love one child more than another. See, I have two *hijos,* children, and there is no way I could decide. I get more frustrated with one than with the other but I do not love him any less. You are asking me what I would do?"

Let's say you have to advise someone else.

"About how old are the kids?"

They were twins, a girl and a boy, one or two years old.

"Actually I do not do anything without praying. I would pray over it and whatever the guidance would be . . ."

But what do you think the guidance would be?

"Let him decide."

If she said, 'You decide,' he would kill them both.

[Silence]

Do you think one choice would be better than another?

"No, it's hard, it's the hardest thing a mother has to do. When it's life, it's so precious that you cannot make a decision like that. When it comes to life you just can't. See my belief is so strong, my faith is so strong that . . . If you were not going to be able to live with it, let him do whatever he has to do."

If you do not decide, you decide by default. Both are going to die.

"This is it, you love them both so much . . . If you have ten you love them so much. I could not tell her what decision to make."

O.K., if you were in this situation, what would you do?

"My faith is so strong that I figure that if that is God's will, that is what it's going to be, if God wanted to take them both, he was going to take them both. If not, God was going to find a way, a way . . . I do not know how God does it."

But God finds a way to act through you; God is going to give you entendimiento, *enlightenment . . .*

"Right, that is what I was telling Sr. Lupe. What blows my mind is that I do my part and he [God] does the rest. The rest . . ."

My abuelita, *grandmother, used to repeat the saying,* "A Dios rogando, y con el mazo dando" *Pray to God at the same time that you strike with the hammer;* "God helps those who help themselves".

"You see, I would not make a decision."

But in not choosing you are choosing.

"Thank God, I hope we never have to be in that situation. Let me put it that way, because as a mother, I could not choose. If they would ask me, which one are you more frustrated about, I could say this one. But that is the one that I put first in my prayer list, he's got more . . . But as far as making a decision . . ."

MARGARITA   "What a dilemma. I would say, 'Take my life and let them live.' I would decide for them, because they are children that still have a life to live and one, well, one already has lived one's life . . ."

The soldier insists that you and only one of them are going to live.

"No, I would tell him he would have to kill me also. 'If you are going to kill my son, kill me also.' How can you destroy the life of a *criatura*, creature, who is without any guilt whatsoever? But I would not let my son die. Look at the Virgin Mary, she struggled and struggled for her son. What anguish, what pain to have one's daughter killed! Let them also kill me because, why would I want to continue to live? Because the decision to terminate life does not belong to man but to God. God gives life and when he calls, then we go. It is a very hard decision."

CARIDAD   "[Long silence] I think I would choose, at least I would have one child left. If not I would have none. It would be very difficult because, if they tell me they are going to take my son away, I would die. So imagine, it would be very difficult, very difficult. I would never want to be in those shoes, never. [Long silence]"[17]

QUESTION
What is the most important decision you ever have had to make and how did you go about making it?

INEZ   "I can think of three: canceling my wedding a week before it was to happen, leaving the convent, and most recently, leaving my job that I have had for over ten years."

Tell me about the last one first. Why did you leave?

"Number one, the racist policy of the office.[18] Number two, when I was a client advocate, I really felt I helped the

17. To appreciate the impact of Caridad's long silences as part of her response to this question, you have to keep in mind the quickness of her style, how well she knows what she thinks and how lightning fast she speaks. Her silence stunned me!
18. Inez had a government related job that combined advocacy and service.

people. I remember that when the people had to go to a hearing to get their social security benefits I would tell them, 'You have to say this and this.' And I felt that I was really helping them. But then they promoted me to coordinator and that meant that I had to support the policies and points of view of the government. Three particular events helped me make the decision. First, we had an advisory board and its members for that agency were considered very radical. They were called "Disabled in Action." They were the ones who fought to have public transportation accessible to the handicapped. They were the ones who fought to have voting places accessible, and they were the ones who wanted to take the mayor and all his administration to court because a bunch of shelters were not accessible—there are a lot of the homeless who are handicapped and cannot get into the shelters. And I was in total agreement with these folks and in disagreement with the racist policies. For example, the city pays $8,000 for a family who is living in a welfare hotel but it will not pay $600 monthly rent for them for an apartment. So, when we were at meetings I would speak out and I would start by saying, 'Look, I am not talking here as an employee of this government related office, I am speaking as Inez.' But my boss found that out and told me I could not speak out, that I was not an advocate any longer, that I represented the official position. Well, things started moving inside my head and I said to myself, 'I am selling out to these people.'

The second thing was when they were going to pass a bill forcing people who have buildings that have commercial use on the bottom floor and the rest is supposed to be for housing but they have them empty—the bill was to force them to fix the housing part and put it to use. The bill did not pass, but I was in favor of it and they did not want me to speak out. I said to myself, 'I have to get out of here.' The third thing was a specific case. There were two old women who were roommates and paid $800 rent. One of them died and the other one kept paying the $400 she always did. She only got $500 from social security so that left her only $100 for food and to get by until the next check arrived. The old woman started receiving notices that she was behind in her rent, and finally she got the seventy-two hours: she had seventy-two hours to pay or she would be evicted! The person who was working as house specialist gave me all the information and I took over the case. So I started by calling the marshal's office and letting him know that this was a handicapped person. That gives an immediate reprieve of twenty days. But no matter how much I argued that they could not evict the woman—you have to remember that the lawyer of the landlord was arguing that she had to be evicted because his client was losing so much money. I got the office to give the woman a lawyer. I personally went to the landlord's lawyer and argued with him. I was supposed as a coordinator just to write memos and oversee the whole thing. But not me, I was right there doing it all myself. I tried to see if I could get for her a special service, that if you are behind in your rent, the government will pay for five or six months if it is a one-shot deal, which means that you have to show that from then on you will be able to continue to pay. Well, this would not have worked in this case but I tried anyway. Well, they finally evicted her. I did not go the day the marshal put her out. I could not stand it. But the old woman called me to let me know that they had thrown her out and she said, 'You see, nothing mattered, they still put me out and the first thing they took out and put on the sidewalk was my Christmas tree.'

"Then to top it all off they started marking us late if we came in after 9:06 in the morning. When you depend on public transportation, it is not always possible to be there at the exact minute. That was when I said, 'Forget it, I am leaving. I will not put up with this any longer!' And when I talked to my boss, she did not care. She had a job to protect. I also wanted to protect my job. It was a good salary. When I started to talk about leaving, my family and friends argued against it, 'How are you going to leave after so many years? And that is a prestigious job, and your pension . . .' There was one thing of which I was very conscious: I could not leave until I had another job because I am the mainstay of my home. In other words, I was conscious of my responsibility because I have to pay the bills. Therefore I could not leave until I found something else. . . . I was disgusted with the whole thing to the point that I knew if I did not leave, I would have a nervous breakdown, because I could not even get up in the mornings to go work. When you reach such extremes, you have to leave. And I was lucky that I found something else."

Did you consult with anyone, talk to anyone else about this decision?

"Oh yes, I talked with my women friends, with someone from that office who had left before I did and who always said to me, 'What are you doing here? You have so much talent.' And that was also another thing. I did not feel I was using my talents because there came the moment when they were really pressuring me because my boss began saying that I was acting like an advocate instead of an administrator. She told me that every time I went to a meeting she wanted a memo, a report, of what I was going to say. So the time came when anyone would say, 'Who wants to continue under such circumstances?'"

Why did you cancel the wedding?[19]

"He lied. He had no intention of coming to marry me and when his brother assured me he would see to it that he came, I said, 'Forget it.' You cannot live with a person you do not trust. You are never going to be happy. You are never going to be at peace. Some members of my family, my aunts said, 'Get married and then you divorce.' You know how people are. They were concerned about the embarrassment of canceling the wedding a week before. But no, people can laugh all they want but I have my values. In other words, for me it is a value that you marry someone because you love him, because you want to live with that person, and you want to share your life with that person. You do not get married knowing that you are going to divorce. In that situation, no wedding!"

What about leaving the convent?

"It became obvious to me, even though I was young, that in order to stay I had to stop being myself. The novices

---

19. Because of space I am only giving here the main reasons for two other key decisions in Inez's life.

were treated like maids while the professed, but especially the superiors, lived the good life."

But did you not think that you could endure such a rough life for a while and then you could have the privileges the professed had?

"No, look, I realized that I was never going to get to be superior, because it was an Italian congregation and I was not Italian. But besides, I saw too much hypocrisy. And then, I was too young. I was not diplomatic at all. I did not think about how I could say things in a less confrontational way. But there was this class system—no, forget it! Besides, I started to get scared because for a year and a half I did not menstruate because of the pressure of the situation. I did not seek much advice. I simply decided by myself."

ADELA   *Adela had recently picked up and moved to another part of the country with her three children. Nobody knew why or how. So during the interview we explored why and how she came to decide to move.*

"I came here because I have a friend with whom I was in the shelter where I first stayed when I came to this country. But I have not gotten in touch with her because if I do she will tell the administrator of the shelter."

So what? He will be happy to see that you are . . .

"Safe and sound? No, I don't know, I simply said to myself, I am going to go. I had been thinking about it. When I arrived I stood there in the bus depot and I said to myself, 'My mother, and now what?' I do not know anyone and if I go to a hotel, I will run out of money. So we called a shelter. I do not speak English so I put my daughter on the phone. She is eleven and my son is twelve. The shelter said they would take us but they had no way of coming to get me. The bus had arrived at 6 P.M. and we were still in the depot at 11:30 P.M. Finally the shelter called the police and we arrived at the shelter in a police car. There we stayed. They gave me a month to get established. They sent for my welfare check. There I became friends with a woman, and we started making all the arrangements to get a place to live together. We found a place to share. I got a job in a nursing home. The children would be alone; they would take care of everything at the house. It was a very hard job, an ugly job to have to deal only with really old people. Then the woman I was living with got back with her husband so she left me. She left me with everything, bills, rent, everything. In a month I moved from that place and went to live with another friend. She lives in government-subsidized housing and she is waiting for her husband to come live with her, so she needed someone to help her pay rent. So I agreed to that. But she did not want the children to go out, to shout, nothing, nothing, nothing. She wanted to have them as prisoners in the room all day long. For me that was not right. Then she wanted to raise my rent. I simply couldn't. So I made many sacrifices, and I moved to a little apartment by myself with my children. Right now I am working with a company that provides health services for disabled people. I visit seven persons, seven old people who are disabled. I help them prepare their meals, clean their apartments. I give them their medicine. I am very happy doing this. They pay me $5.35 an hour. I feel good about my job.

Did you talk to anyone about this move?

"No, only I know...My mother does know. She is in Mexico but after two months here I could not stand it any more and I called her. . . .

"I did not tell anyone I was coming here, I did not consult with anyone. I had problems with the landlord where I was. They broke into my house several times so I sued him because I am convinced he was involved. So then he sued me, so I left. We brought two or three things and a big box. I did not consult with anyone because I knew they were going to try to dissuade me from leaving. And I knew inside me that I had to go, I and my children. When I have something to decide, I decide by myself for me and my children. God puts one on the right road. As the saying goes, 'God is never away from his son.' And he puts in our thoughts which way one is to move to solve a problem."

How come you have so much courage, such an adventurous spirit? Is your mother like that?[20]

"No, my mother is not like that. My father was also very calm, and a first-rate father. No, I do not know where this sense of adventure of mine comes from. I think that it comes from all the suffering that I have lived through, all the silence I have had to keep, all that I have seen in my life. In the fifteen' years I have been in the U.S.A. I have seen so much, and so much has happened to me, and I have suffered so much. I think this is what has made me be this way. Life made me this way. But I still have my heart, my same sentiments. But I feel strong, I feel that when I say, 'I am going to do this,' I do it. And I do not rest, I do not rest until I do it. I always go; I am going to do it because it is good for me, something moves me to do this. What is going to happen? I will see when it happens. What I hope for will happen, don't ask me how."

MARTA   "When I got divorced, I had to come to the point of forcing my husband to leave. For me at that moment, for him to stay and torture us emotionally did more damage than having him leave the family nucleus. So, it came to the point that the damage was so big that there was no way of justifying postponing the decision. Of course you also then have to weigh the decision. You think, 'If I do this, maybe he will react and act differently.' In my case my decision, my reasoning was, 'It is not worthwhile for him to stay, given the Chinese torture he is putting us through,' because he was torturing all of us, and at least in my case, he was torturing me in a way that could have been harmful to my own children. If I had lost all personal control, I would go crazy, and the children were not going to be in much better condition than I. The children, even if they did not know what was happening, were being affected by all that was going on around them. And he was going to do whatever was necessary to force me to be the one to make the decision. I have seen this often, that women are forced . . . In very few marriages nowadays are women not the ones who forced the divorce or the separation. Very few

---

20. At the beginning of our conversation Adela described herself as an *aventurera,* an adventurer.

men are the ones who take the decision and say, 'I am going to leave.' They almost always force the women to throw them out. Of course, the throwing them out is because of the deterioration of the relationship, of the Chinese torture, as I say, to the point that forces the break. But you begin to think, and that one thought comes back time and again. 'Maybe forcing him out is my last chance of reconciliation, because it might force him to react and change his behavior.'

"For myself it came to the point that I was going crazy. I thought, 'If I continue this way I am not going to be able to carry on, and the children will be affected very much.' Did I think more of myself than of the children? No, I do not think so. For me I was doing it for the children. Was I in reality using them to justify to myself what I was doing, saying that it was for the sake of the kids but in reality was it for my own sake that I did not want to continue in that situation? I don't know."

Was it an either-or question, either for your good or for the good of the children?

"I would not have minded going crazy if the children had not been involved. That is, 'What is going to happen to the children if I lose my mind?' If the father is letting go of family responsibility and I go crazy, then we will really be in bad shape. It was responsibility for the children that always made me take a whole bunch of decisions, and looking back upon them, one can always say, 'Maybe I should not have done this.' You know you can always say, 'I should have done it a little bit different.' But there are many women who withstood more aggravation, more humiliation, and they were able to save their marriages. I do not think that I would have been able ever to save mine, and, anyway, maybe it was not worth it. But the doubt always remains, would it not have been better for the children if I had done differently?

"I think things worked out very well for me. But later on when there are problems with the children, the thought comes back, what if I had done it differently? It is a question mark. In one's life everything is a question mark.

"Yes, I sought the advice of my sister. My parents were

living abroad and they had nothing to say about it. Besides, I was convinced, well, maybe not one hundred percent, but I was quite certain that they were going to side with him because for them he always was the perfect one. Everything he did was perfect. So imagine, I was too weak emotionally to understand that as soon as they knew the facts . . . Now I realize that it was stupid for me to think that way, and if I told my mother and father they would be insulted that I could have had *la más mínima duda*, the most minimal doubt, that, knowing all the factors . . . Besides, I did not want to cause them pain. I kept saying, 'Maybe this can get fixed! Maybe he will react and change. And then they will never forget, especially my father.' So they did not advise me at all. Later, yes, after the separation. But then, not really because they were as lost as I was. My sister, yes, my sister, for example, was the one that helped me to get psychological help. She would say, 'You cannot continue this way. You cannot go into total depression because you will not be able to do anything. If this is what you were avoiding, the fact is that now we are worse each time.' She was the one that always pushed me to do certain things, and also, to get control of myself, to get a hold of myself."

Do you now feel good about the decision you took?

"Of course every time you evaluate something you measure the pros and the cons. Yes, I feel good because my ex-husband is a person who still has not gotten rid of the problems he has that cause him to behave in a way that does so much damage to those around him. Then, to live with a person like that, to be in a relationship with someone that brings suffering. I can see it and I know that I have gotten rid of that source of suffering."

LUPE   *You recently decided not to apply for the position of CEO of your company. Take me through that process of decision making.* [21]

"I was thinking of applying for the position, and my decision not to do it has overshadowed the event in my life that I

21. In the company in which Lupe works, the whole board votes for the CEO and those interested in the position lobby actively for endorsement by the board members. The board members are also lobbied by the consumers.

used to consider the saddest and most difficult decision I had had to make . . . My husband wanted so badly for me to apply, and to see it in his face that he wanted it so bad and to have to say no . . . I decided not to apply for the position because I did not think I would be chosen. But what made it worse was that the people who traditionally had been helping me, fizzled. My closest advisors fizzled. 'If you want it, we will be there of course,' they would say. But when people start saying that, then all the *ánimo*, fortitude, hardiness, has to come out of me, everything has to come out of me. It was going to be real hard and we all know it. Those who know the board well told me, 'Wait for the next opportunity.[22] Meanwhile, let's get ready.' But I was saying, 'No, it's got to be now, I have to do it now or never.' My friends were saying, 'If you want to apply I would support you but . . .' The pain I had was to be left alone, because at the end, at the very end, it was me and my secretary; she was the only one whose thinking was, 'Whatever you do, I'll be there.'

"Everybody thought I was going to apply for the position. Some chicanos on the board had already indicated that they were going to vote for someone else. I would have had to mount a huge campaign among the members of the community so they could pressure the board. But even the people of the community with whom I have worked for so long, were not clearly behind me. Even the *viejitos*, the old folk, would not support me. 'Lupe has done so much, but she is too young.' They were favoring another person who had applied for the position, one who is much older and in their eyes, because he was older, would know better how to run the organization. Faced with all of this, I did not have it in me. I did not think I would be able to do it by myself. And it would have been something I would have had to do by myself, at least when it came to making the decision and, at the beginning at least, start lobbying the board members. And that hurt a lot. What I learned, and it is not a bad lesson to learn, is that people outgrow each other. Not as friends, but if I am going to be in that kind of position, the people who are going to be with me have to be there because they

22. People knew that the person who would most probably get the job this time around would only take it for a short time because of his age. So "the next opportunity" to apply for the CEO position was not so far away.

want to help me. Somebody has to help me openly. They have to be out there in the front lines, and I learned that they will be people that are not themselves so high up. Your frontline workers are the ones that do not have anything at stake themselves in what I do.

"I feel that they failed me. Maybe that is harsh. I wanted to apply because I think one owes something to people and not just because I think I could do the job. I could not please my husband, and that hurts a lot because he never asks for anything. I have to say, here take some, take more . . .

"In order to apply, you need to think that you can get the job. Unless you think it would be worthwhile to give the other people applying a good fight . . . For two weeks I decided, 'What the heck, let's do it. We are going to get publicity galore and I am going to make a name for myself. I am going to make of myself a Hispanic leader in this country.' But then I started to listen to the *viejitos*. One man came in and said, '*Oye, Lupe*, what is this that you are going to apply for the CEO position? What are we going to do without you?' I said to him, 'Ay, Mr. García, do not worry. You are all very shrewd and you will get someone to replace me in my job who will help you all.' But the person who applied for my job is someone I do not trust. So then I thought, 'Forget it, I might not get the CEO job and I will also lose my present job.'[23] I asked myself, 'What do you want to do, stay in your present job so you can continue to be a thorn in their side by not shutting up, or what?' The fact that I did not have people really behind me, ready to help me lobby the board. . . You can go and hire professionals to do that but I did not have that kind of money. I did not have enough inside me to make up for all those negatives. That is what hurts. It makes me feel very very bad. So what if I am a great Hispanic leader? Who is going to take care of the *viejitos*? And if I do not get to be CEO, I will have lost my present job, and people listen to me now because of the job I have. I hurt a lot and I am trying to learn from it. The other thing is this. What I do, the job I have, is for a purpose. It gives me the opportunity to do with my life what I have to do. Things will work out because

23. The company had made it known that in order to make this an open search it would not give serious consideration to an insider. So the few from within the company who applied for the position had to start by leaving their jobs.

I am doing what I have to do. I think the people need leaders who belong to them, not leaders who sell out. The people need leaders. And how are we going to have more leaders who remain true to the people if we beat them so much? How do I go and talk to other people to do the kind of job that I do? It is such a difficult job. Does it work to do it my way?

"I consider myself the property of the people. Other people point out that I am being used. And I say, *¡Pues qué bueno! ¡Que me usen los viejitos, que me usen!*, it's all right! Let the old folk use me! They want this or that, sure I will fight for them. They are little things, they are good things. I am very proud to say I am the property of the people, and I want other people to think the same. It is not just me; we need to find leaders from among the people. And if we find this guy who says he is going to do it, well, what am I going to do but help him, because he is like a community asset? I have to think that way or *me volviera loca,* I would go crazy. It is very good and very important for me to feel anchored to my community. It is very good and it is very important. I mean, that is what it is all about."

So one of the elements in choosing is to consider how the choice is going to be implemented?

"Yes. In the end it was my choice. I was saying, 'I know I can get the job,' but I was saying it without it being inside of me. And I have a very difficult time acting when it is not inside of me. I pretended, but it was only possible to carry on like that for a little while and then I had to decide against it.

"In my present job I like it when I am out there giving a speech. I identify for the people what it is that they need and explain to them what I can do for them. I like it because I like to be out there with the people."

Now as you look back, was it a good decision?

"Yes, other situations have come and I have taken a position different from that of the majority of the board and we have divided the community. I do not say that in the future I will not apply for the position, but I need to be more ready.

"I think it was a good decision because I know now that I would not have gotten the job. If I had seen that it would have been of great value to people, to people I care about, then doing it, even if I had not gotten it, would have been O.K. But it would not have been a fair fight. I was out-gunned, it would not have been a fair fight.

"I feel sorry I did not apply for the job, but I do not regret it, I do not regret it. When I was making the decision, God was with me and I think, I hope, I was with him. . . .

"In two years I will have to make that decision again. I have started to do different things. First of all, I have started grooming a different group of people. I am not going to depend on the same ones ever, for that. I'll have them do big things . . . but not help me at the level of lobbying and pressuring the board because we outgrew each other at that level. Their support is at another level, and I have to understand that.

"I am good at grooming other people. I am good at that. Because the reason why some of these people are where they are is because I helped them along and I put them in places. I did not give them anything. I have a job that gave me a chance to appoint them, and they have taken advantage of it. So during the next two years I have to open my circle more, bring more people in and actually ask for help. That is something I had never done. I have never asked the people in the community to help me move up in my job. I will now and we'll be more ready. I feel it was the right decision for this time but I am not happy about it.

"I feel bad about the friends who pushed me not to run, even if it was the right decision, because they did it to ad-vance their own agenda. . . . Their advice was not out of their concern for me but because they had their own agen-da. I feel bad also because it is no fun to feel all alone."

But when push comes to shove, we stand alone.

"And I have come to understand that in my head. But I care about people. They are my friends and I care for them. I have cared for years and years and years. . . .

"One thing I have done is I have kept the board straight. I sit there and watch. To me it is very important when there is something that is not helpful for poor people, even if they have the majority of the votes, not to let them have a unanimous vote. I have often been the only "nay" vote and it feels so good. The reason I talk so much is because I want it to be on record that when such and such was approved, there was one person who talked a lot and opposed it. Let history show that it was not a unanimous action. No matter what the issue is, always to bring out a certain point of view is very important. I am very process oriented and I want to see that the process is fair, and that it takes into account the little people. That is my philosophy and it is injected into everything that is happening, and this is very important for me. Public accountability is very important. One has to be accountable to the people . . . Like the church is not accountable to the people. . . .

"I have a great need to know that what I do counts. Maybe it is because I do not have children. I want to leave something behind."

MARÍA   "When my husband got sick, he began to feel ill here, and especially he was very depressed. He had just retired. . . . So I took him to several doctors and none of them found anything wrong with him. All of them told me the same thing, that it was depression, that this happened to many men, that after they stopped working, they felt they were not useful any longer, that they were not needed, and so on, and so forth. . . . Then I called the children in Texas and told them what was happening. And I asked them what they thought about my sending their father down there, because he liked the countryside very much. He liked to plant. And they thought it was a good idea. 'Maybe here he will stop being depressed.' So my oldest son came to get him and take him down there, but he continued with the same depression. One day my daughter called me and said they were going to take him to emergency because all the household remedies for constipation had failed and he was not doing well. I reminded them that this was a problem he had had before. See, he left in May, and my plans were that as soon as the school year was over in June, I would go down to join them.

"My daughter called me from the hospital and told me that they had removed the blockage and that he was feeling well and they would call me from the house. Time went by and they did not call and I was all worried so I called them. But my son-in-law said they were not back yet. Finally my daughter called me and said that they had left him in the hospital. They had asked if he had back problems because they said that back problems and constipation at times go together. He had had problems with a disc before, so they took an x-ray and they found a mass. I immediately said, 'Ay, don't talk to me about a mass, that is cancer.' She told me not to be so fast with a diagnosis, to allow the doctors to do their jobs. I told her I was catching the next plane and I did just that.

"When I got there they said it was cancer but it did not appear to have spread beyond the lung and that he was healthy. They thought that if they operated, his life could certainly be prolonged. That same night he had a heart attack. So that was the end of that, you know. The efforts from then on were to keep him alive. He was like that for three months, each day worse. It was September and the school year had started. I had to make a decision: should I stay with my husband who needed me or come back here to my job that I needed?

"His sister had come to see him and she said, 'Vete en paz, go in peace, you need your job and they need you there particularly at the beginning of the semester. Leave him here. His children will take care of him and you can come see him every other weekend.' I really had to struggle with this decision. I would tell my daughters, 'You are not helping me to decide.' I even got a bit hysterical. My daughters said to me, 'Mom, the decision has to be yours. We will support you in whatever you decide, but you are the one that has to decide.'

"One night I came up with the solution, obviously because I was thinking with my heart and not with my head. I said to myself, 'I am going to take him up north with me. I can find there someone to look after him. I can rent a hospital bed, and I'll do this and I'll do that, and I will take him with me.' So he was just this size; he weighed seventy pounds. I talked to the doctor, and he said I could bring him if the airline allowed it. But he had to travel with an IV, and I also had to get an oxygen tank in case he needed it on the plane. Nothing frightened me, nothing made me change my mind. When I called the airline, they placed many obstacles in my way. So my youngest son said he would accompany me. Finally the airline gave in. I went and I bought my husband a pair of trousers in the children's department and fixed them for him, and everything was ready. We were set to go the next day. I was about to leave for the hospital to pick him up on the way to the airport when they called to say he had taken a turn for the worse and I was to go right away. The truth is, he was already dead.

"That decision I had to make with my heart instead of my head. Afterwards I thought, 'How foolish I was! How could I imagine I was going to be able to manage all of that by myself up north, when he was so sick?'"

When you say you were thinking with your heart instead of with your head, what do you mean?

"I felt sorry about leaving him, even if his own sister was telling me to do it, that he would be all right with his children."

Were you thinking that he was going to think you were abandoning him?

"No. It surprised the doctors that he was not very lucid. Even if the cancer did not affect his mind, he had such a loss of potassium that he was confused, out of it, you understand? So he would not have noticed that I was not there, but I would have known that I was not carrying out my obligations as a wife, that when he needed me I was going to abandon him and keep going on with my life. Yes, because here I would have not only gone to my job, but I would have continued to participate in the many things I have always been involved in. I say with the heart instead of with the head because I had other options that I never thought of at the time. First of all, I could have called my job and asked for a leave. But above all, I thought that the logical thing to do was to have my husband with me and that he was my responsibility and not that of the children. I made all the arrangements to bring him here. Maybe he would have even died in the airplane, and how difficult it would all have been for my son who was coming with me."

You came back and you have lived here for ten years by yourself, but now you have decided to move to Texas.

"Yes. I remember ten years ago the night that we buried him the children said to me, 'Mom, what are you going to do? You have to decide, and you cannot stay in the north alone. Are you going to come live here or are you going to go live in Miami?' where I have one of my children. And I answered them, 'Right now I am not going to do anything. I am fine in the north, I love to be there.' They started to argue with me. You know I had just buried my husband and I was traumatized. My oldest daughter was the one who said, 'Leave mother alone, let Mom decide whatever she wants. She can live wherever she feels the happiest.' So ten years ago they were pressuring me, almost obliging me. And now ten years later I am deciding on my own. They were surprised when I called to tell them I was moving down there but I did not want to live with any of them. I want my own place. Near them, yes, but not with them. . . .

"Many different things are making me decide to leave. Maybe, in a special way this last incident [being mugged in the elevator of her own apartment building] that happened to me pushed me to this decision."

OLIVIA   "The latest big decision I have had to make was when my husband got laid off. He was offered another job, but it was going to be three hundred miles away from here. We had to make a decision because the job was his if he wanted it. So I said, 'Well, we have to make the decision but it has to be God's will, not what we want but what He wants for us,' because He guides the way daily. For us that was very hard because first we had come two thousand miles, from Texas to Michigan. So I go, 'Lord, I know that three hundred miles to you is nothing but for me and my children and my grandchildren it would be a very hard decision. But if that is what you want us to do we will do it.' After praying for two weeks . . ."

Did you ask advice from someone?

"No, the advice I get is from the Psalms, from the Scriptures. He talks daily to each one of us, you know. And no matter what the circumstances He gives you the answer. Sometimes you go through something, and you realize, Wow! Here is the answer!"

And how did you come to decide to stay?

"After two weeks of praying, I told my husband, 'Let us not talk about the job at all. There is going to be no conversation about the job at all. There is going to be prayer and listening, listening to what He is going to tell each one of us.' At the beginning of the two weeks I said, 'Lord, if it is thy will that we stay, let my husband's opinion and mine . . . let us both be thinking the same. And that would be a sign that you want us to stay here because he would be getting his job back. But if he has a different opinion, if he wants to go and I want to stay or the other way around, it means that we have to go, because we are not in agreement.' I told my children also, 'I am going to need the votes of all five of us to see what your decision is. Each one has to decide what is best, because God will be talking to each one of us. There are five, if there are three with the same answer, we are staying.[24] So for two weeks we did not talk about anything. On a Sunday morning, I asked my husband what he wanted to do. And he said that he wanted to stay, that God would provide. On Friday night I had written my answer, so when I asked him, my answer had been written down because I had been guided to an answer. My husband said, 'I want to stay and I will get my job back.' So we went to church and I told Father we were going to stay. He was happy about it and asked if my husband had gotten his job back, and I said, 'No, but he will!' A month after that he got called back to work. The younger one of my kids had decided that whatever we decided he would go with us, but he preferred to stay."

Did you read a specific part of Scripture . . . ?

"Let me show you what I read." [Olivia showed me several books and magazines. One was by Billy Graham, one was

---

24. I think Olivia meant that they would do what the majority decided, but she did say what is written here.

the story of Mother Teresa, also, "The Official Magazine of Life," by the Study Fellowship of Northern Connecticut, and the New International Version of the Holy Bible.]

Do you work mostly with the Psalms?

"I have different prayers that I work with. I read them over and over."

Do you remember specific Scripture passages that helped you during the two weeks you were praying?

"What I do is I stop and think of the people He has helped in Scripture and then I try to look them up and—look what Job went through, Daniel and the lions, Noah and the ark—and I read the stories of how they trusted in Him and He guided them to the right way, the right decisions. I read the Psalms, I mean I just love to praise Him and glorify Him. I got music . . . every day before I get to the Scriptures I play three songs. I do not know why He has chosen me, but I say, 'Whatever you will, I will it too. I praise you, I thank you.'"

When you say "he," are you talking about God?

"Yes."

You are not talking about Jesus?

"Well, I have to believe in Jesus in order to know God. I know that God sent His son. Jesus said, 'If you know me you know my father.' If God had not sent His son we would not be saved, there would be no hope for us."

I ask because the examples you have given me are about the time before Jesus.

"Yes. How about the miracles? They are Jesus'. Look at the blind man, all that Jesus did to him, he put mud on him, you know. Look at the lady that had been bleeding for seven years. She just touched his garment and right away she was healed. And I went through a lot myself. I imagine I have

a better chance than people from the Old Testament because
he came down, he has proven that it can be done, but he
has to do it. We do what we have to do, and he does the rest."

MARGARITA "For me it was not difficult to leave Cuba. I was really young,
it was not difficult. And the situation was not as precarious
as it is now. I came out—not bad, my aunt sent for me, and
I came over here fine. I have not had any difficulty since
I arrived in this country. I worked, then I decided to go to
school at night, which was quite easy to do. It was a bit more
difficult once my children were born because I had to bring
them up. When they were a certain age I was able to start
evening classes because I wanted to become proficient in
English. I took that decision. It was not difficult after that.
I decided to pursue being a nurse, which I had liked ever
since I was small and since I could not be a nun."

Why could you not be a nun?

"Well, you know the difficulties the poor had in Cuba.
Frankly, you know that in our Cuba—since we are both
Cubans I will tell you—there was also some racism. That
we know for sure. I continued to go to church, I paid no
attention to not being able to be a nun. Then I thought I
would like to follow a medical career. And that is what I
have done and what I enjoy. I like my career. It is true that
at times I have difficulties on the floor. But I continue to
do it because it is something I like very much. I am responsible for my floor at night."[25]

JULIETA "The most difficult thing for me was to decide to leave my
first husband. Because when I came from Mexico he made
me work in a place where I had to dance, I was not a
prostitute but a dancer. And I left him because I felt so bad
that he was making me work in things that I did not want.
It was difficult to leave him because I thought that my

25. Margarita has a very positive attitude towards life and it did not surprise me that she
could not think of any serious or difficult decision she had made in her life. In the previous
interview I had done with her, it was hard for her to think of the best thing that had ever
happened to her because so many good things had occurred in her life. And when it came
to talk about the worst thing that had happened she could not think of any except not being
able to go back to Cuba to see her dying mother. See *Hispanic Women*, 88–90.

children would suffer as a consequence of leaving him, because they loved their father very much. And up to now at times I think that it was a decision I took for my sake, but not for the good of my children. Still now they miss him and they ask me why I left him. And I cannot tell them. The oldest one does know and he does not think that I am a bad mother; he understands me. Maybe it is because he now is suffering with his wife and his daughter going from one place to another."

When you made that decision did you think about it for a long time? Did you discuss it with other people?

"I did not need to talk to others, because I knew they would not understand me. They did not know how I felt. I felt really ugly. I thought, 'If I leave my husband, my children are going to suffer.' But I like . . . Whenever I feel something like that I go to God, I go to church and I pray and I feel relief. Maybe I asked God to help me, to give me strength to be able to do it and then to resign myself to it. Because I loved my husband very much, but I also love my children and a life like that one was not going to be good for me.

"I left him because of my children. Because I think that if it had been only he and I, I would have stayed. The only thing he liked was for me to work. He also worked. For me it was difficult to do it, but I did it and God has given me resignation."

And the decision to have to work in prostitution when you went back to Mexico?

"Oh, that was the hardest decision of my life. Because I thought and would tell myself, 'If someday my children find out about this, they will never forgive me.' But every time I arrived home—I lived with my mother and father—I saw one of my brothers—by the way, he is the one living with me now—hiding the tortillas from my children. I think maybe he was just kidding around because I could not think he was doing it because he is bad. But I would always arrive and my children would have their little bellies empty, without shoes, sick, and I had nothing. I looked for work in a factory and I got a job that paid 80 pesos a week, and that did not cover hardly anything. I had three children, food for me, food for them, and I would give the money to my mother but it was not enough for her. I understood that it was not enough. 'What should I do? What should I do? For me it is very difficult. I work all week long to give my mother 80 pesos and it is not enough. What am I going to do?' And a friend told me about this place, 'Look, you can make . . .' 'I don't want to,' I told her. 'I have my children and if I get involved in that, they are never going to forgive me. If I want to marry again, the man is not going to want me because he is going to know what I was.' It was a decision about which I thought and I thought much, but I decided to do it for my children. Because I say it is like this: if I am not going to make headway for them, who is going to do it? And they would ask me for shoes to go to school, for books, and I could not buy them anything. And I had always suffered from that. I had suffered hunger; I had to do it.

"I was not there very long, three or four months. I met my present husband in the street, not there; but I have never wanted to hide anything from him and I told him. Maybe that was my mistake, to have told him. But then I felt more at peace, but now I am paying the consequences. He makes my life impossible. He tells me very ugly things. Yes, he is the one who has told me that God will not forgive me, 'You think God is going to forgive you those things?' But I tell him, 'But God even pardons those who kill, those who steal. How can he not forgive me what I did when I did it for my children? You think He is not going to forgive me?' 'Who knows?' he says; 'You are always sick and sick and that is God's punishment.'"

And you think God punishes you?

"No, I don't think so. God has given me many good things. If I think that He was punishing me, He would not give me all that He gives me. At least I am not missing a hand, a foot. I am not missing anything. I have the main thing, my health, the health of my children, my children that are mine. If God had not pardoned me He would not send me children. I would not be here, I would be suffering. . . . I don't think so, I am sure God pardons me. Even if my husband does not forgive me, with God forgiving me, I am at peace and satisfied. God knows that I did it for my children, I did not do it for no good reason. If it was for no good reason I would be doing it now, I would still be doing it if I had done it for no good reason. I did it because I had great needs."

CARIDAD   "One of the decisions was marrying my present husband.[26] I met him at a part-time job I had on Saturday as a manicurist at a barber shop. I had gone out with only one other client about my age. My present husband invited me out and I said no, I was very tired. He insisted on asking me to go with him to eat, and I agreed to that. At the time he did not have the final papers of his divorce. When he had them, he told me that I was the woman with whom he wanted to re-do his life. I told him I was not getting married with papers and everything one more time so fast. I was the one who made the proposition—this is usually done by the man—'If you want, we can live together. We can live together for a year and then we can see, and during that year we will have no children.' Because I am a daughter of divorced parents, and I have gone through a lot and I do not want to have a child and have that child go through what I have gone through. He said, 'That's fine if that is what you want. Those were not my intentions but . . .' I called my mother because I was living alone at the time. That was another big decision I had made. . . ."

What process did you follow, how did you decide to live alone?

"The decision to move out and be on my own? I put it in front of me, and I decided. I told my mother, 'I want four walls for me alone, where I am the one who decides, a place I can call my own, my own house, my own closet, my own kitchen.' My mother told me that I was crazy, that the money I made would not cover my expenses. 'Mom, you are right, it is not enough money but I have two arms, and I am strong, and work does not frighten me.' And I worked in a factory and at another job and part-time in the barber shop, and that still was not enough. I had no insurance, no telephone, nothing, but I did it."

26. I do not think the written word, no matter how gifted the writer, could ever convey the absolute matter-of-factness and the decisiveness of the analytical account Caridad shared with me.

Do you ever think of the consequences your actions can have?

"Never, never in my life have I thought about the consequences of my actions. When the consequences come, I deal with them but I never think about consequences when I decide to do something."

Have you ever made a bad decision, a wrong decision?

"Yes, I made a decision and the outcome was not good. I think, 'I took this decision and things turned out bad.' I analyze it as an experience, and I keep it in mind so I do not do it again. I cannot live thinking of consequences."

Latinas' Understanding of Themselves

The material presented above shows unequivocally that Latinas produce practical reality as they struggle to survive. It also shows that their lives are self-descriptive, that is, Latinas are aware that their lives happen within a certain context, a given social reality constituted by a historical-political situation, economics, religious-cultural background, and personal decisions. Their telling of their stories shows how their struggle to survive includes praxis: reflective action.

In this section we will look into how Latinas understand what they have shared in their stories. Our attempt here is to go further by translating into one another some of their accounts and other explanations about the process they shared. This is a process that steers clear of reductionism and generalities while attempting to elucidate the relationship between the different texts. The goal here is not to create an explanation of "what they mean." The goal is to throw light on Latinas' exercise of their moral agency in order to advance it further.

The purpose of the interviews was to look at Latinas' moral agency by eliciting the process they use in making decisions. Since I could not perceive, nor did they identify, any process per se, initially I concluded that they had not reflected much on their ability to be self-determining and still less on their right to be so. But after the third interview I began to see the responses differently. These women found it difficult to deal with the "process" because they see and understand it within the much broader scope of what constitutes the fiber of their moral being. They quite appropriately resisted dissecting their experiences in order to identify the process of decision making. However, they were eager to share their experiences and give their opinion about how to proceed in hypothetical situations. Their common sense, formed within the Latino cultural ethos and sharpened by the struggle for survival, provides them the moral wisdom they need in their everyday lives.[27]

Margarita seems to go through life calmly, thinking that, in general, she has not had to take many decisions, thinking that things have fallen into place nicely for her. Her sense that she has had to make no momentous decisions seems to indicate a strong inner core which she intuitively trusts. Her life story reveals that in her own quiet way she has been able to find alternatives when things have not gone the way she wanted. She could not be a nun, so she became a nurse. As a poor person in Cuba her possibilities were extremely limited so she decided to accept the invitation of her aunt and come to the U.S.A. Margarita believes in doing for oneself. "The first decisions are learned at home and at times what one hears preached in the church helps. But I am going to tell you the truth; one helps oneself."

People have been there for Margarita, even her in-laws after she and her husband went separate ways. So it is inconceivable to her that anyone would need to steal to feed her child: "There is always a good soul who gives you something." However, in the face of having to decide which of two innocent children should live, she will die rather than decide for one or the other. She talks about how God helps us to make decisions. "God gives us strength to go on, to know what it is that one has to do. Right now I have a friend who is having a thousand and one difficulties with her daughter. I advise her, 'Do not get desperate. Pray to the Virgin,' and she does and then when her daughter arrives they sit down and talk."

In her interview she talked about being in charge of her floor during the night shift in a hospital. Part of her responsibility is to take care of people hooked up to respirators. No, she would not disconnect them in spite of the cost and all the talk about the lack of quality of life for these persons. "No," she jumps in to say, "money is nothing; what is important is life." Twice she reminded me of the oath to defend life that she took when she became a nurse. It is not surprising, therefore, that Margarita thinks the best thing that has happened to her is to have survived being run over by a car. And the worst thing going on in the world today is the drug problem, because to use drugs is to toy with death.

But Margarita is no pushover. She angrily told me about the times when drug addicts tried to attack her in the hospital. "They insult me and at times they try to hit me. Last night I said to one of them: 'Let me make it perfectly clear; you hit me and I'll hit you back.' I'll lose my job but I am not going

27. Their discomfort in talking about the process of decision making as something separate from their moral being reaffirms the understanding that process and content simply cannot be separated, that the process affects the content and the content should be part of determining the process.

to be looking at patients' rights. Like I said to my supervisor, 'Sure, patients' rights, but where are the rights of the nurses?'"

Neither is Julieta a pushover in spite of her trying life and most difficult present circumstances. Her decisions are basic ones: she left her first husband because the kind of life he was insisting she lead was not, in her opinion, something she considered good for herself. She wanted her children to look up to her and for that to happen, she needed to do what she thought was right even if she worries that it might not have been good for the children, "And I left him because I felt so bad that he was making me work in things that I did not want. It was difficult to leave him because I thought my children would suffer as a consequence of my leaving him. . . . And up to now at times I think it was a decision I took for my sake, but not for the good of the children." But when the situation became desperate and it was a matter of the survival of her children, she went ahead and worked as a prostitute. Her decision made after long deliberation convinced her at the end that she had to take this course if her children were not to suffer what she had suffered: hunger. She thought about it for a long time, she says. It was not the easy way out because if it were, she insists she would be doing it now.

Julieta does not complain. When her present husband puts her down by telling her God may not have forgiven her for what she did, Julieta rests assured that God has forgiven her because she did it for the sake of her children. She insists that God has given her many good things, her health, her children, and for her these are signs that God has forgiven her. "I am grateful to God for having my children. I always thank God for being the way I am. As I say to my husband, I am a good mother and I feel, I feel that I am somebody even if they say that I do not do anything. I think I am somebody of value, because I am valued by God even if I am not valued by anyone else. I am also valued by my children, who love me very much."

Unlike Margarita, Julieta has had to depend mostly on herself for her survival and that of her children, despite some small help from her parents. The men in Julieta's life, like the man in Margarita's life, have not been very helpful. "If I leave this one, I do not think I am going to take up with anyone else." And also like Margarita, who stands up for her rights against abusive patients because she has rights too, Julieta is adamant about her self-worth: "This is what I tell my husband, God knows that I have always had enough to eat and for my children to eat. . . . God says, 'Help yourself and I will help you.' I cannot expect God to give me everything. God says, I will help you, but you have to do for yourself."

Like Margarita, Inez is not willing to admit too quickly that in order to feed her child a woman can steal. Margarita was adamant about saying that there is always another way of coping. Inez did finally give in and say that "if there is no other means, then if she has to steal, she has to steal. But it is a very drastic measure . . . maybe she can give the child up for adoption." Like Margarita and Julieta, Inez is determined to do what is good for her. In order to be faithful to her own self she left the convent because, as she says, in order to stay, "you had to stop being yourself." And she preferred to be embarrassed, to lose face and cancel her wedding a week before it was to happen, rather than live a lie.[28] Finally, when her job of many years kept her from being directly involved with her people, an intrinsic part of what she considers to be her calling in this life, she knew she had to leave. "I feel most fulfilled when I am about constructing community; that happens when you are with the people, when you share what you know with the people. . . . What satisfies me most is to see that I have done something with the people and they have responded. . . . It satisfied me when I went to preach in that Catholic church because I was able to communicate well the message I wanted. . . . It satisfies me to see what the people can accomplish, because if you are supportive, the people can grow and better themselves."

Though Inez is deeply involved in church activities, her relationship with God seems to be different from that of Margarita and Julieta. The latter pray to God and advise others to pray to God. Not Inez. Her relationship with God is identified with her relationship with her people. For her, God is present in her struggle to keep the old lady in her apartment. Inez called me recently to share with me what happened in her parish church on Holy Thursday, 1990. After the traditional Eucharist, Inez had prepared an *agape* in the church hall. She could not contain her excitement as she told me that over two hundred people came to the *agape* after the church services ended. "The people really shared what Eucharist means for them. I could have stood up and given a speech, but no, we went around and people said what it meant for them. And then, since not everyone had talked, I said, 'Now we will go around and let us hear in just one word what the Eucharist means for you.' And the people started to shout, 'Joy, hope, resurrection, love. . .' I was crying and if you had been there you also would have been crying."

This sense of her people, of the possibilities in her people, of the role that the church could play in the lives of her people, is the core of Inez's life. To finish the interview I asked her what she would ask for if she were "Queen for a Day." "I would ask that the Puerto Rican people stop having such an identity crisis. And I would ask that conscientious

28. This was no small wedding. It was going to take place at the cathedral of the archdiocese with the cardinal officiating. Inez had taken a loan of several thousand dollars to cover all the expenses.

Catholics, men and women who understand their Catholicism as building community, be allowed to take over the church just for one day, just for one day, because they would spend it on human things and not on so much nonsense."

Like Inez, Lupe's commitment to her people is intrinsically linked to her understanding of herself and of God. "There is the journey to the inside . . . But I have to reconcile more my two lives, my two worlds as I call them. The world of action as a Christian, what you do, which always has been there, but there is more meaning to that now. . . . And then there is the journey inside, a very personal journey, but that has everything to do with what I do outwardly. . . . God is in me, God is in me. That is why I like myself. . . . I am beginning to understand what I have heard for many years, for many years. God speaks more through the poor and in the poor and with the poor than in anybody else because they do not have anything." Vehemently Lupe insists that if the *viejitos* use her, that is good.

Unlike Inez and Margarita, Lupe very quickly says that if a child is starving, the mother has to find food wherever she can. "Whatever value is in anything else is overshadowed by the necessity of the mother to see that the child is fed. She'll have to accept the consequences if she is caught."

In this Lupe resembles Caridad, who insists that she never thinks about consequences when she is deciding what to do. She does it and that is that, she insists. Caridad's "electrical style," as she describes herself, is very different from Margarita's, but the underpinnings of their moral character seems to be the same: a self-affirming, self-valuing that significantly limits the weight they give to what others say or think about them.

Lupe is in a stage of her life in which she finds that in herself the inward and the outward are interconnected. Although on the surface she may seem to resemble Olivia, closer examination shows that there are significant differences. Olivia prays to find guidance and waits for that guidance from God to be very specific. She tries to find ways to be perfectly sure of what God wants her to do. Lupe, on the other hand, has come to realize that God is in the poor, and that she will know what God wants from her by advocating and working for the poor. But like Olivia, Lupe is convinced that through all of this she is following what God wants from her, "though I am still not there." Olivia finds great joy in getting down on her knees and praising and thanking God daily. Julieta thanks God for all that she has, her health, her children, even in the midst of a life so insecure that she does not actually know how she is going to get something to eat each day. She lives, nevertheless, convinced that "God does not leave us. . . . God is here already. I do not think that God is going to come, but that God is here with us. We are the ones that do not see him because of our sins."

Like Olivia and Julieta, María's trust in God is unflinching. Asked what elements play a role in her decision making, she answered, "Maybe my trust in God. I always think that what one does in life is because they are part of a larger scheme. And I always think that when I make a decision, it is because God is taking me towards that decision." But this does not take away her sense of responsibility. "My sense of responsibility is very great, not only for my children, but in all matters. . . . My sense of responsibility, maybe it is because of all that I did not have, but also because I am a bit demanding. . . . I have a sense of keeping my word. For example, some musicians in my parish did not do what they said they were going to do. And I say, 'How can they call themselves men? They have no money but at least they could have the honor of their word.' Because I think one's word is of great value and we should be responsible. . . . I do not consult with anyone. Maybe that is why I am so strong in my decisions, maybe because I think, when I was small I did not have a mother to whom I could go and ask, 'What do you think?'"[29]

Like Inez, when asked what she would wish for if she were "Queen for a Day," her requests have to do with the good of the community. First, she would ask for love in the community. "By that I mean that we would share, that we would take each other into consideration, that we would be more sensitive. . . . Then I would like to see this world free of drugs because I believe that if we got rid of drugs we would get rid of many other things. . . . One can be happy being poor but people feel inadequate, they do not value themselves. . . . These kids need role models. . . . The drug situation is totally out of control. In the beginning, when all of this started, Puerto Ricans and blacks were the ones who were taking drugs, the ones who were dying and killing, and the government did not pay much attention. But when the people from the suburbs and the whites began to come to Harlem for drugs, the government tried to do something, but it was too late to try to control the situation. When one building is burning, the firefighters can get control of the flames, but when it is a whole block of buildings, it is impossible for anyone to control it. . . . And the last thing I would ask is that my children be happy." María's last words to me were these: "The other day I read somewhere a phrase that I like very much, 'I love my God and I love my people and I hope to serve them both.' I'm going to use that in one of my speeches someday because it is exactly what I think."

Like María and especially like Julieta, Adela's children are central. She had lost a baby in Mexico before she ever came to this country. At that

---

29. For reasons María has not explained to me fully, her mother gave her to a cousin to rear and, as a result, María did not see much of her mother. María has found this very difficult to live with and she says laughingly that she has overcompensated by loving her children to excess.

time the doctors told her she would never have another child. But she never doubted that she would. When she got pregnant with her son she was overjoyed. And then she said to God, "You have given me a son, if you could please give me another child. And when I found out that I was pregnant a second time, I was the happiest person in the world." No wonder that putting herself in the shoes of the mother who is asked to decide which of her two children she would hand over to be killed, Adela immediately thinks of death for all three of them. For Adela, her children are a cause of personal satisfaction. "Oh, yes! It is such a great satisfaction for me to have these two children. I want nothing, nothing, nothing, nothing, in this world but to live. I do not want wealth, I do not want luxury, I do not want anything. I only want what is sufficient for me and my children to live. I tell them: 'When I am gone I want to have left you with a little base so you can build upon it, and above all I want to leave you with the greatest thing, an education.' I tell them: 'What pleases me most is to see you going to school. I do not want you saying to me one day you do not want to go to school.' I see how they get up in the morning eager to get going, they clean up, get dressed . . ."

Though Marta's circumstances are very different from Adela's and Julieta's, she also made her most difficult decision in life, to ask her husband to leave the house, because of the children. For her, her own mental health and the safety of the children were all linked together. "It came to the point that I was going crazy. I thought, 'If I continue this way I am not going to be able to carry on and the children will be affected very much. I would not have minded going crazy if the children had not been involved. That is, 'What is going to happen to the children if I lose my mind?'" Unlike Julieta, who in spite of her husband's harassment believes that she is of value, Marta has doubts about herself. "I am very insecure and I am near the edge of not being very healthy. People do not notice because I fight tooth and nail for the sake of those I love. But I have a very low self-esteem. People do not see it because I put up a front. It has nothing to do with good. Capable, I am not capable. It has nothing to do with good or bad. I am not bad, I am very good. I am not capable. I cannot do things in a way that obtains for me what I want. I'm talking about what I want emotionally because in my business I am an ace. I have accomplished so much in my business but I do not get the highs that I see my son and my father getting when they do a good business deal. I can't. We as women—well, one has accomplishments outside—so what? But it comes down to the fact that I am not married and outside accomplishments are worthless."

Marta stopped going to church once she could not agree with its position on birth control. "But I have all my convictions, and my religion is a matter between my God and me. I have my religion and my God, very,

very, very, very much in mind. . . . I do not go to church because the
church is against remarrying. So, since I have always said that if I find the
right man I will marry him, I do not go to church." Inez feels free nowadays
not to go to church every Sunday. The priests and the way they treat the
people make her angry. But like Marta, not going to church does not take
away from her relationship with God. Julieta goes to church to be near
God; for her the church is a place of refuge when she needs to think, to
get rid of her frustration. But she does not go to Mass on any regular basis
and does not partake of the sacraments. Margarita finds, when she has to
make a decision, that she can use some of the things she hears in sermons.
Lupe, on the other hand, feels that her relationship with God is growing
as she goes deeper into herself and connects that with what she considers
her vocation: to serve her people. She says, "The more I travel into me
and come to know who my God is, the more separated I become from
my church. It's now to the point that just seeing certain people offends
me, just seeing representatives of the institution offends me because they
are with power and they are with money, and they are now with the people. And they leave us alone, those of us who stick our necks out, they
leave us alone. They do not want to touch us with a ten-foot pole. I think
the church is going to fall apart. I do not know how long it is going to
take. . . ."

Generative Themes Central to Latinas

Mujerista social ethics seeks to discover the themes that are important to
Latinas, the ones they feel strongest about, the ones that motivate them.
In the process of identifying some generative themes from the "translations" just made, more comes into play than the information gathered
through the ethnographic interviews. The information produced by the
socio-economic and the cultural-religious analysis is also a very important
part of this process. Likewise, the understandings and perspectives of the
meta-ethnographer are also of great significance at this point, and this is
why I have argued that this person should be an insider.[30] Also of importance here is a factor that cannot be translated into either oral or written
language—the modulation of the voices of the women during the interviews, their gestures, the knowledge the researcher has of them, all of which
goes well beyond the actual recording of the interviews.[31] Aware of all
the different factors that play a role in this next step of the process, here
are two of the key themes that have emerged from this study.

30. See pp. 70–72.
31. And, again, in order to be sure that this exercise does not result in just the viewpoint
of the writer, the reader can check to see whether these themes are found in the accounts.
The writer also takes the responsibility of having at least a few of the women read the materials
to see whether they are true to their understandings and perspectives.

Above all else, there is a sense in these Latinas that they have to act, that whatever is going to happen is going to happen because they see to it that it happens. But their doing is not a thoughtless process, a routine kind of action, empty of reflection. On the contrary, the more critical the action becomes, the more reflection it requires. Even behind Caridad's assertion that she decides "just like that" is a vast amount of reflection on past experience which leads her to know almost intuitively what she must do for her own sake.[32] And Julieta insists that she never stops thinking, trying to find ways to feed her family. In her shines forth that extraordinary creativity of the people, that finds thousands of ways of surviving. For Lupe, her way of coming to know herself and her God is to "*dale y dale y dale*" (an expression which combines the sense of being engaged in doing something, doing it repeatedly, and doing it over the long haul). All of them insist in their own way that only if they depend on themselves can they depend on God.

Second, there is in these women a strong awareness, almost a passion, for claiming and asserting their value and their self-worth. Even Marta, who claims to have low self-esteem, struggles valiantly to separate that negative image from her belief, her knowing, that she is good, very good. Julieta's husband tries to control her by insisting that God might not have forgiven her working as a prostitute, and at times he seems to succeed in planting in her a seed of uncertainty. But then, almost out of nowhere, comes Julieta's assertion that she knows she is of value to God, that she is a good mother, that her children love her. Adela is more than pleased with her adventurous self and the way she has succeeded in providing for her children. She makes plans to have a small business in the near future because she believes in herself. Margarita defends herself against abusive drug addicts even if it means risking the loss of her job just before retirement. Caridad emphasizes that she is indeed a good mother for her young son. She ended the interview by saying she wished she could convince her husband to have another child so she could prove herself once again as a mother. Lupe is sad about not having applied for the CEO position in her company, but she is immensely consoled by her reason for not doing it, namely, that it was not worth the risk of her present job in which she can do much for the welfare of her people.

Even the circumstances surrounding the interviews show how they value themselves, how self-determining they are, and how they do want their

---

32. Caridad's quickness of reasoning and action reminds me of what Aquinas calls *solertia*, an easy and prompt response to sudden and unexpected situations, a certain nimbleness and adroitness in reaction to new situations. *Solertia* seems to build on *habitus*, which leads one to know from within, as through a disposition that one has, instead of from without, as one usually knows an object. See Daniel Maguire, *The Moral Choice* (New York: Doubleday & Co., 1978), 281–308, 375–76.

voices to be heard. Most of them had participated in the weekend gatherings we conducted around the country a few years ago to gather the materials found in the book *Hispanic Women: Prophetic Voice in the Church.* At that time they had all felt that the process was very valuable for them personally. Therefore, in choosing to participate this time, they were doing so not only to help me, but, as most of them verbalized, to help themselves, in spite of the fact that the time set for the interviews was not very convenient for most of them. Olivia gave this project the best part of Mother's Day. In order to be interviewed when I was in the city where she lives, Marta had had to work late the previous evening and then shuffle her schedule to make time for our meeting. Lupe canceled appointments and took the whole day to participate as fully as she could. Julieta materialized out of nowhere at the women's shelter where she had agreed to meet me, and when her husband dropped by during the interview and tried to get her to leave, she firmly told him he would have to wait until we were finished! Adela got in touch with me after meeting by chance with someone who knew I was looking for her. That meant that she had to write to me, and writing is definitely not one of her strengths. Margarita was willing to be interviewed in one of her few precious weekends when she is not working at the hospital. Caridad went without lunch the day of the interview since that was the only time we could find. María had to arrange for us to meet at her church since there was some kind of construction going on at her house. Inez insisted on finding time one Saturday morning before going to an important meeting. By the time I interviewed the last of them, I was more convinced than ever that these women want their voices heard, that they believe they have a contribution to make to the doing of *mujerista* theology.

In the language used by liberation theologies, two of the main generative themes that emerged from our interviews with the women are praxis and moral agency. These are the themes that we will elaborate in the next two chapters.

⊡ SÍNTESIS DEL CAPÍTULO 4: En Sus Propias Palabras: Latinas como Agentes Morales.

Son cuatro las razones principales que me llevaron a estructurar el proyecto de investigación que presento en este libro en la forma en que lo hice. Primero, sabía que el entrevistar a las mujeres cuyas voces se escuchan en este capítulo les daría a ellas oportunidad para fortalecer y ampliar su rol como agentes morales al reflexionar sobre cómo es que ellas tratan con su mundo cotidiano y cómo es que ellas se auto-definen en la lucha diaria. Segundo, sabía por experiencia propia que, dada la influencia de catolicismo en la cultura latina, las mujeres latinas usamos la palabra "conciencia" para referirnos a nuestra habilidad y esfuerzos por decidir por nosotras mismas qué hacer, quiénes ser. Tercero, yo había notado que las iglesias institucionales usan a menudo *la conciencia* como instrumento de dominación y control. Cuarto, la reflexión que este proceso hace posible, ayuda a comprender la opresión en nuestras vidas y, como explicaré en el próximo capítulo, cuanto más conscientes estamos de ésto, mejor podremos luchar por nuestra liberación.

Presentamos las voces de nueve latinas en este capítulo para que sean un recurso en nuestra lucha por ser sujetos de nuestra propia historia. Y para ser sujeto tenemos que hablar por nosotras mismas—otra de las razones por las cuales la teología mujerista es un foro para las mujeres latinas en vez de contar acerca de ellas.

Hay otras cuatro razones para incluir aquí las voces de las mujeres latinas. Primero, es imposible decir en forma más elocuente, más simple y de mejor manera que en sus propias palabras lo que las mujeres han compartido conmigo. Segundo, en el mundo de la teología las mujeres latinas no hemos tenido oportunidad de hablar y ser escuchadas. Esperamos que las voces que aquí escuchamos hagan que ésto cambie. Tercero, necesitamos escuchar a las latinas para entender cómo es que la religión es elemento vivificante de la cultura latina, cómo es que la religión funciona como "empuje revolucionario" en la lucha por sobrevivir, por nuestra liberación. Cuarto, la teología mujerista desea respetar las variaciones en maneras de entender y practicar la religión entre las latinas. El presentar diferentes voces hace ésto posible.

Al presentar aquí las voces de las mujeres no estoy diciendo que el material de este capítulo es objetivo, libre de interpretación. Aunque he tratado de no imponer mis esquemas interpretativos en lo que dicen las latinas, sé que el proceso de seleccionar y organizar lo que ellas han dicho constituye en sí una especie de filtro. Aún el escribir lo que dijeron y al traducir del español, "espanglish," o mejicano al inglés—todo ésto ya constituye adaptaciones de acuerdo a lo que yo, la autora, pienso. La única corrección que podemos presentar aquí a ésto es el hecho que como autora he tratado de identificar mi subjetividad para que los lectores sepan el lente que uso en mis interpretaciones, mi perspectiva en general.

Después de las voces de las latinas en este capítulo, voces que por falta de espacio no podemos incluir también en español, presentamos la parte del proceso que en meta–etnografía se llama "síntesis del conocimiento." La síntesis del conocimiento tiene un fin triple: apunta diferencias y similitudes, facilita el descubrimiento de temas generadores—los cuales explicaremos en detalle más tarde e impide que se impongan esquemas analíticos ajenos a la realidad de las latinas—a nuestra lucha cotidiana por sobrevivir. El propósito de la síntesis del conocimiento no es establecer normas y valores, sino elucidar para las latinas nuestra manera de pensar para que podamos fortalecer nuestro rol como agentes morales. El propósito de la síntesis del conocimiento no es hacer el análisis de lo que dicen las mujeres latinas, lo principal en la teología mujerista, sino ayudar a oír mejor sus voces simplemente porque las latinas tenemos el derecho a ser escuchadas. El propósito no es instrumentalizar, objetivizar las experiencias de las latinas sino el reconocer el derecho que tenemos de expresar nuestro punto de vista y nuestra manera de entender la realidad. El propósito de la síntesis del conociemiento no es construir un discurso teológico acerca de la realidad de las latinas, sino presentar sus voces como elemento clave de una hermenéutica de la sospecha que usamos en analizar el papel que la religión y la teología tienen en nuestras vidas.

¿Quiénes son las latinas que nos hablan?

Inez, de clase trabajadora, nació en los EE.UU. y creció en la casa de sus abuelos en la campiña puertorriqueña. Al principio de la década del '70 entró en un convento pero después de un año muy difícil, colgó los hábitos y se vino a vivir a los EE.UU. Su lucha y su trabajo tiene como foco principal los derechos de las mujeres, sobre todo en la iglesia católica en la cual está muy involucrada a nivel local, regional y nacional. Inez trabaja en relaciones públicas para un hospital. Hace poco recibió su maestría en comunicaciones y su ambición es trabajar en radio o TV. Inez se siente muy a gusto consigo misma y es una persona muy amigable. Ella prefiere hablar en español no sólo porque le es más fácil sino también porque ve la necesidad de hacerlo para preservar su cultura. Inez no pierde las esperanzas de que algún día Puerto Rico será una nación independiente.

Adela es madre soltera de una hija y un hijo. Nació y vivió en México los primeros 15 años de su vida. Después, hasta hace poco, vivió en Texas. Al hablar con ella uno enseguida se da cuenta de que está acostumbrada a lidiar con situaciones muy difíciles y tiene gran habilidad para salir adelante a pesar de muchos obstáculos. Las injusticias que ha sufrido en los diferentes trabajos en que se ha ganado la vida la han llevado a soñar con tener su propio negocio: una panadería. Sus hijos son la cosa más importante para ella y los empuja constantemente a que estudien diciéndoles que ésa es la única herencia que les puede dejar.

Marta nació y se crió en Cuba. Es madre de una hija y un hijo, los dos casados y ya es abuela por segunda vez. Marta lleva como 8 años divorciada, aunque preferiría estar casada y vive con su hermana soltera. Marta es sumamente trabajadora y es la dueña de un negocio bien lucrativo. Marta es de clase media alta; ella es dueña del condominio donde vive, tiene un bote, viaja durante sus vacaciones y disfruta de muchas otras amenidades. Marta se expresa muy bien en una mezcla de inglés y español y disfruta al poder compartir lo que siente, lo que cree, las razones por las cuales es como es.

Lupe es méxico–americana y toda su vida ha vivido en la ciudad donde nació en el suroeste de EE.UU. Ella es la mayor de una familia que era muy pobre y ayudó a criar a sus hermanas y hermanos. Ella terminó sus estudios en college ya algo mayor, está casada y no tiene hijos. Cuando la entrevisté, Lupe era parte de una corporación grande y en su trabajo lidiaba directamente con gente de la base. Su trabajo le ha dado gran visibilidad en la comunidad y ella trabaja como voluntaria en muchas organizaciones cívicas y en grupos relacionados con su iglesia. Lupe piensa bien las cosas y pone mucho empeño en tratar de determinar qué hacer con su vida.

María nació en Puerto Rico pero vino a los EE.UU. cuando era niña. Ella es la menor de once hijos y su mamá la dió a una tía para que la criara. María es viuda y tiene doce hijos—tres de los cuales se murieron cuando eran jóvenes. María ha estado involucrada con la iglesia y en política a nivel del barrio por muchos años, habiendo sido elegida miembro de la junta escolar. Aunque vive sola, María está muy apegada a sus hijos los cuales le siguen causando preocupaciones y sufrimientos al igual que consuelo y alegría. Hace poco se mudó a otra ciudad a vivir cerca de una hija pero no resultó el arreglo y ahora se ha vuelto a donde había vivido casi toda su vida.

Olivia es méxico–americana nacida en Texas y ha vivido la mayor parte de su vida en la parte central de EE.UU. Está casada hace más de 30 años y tiene varios nietos. Cuando la entrevisté, estaba trabajando en una panadería y estudiando para graduarse de secundaria ya que quiere ser ayudante de maestra. Olivia ha disfrutado participando en este proyecto y ha insistido en que use su nombre verdadero. Olivia habla con gran entusiasmo acerca de la religión y de Dios en su vida.

Margarita es cubana y ha vivido en la ciudad de Nueva York por muchos años. Vino de Cuba hace más de cuarenta años invitada por su tía. Margarita se casó con un hombre nacido en Tampa de padres cubanos pero el matrimonio no duró mucho. Su hijo está casado y tiene mellizos varones; su hija es soltera y vive con ella. Margarita es estricta acerca de la religión. Cuando era joven le hubiera gustado ser monja, pero dice que nunca encontró cómo seguir ese llamado ya que era pobre y negra. Después de mudarse aquí, estudió enfermería y ha trabajado el turno de noche en uno de los hospitales de Nueva York los últimos 19 años. Cuando la entrevisté, Margarita estaba a punto de retirarse.

Julieta es, de las latinas que entrevisté, la más pobre. Es mexicana y ha vivido en EE.UU. por 12 años. Su mamá tuvo 21 hijos de los cuales sólo la mitad sobrevivieron. Julieta tiene 6, el mayor tiene 18 años y el más pequeño, que estaba con ella durante la entrevista, tiene 5. Uno de sus hijos murió de bronquitis. Ella va de vez en cuando a México a ver a su mamá. El día que entrevisté a Julieta me dijo que ni ella ni su marido tenían trabajo y que el día anterior habían recogido por las calles unos colchones viejos y los habían vendido para tener dinero para la comida. Ella es indocumentada y no puede arriesgarse a trabajar en una fábrica ya que la "migra" (el Servicio de Inmigración y Naturalización) la puede encontrar y deportar a México.

Caridad nació y se crió en el campo en Cuba, en condiciones de gran pobreza. La bautizaron al nacer pero no ha participado mucho más que eso en nada que tenga que ver con la religión. Ahora se ocupa más de ir a la iglesia ya que tiene un hijo, el cual ella quiere que sí vaya a la iglesia. Cuando va a la iglesia hoy en día no es porque crea sino porque, según ella, alguien más allá de este mundo tiene que existir y "tengo que dejar de andar sin rumbo en esta vida y creer en algo." Caridad es muy honesta consigo misma y ha salido adelante teniendo a veces hasta tres trabajos. Ella misma dice que es "eléctrica", hablando con una rapidez increíble y no reservándose ninguna opinión.

Cómo las latinas entienden su propia realidad

Las entrevistas con estas mujeres muestran cómo las latinas construyen su propia realidad a través de la lucha diaria. Estas latinas se dan cuenta del contexto dentro del cual se desarrollan sus vidas; ellas están conscientes del papel que juegan en su realidad social, la situación histórica, política y económica, el trasfondo religioso–cultural y las decisiones personales. Es obvio cuando uno habla con ellas que la lucha cotidiana de estas mujeres en una verdadera praxis: acciones premeditadas sobre las cuales después reflexionan.

Estudiamos lo que dijeron estas latinas en las entrevistas comparando lo que dijo la una con lo que dijeron las otras, no para explicarlo en nuestras palabras, sino para ver cómo es que se van auto–determinando en el quehacer cotidiano. Una de las cosas que queríamos aprender de estas latinas era cómo es que deciden, qué proceso emplean para tomar decisiones. Lo que vimos fue que las decisiones no surgen de un proceso específico, algo aparte, sino que estas latinas toman decisiones dentro del ámbito general de sus vidas en el cual se desarrollan como seres morales. Es el sentido común que han ido desarrollando usando elementos de la cultura latina perfilados por la lucha por la vida, lo que les da la sabiduría moral que necesitan en su vivir cotidiano.

Temas generadores

La teología mujerista trata de descrubrir los temas que le son importantes a las latinas, los que conllevan gran carga emocional y nos motivan. Estos temas se descubren no sólo analizando lo que dicen las mujeres. Para ésto también hay que tomar en consideración la información que se adquiere de los análisis socio–económicos y culturales-religiosos de sus vidas. En este proceso también juega un papel muy importante la persona que está haciendo el estudio y algo que no se puede poner por escrito: la información que uno recoge al estar con estas mujeres, la información que nos dan sus sonrisas y lágrimas, la inflección de sus voces, la postura de sus cuerpos. Teniendo todo ésto en cuenta presentamos dos de los temas generadores que han surgido en este estudio.

Primero, más que nada hay un sentido en estas latinas de que tienen que actuar, de que lo que va a suceder, va a pasar porque ellas actúan. Y el actuar de ellas no es algo que hacen sin pensar, no es rutinario, sin reflexión. Al contrario, cuanto más crítica es la situación, más y más piensan y reflexionan. Aún Caridad quien nos dijo que ella decide "en un abrir y cerrar de ojos", reflexiona muchísimo sobre sus experiencias pasadas y ha aprendido tanto de ellas que le parece instantáneo o intuitivo cómo decide y actúa. Y Julieta insiste que ella nunca para de pensar, tratando de ver cómo va a alimentar a sus hijos. En ella brilla esa extraordinaria creatividad del pueblo que se manifiesta en la ingeniosa manera en que inventan miles de maneras de sobrevivir. Para Lupe la manera en que ella ha llegado a conocerse a sí misma y a su Dios es a través de "dale y dale y dale". Todas ellas insisten que sólo pueden depender de Dios si dependen de sí mismas.

Segundo, estas mujeres están muy conscientes de que tienen que afirmar apasionadamente su valor como personas. Aún Marta, quien insiste en que no tiene mucha estima personal, lucha por separar la imagen negativa que tiene de sí misma, de lo que sabe intelectualmente, "que yo soy buena, muy buena". El marido de Julieta trata de controlarla, insistiendo que Dios no le perdona que haya trabajado como prostituta para darle de comer a sus hijos. Ella confiesa que a veces él le hace dudar; pero, en el fondo ella siempre sabe que ante los ojos de Dios ella tiene valor, ella es una buena madre. Adela está más que satisfecha consigo misma, con su espíritu aventurero y la manera en que ha logrado proveer para sus hijos. Ella no duda que en el futuro podrá tener su propia panadería porque confía en sí misma. Margarita se defiende contra los drogadictos que vienen al hospital y vituperan a las enfermeras aunque sabe que al hacerlo corre el riesgo de que la boten de su trabajo. Caridad afirmó muchas veces que ella es una buena madre y lo quisiera probar teniendo más hijos, cosa que su marido no quiere. Y Lupe, está triste por no haber solicitado al puesto de directora de la compañía donde trabaja, pero le consuela el no haberlo hecho porque no merecía la pena correr el riesgo de perder su posición presente en la cual puede ayudar a la comunidad hispana.

Cuando terminé de entrevistar a estas mujeres latinas yo estaba más convencida que nunca que ellas se valoran, que quieren ser escuchadas, que creen que tienen algo importante que contribuir a la teología mujerista.

Usando el lenguaje de las teologías de la liberación podemos decir que dos de los temas generadores que surjen de las entrevistas con estas mujeres latinas son "praxis" y "agencia moral." Estos son los temas de los próximos dos capítulos.

CHAPTER 5

Conscience, Conscientization, and Moral Agency in *Mujerista* Theology

ONE OF THE main goals of *mujerista* theology is to enhance the development of the moral agency of Hispanic Women—a theme usually studied under what is called moral theology or ethics. In order further to enable the moral agency of Hispanic Women, it is important to understand the significance and role that conscience plays in the lives of Hispanic Women. Our starting place is Hispanic Women's fundamental assumptions in this regard—assumptions evident in our language and experiences. It is necessary also to show how these assumptions, because of the symbiotic relationship between Hispanic culture and Roman Catholicism, are grounded in the appreciation of conscience in this tradition. An understanding of conscience in Roman Catholicism will help clarify and reinforce its significance for Hispanic Women, and point out the part it plays in *mujerista* social ethics. Our brief analysis will be especially useful in helping us guard against the corrosion of the primacy of conscience being attempted by some of the Catholic hierarchy as well as in combating certain forms of fundamentalist biblical perspectives and influences to which Hispanic Women are exposed.

"Mi conciencia me dice," my conscience tells me, is a phrase often heard among Hispanic Women. Appealing to one's conscience in regular conversations, in discussions, and even arguments of small consequence, is not unusual for us. In the Hispanic culture conscience is not something that comes into play only when considering matters of grave importance or when making critical decisions. Conscience is invoked frequently but not lightly. Advising others, appealing to them to act according to their conscience, *"haz lo que tu conciencia te indique,"* do what your conscience tells you, shaming others for what they have done or have decided to do, *"parece mentira que no te remuerda la conciencia,"* it is a shame you have no remorse of conscience, indicating disagreement or condemnation of what another

person has done by referring to conscience, or *"la conciencia no le va a dejar tranquilo,"* her conscience is not going to let her have any peace—this kind of usage of "conscience" in our conversations is a daily occurrence. To make known that in small as well as in important issues conscience plays a role lets others know that you have considered the matter, that you are not talking off the top of your head, that you are investing yourself in what you say. It is also a way of giving yourself some importance, of making it known that you can think, have an opinion, decide.

The fact that we readily recognize the importance of conscience and the role it plays in our lives makes it all the more difficult to act *"a pesar de lo que mi conciencia me dice,"* in spite of what my conscience tells me, because of circumstances beyond our control. An awareness that we are repeatedly obliged, for whatever reasons, to act against something as central as our conscience contributes greatly to the sense of being oppressed. It is obvious to us that the violation of our conscience impinges on our honor, and such a violation is all the more painful since honor—a term we use to connote our personal worth as human beings—is another basic understanding and value in our culture. To act against one's conscience is to destroy one's integrity: How can you be a person of honor if you do not act according to what you know in the core of your being, in your conscience, is right?

In the context of Hispanic Women's religious experience in the U.S.A., the increased influence of the official Roman Catholic Church on Hispanic Women—or even its possibility—worries *mujerista* theologians because of recent blatant attempts by the Roman Curia to stifle opinions and understandings in the church to the point of threatening primacy of conscience (that is, threatening to subordinate conscience to obedience to Rome in ethical matters as well as in matters of church discipline).[1] This, we believe, disempowers Hispanic Women in our attempt to strengthen our moral agency, an essential component in our struggle for liberation.[2]

If Hispanic Women related very loosely to the official church structures in the U.S.A. as we do in our countries of origin, the task of *mujerista* social ethics in this matter would be only to enhance our sensitivity to conscience

---

1. I mention here just a few cases in different parts of the world which substantiate this statement. Starting with the U.S.A., which probably has the largest number of incidents, those best known are: Charles E. Curran, Agnes Mary Mansour, Liz Morancy, Arlene Violet, Ardith Platte, the Vatican 24 + 1, Mary Ann Sorrentino, Geraldine Ferraro, Mario Cuomo, and so forth. In Latin America: Leonardo Boff, the Cardenal brothers, Miguel D'Escoto, Gustavo Gutiérrez, Bishop Pedro Casaldaliga, and so forth. In Europe: Edward Schillebeeckx, Hans Küng, and so forth.

2. I am neither proposing nor endorsing the legitimacy of all dissent from what the Roman Catholic Church calls noninfallible teaching. My concern is with how the corrosion of this principle impinges negatively on primacy of conscience and the development of moral agency.

and to show how prominently it figures in the development of moral agency. But in the U.S.A., the Roman Catholic church tends to have much more influence and control over our lives for two reasons. First, the Roman Catholic church is operative at the neighborhood level through well organized parishes that provide a strong presence of the official church among the people. This is quite different from the situation in our countries of origin, where, because of lack of priests and because the concept of belonging to a parish is not operative in most cases, the church lacks tight organization and is not able to exert significant control. Second, here in the U.S.A., because of the availability of means of communication, the church reaches people much more frequently than in Latin America and the Caribbean. Thus, the church has more opportunity to influence what people think and believe. Therefore, our task as *mujerista* theologians is much more extensive in regard to encouraging the growth of moral agency. Not only do we have to support and enhance its development but we also have to argue for it and help Hispanic Women to defend their right and duty to develop their own moral agency. This task is made obvious by the present practices of the Catholic hierarchy which we now examine briefly.

Catholic Bishops' Understanding of Conscience Today

Although the teaching of the primacy of conscience has a long tradition in the church and is firmly entrenched in Roman Catholic theological under-standings and teachings, in general it has been kept a secret from the faithful and does not enjoy much respect today among a significant number of members of the hierarchy. Their understanding of conscience, of its nature and function, is closely related to their understanding of the role they have in determining what is truth and their authority in imposing that truth. More and more, those who belong to the hierarchy of the church insist on making the authoritative hierarchical magisterium[3] the decisive factor in the teaching function of the church. Their claims do not stop there, however, but go much further. Addressing moral theologians in 1988, John Paul II stated that "conscience is the 'place' where man [*sic*] is illuminated by a light . . . [coming] from the Wisdom of the Word. . . ."[4] He then goes on to claim that since "the magisterium of the Church was created by Christ the Lord to enlighten conscience, then to appeal to that conscience precisely to contest the truth of what is taught by the magisterium implies rejection of the Catholic concept of the magisterium and moral conscience."[5] Here

3. Magisterium has to do with the teaching authority of the church. Since the bishops, with the pope—the bishop of Rome who is "first among equals"—usually are the ones to voice such teachings, the word has come to refer to them. However, as explained later in this chapter, theologians and the faithful in the church do play a part in the magisterium of the church.
4. John Paul II, "Truth in the Magisterium," *The Pope Speaks* 34, no. 2 (July/August 1989): 99.
5. Ibid.

John Paul II is claiming that the magisterium of the church enlightens the Wisdom of the Word or at least he is equating that magisterium with the Wisdom of the Word.[6] This is in keeping with what one of his delegates had claimed a few years earlier when he said that there is "no substantial difference between the word of God and the word of the pope."[7]

This mode of reasoning by the hierarchy results in an amplification of the dogma of papal infallibility.[8] If what the magisterium says, even when not speaking in its official capacity of teacher of the faith—*ex cathedra*—has the same authority as the word of God, then what is to be the response of Catholics but total assent in all circumstances? Until now the hierarchy has not claimed that infallibility can be applied to moral issues for, though there are universal moral principles, the application of those principles always involves a particular situation and, therefore, there cannot be a universal application.[9] Furthermore, in moral matters the Church's role is limited by the possibility of inadequacy. This has to do with the fact that as temporal beings persons are subject to evolution and change:

> It is distinctly possible that what once was good, truly helpful to persons, truly serving this humanization and spiritualization, may someday become the opposite. Thus, while a Church teaching may well have been both adequate and accurate at one time, it does not follow that it will always be so. On the contrary, there may well be need for revision and rearticulation. What was once adequate teaching has become inadequate. And we ought not to be surprised.[10]

The hierarchy, like everyone else, can certainly have opinions about moral issues and no one disputes their right to make them public. However, what is of concern to moral theologians and Catholics in general is the hierarchy's vesting their opinions with the same authority as the word of God. This amplification of infallibility leaves no room for dissent regarding noninfallible matters, including moral issues one has to decide about, issues for which one is responsible. This position by the hierarchy violates the moral obligation to follow one's conscience.

6. I am grateful to Ann Patrick Ware for sharing this insight with me.

7. According to the *National Catholic Reporter* for 25 July 1985, this was said by Archbishop Vincenzo Fagiolo, the papal delegate to the general chapter of the Franciscans in Assisi when he asked them to meditate on a letter from the pope; quoted in Anne E. Patrick, "Conscience and Community: Catholic Moral Theology Today." The Warren Lecture Series in Catholic Studies (Tulsa, Okla.: Univ. of Tulsa, 13 February 1989).

8. This dogma teaches that when the Pope purposefully speaks officially in matters of faith, he cannot err. Noninfallible teaching is all other teachings of the Pope or of the hierarchy of the church—teachings that Catholics are taught to consider seriously but which we know do not obligate us.

9. Timothy O'Connell, *Principles for a Catholic Morality* (New York: Seabury, 1978), 95.

10. Ibid., 96.

Curtailment of Freedom of Conscience

To deny the possibility of dissent from noninfallible church teaching results in curtailment of freedom of conscience. When church authorities are pressed on this matter, they defend themselves by indicating that the issue is not the right to dissent from noninfallible teaching, but the right to dissent publicly.[11] But their insistence on obedience and their threats of punitive measures against those who do not abide by what they say, their emphasis on knowing and keeping the laws, all results ordinarily in an "authoritarian" conscience (the internalization of an external authority). The "authoritarian" conscience follows the law because it is where authority resides, not because it reflects or embodies one's own value judgment.[12] The main sin of an "authoritarian" conscience is disobedience. It has no right to question or to criticize. "If there seem to be reasons for criticizing the authority, it is the individual subject to the authority who must be at fault; and the mere fact that such an individual dares to criticize is *ipso facto* proof that he [*sic*] is guilty."[13]

There are two important corollaries to this discussion of "authoritarian" conscience that help to explain the present self-understanding of the Roman Curia and their insistence on not allowing public dissent. First, if obedience is the main virtue of an authoritarian conscience, then it is "blind" obedience that the hierarchy of the church believes it has the right and duty to demand from Catholics today.[14] Second, one of the main tenets of the authoritarian conscience is the fundamental inequality between the one in a position of authority and the rest of us. The one in authority has "the privilege of being the only one who does not follow another's will, but who himself [*sic*] wills; who is not a means but an end in himself [*sic*]; who creates and is not created."[15] This tenet may explain the unwillingness of the hierarchy to accept the role of theologians in the magisterial function of the church; the hierarchy will not see themselves following nor even being influenced by anyone else.

This insight into authoritarian conscience also helps to explain the hierarchy's attempt to ignore the centuries old Catholic belief in the *sensus fidelium*—"the body of the faithful as a whole, anointed as they are by the

11. Charles E. Curran, *Faithful Dissent* (Kansas City, MO: Sheed & Ward, 1986), 47.

12. Erich Fromm, "Conscience," in *Moral Principles of Action*, ed. Ruth Nanda Anshen, Science of Culture Series, 6 (New York: Harper and Row, 1952), 179.

13. Ibid.

14. "Blind" obedience is used here not only in the popular sense of obeying no matter at what cost, but also in the sense of an obedience that demands not only complying because a superior says so but of requiring the person to believe that what the superior says is right, and therefore one must comply. It is a concept geared, I believe, to circumvent the accusation that religious and church superiors are promoting the development of "authoritarian" conscience.

15. Fromm, "Conscience," 182.

Holy One (cf. Jn. 2:20, 27), cannot err in matters of belief."[16] The *sensus fidelium* certainly does not assert the inerrancy of the faithful apart from the hierarchy. Nor does it provide, I believe, for the inerrancy of the hierarchy apart from the faithful unless the hierarchy considers itself as separate from the People of God: "Thanks to a supernatural sense of the faith which characterizes the People as a whole, it manifests this unerring quality when 'from the bishops down to the last member of the laity,' it shows universal agreement in matters of faith and morals."[17]

The "authoritarian conscience" that the Church hierarchy is promoting feels good to one who is obedient, feeling dependent, powerless, and sinful. On the other hand, the "authoritarian conscience" feels guilt whenever a person has a feeling of strength, independence, productiveness, and pride. Paradoxically, then, the "guilty conscience" becomes the basis for a "good conscience."[18] The "good conscience" helps one to move away from understanding conscience apart from the rest of the person by making it possible for one to see conscience, not in relation to an external norm, but as a revelation of who the person is. One then begins to understand that

> not only are actions expressive and revelatory of the person, but by one's actions the individual shapes and constitutes the self as agent. . . . Truly the individual human person has the opportunity and the destiny to create one's own moral self.[19]

This is the understanding which is common, though mostly not consciously cultivated, among Hispanic Women, as witnessed by the examples given at the beginning of this chapter. The understanding of the "good conscience" is also an understanding we claim is faithful to the more traditional view of conscience in the Catholic tradition.

---

16. *The Dogmatic Constitution on the Church*, n. 12. For an English translation of the Vatican II documents see Walter M. Abbott, ed. *The Documents of Vatican II* (New York: Guild, 1966), 29.

17. Ibid. The text here is from St. Augustine, *Liber de Praedestinatione Sanctorum*, 14, 27, in *Patrologia Latina*, ed. J. B. Migne (Paris: J. B. Migne, 1841), 44: 980.

About ten years ago, I participated in a panel discussion on dissent with Charles E. Curran and an Archbishop of the Roman Catholic Church. The Archbishop and I reached an impasse exactly on this point. He insisted that the *sensus fidelium* did not mean that the faithful could disagree with the hierarchy even in noninfallible matters like the ordination of women, which was the subject of this panel. I insisted on asking him for his understanding of what it did mean but he would only assert what it did not mean. I remember asking whether the hierarchy was not part of the People of God. When he said it was, I then argued that the *sensus fidelium* did not provide space for the hierarchy to disagree with what was a generalized belief among the laity and a significant segment of the hierarchy. Curran tried bravely though unsuccessfully to break the impasse. This episode taught me firsthand much of what I argue here.

18. Fromm, "Conscience," 183.

19. Curran, *Directions in Fundamental Moral Theology* (Notre Dame, Ind: Notre Dame Univ. Press, 1985), 232.

Historical Developments in the Catholic Tradition

Unfortunately, for several centuries—from the sixteenth century to the second half of this century—moral theology in the Roman Catholic tradition became

> a very practical discipline concerned with training confessors for the Sacrament of Penance especially in their role as judges about the existence and gravity of sin. Moral theology was cut off from its speculative roots as well as from dogmatic and spiritual theology. [20]

This shift had to do in great part with the Reformation and the Counter-Reformation. [21] It is beyond the scope of this work to analyze at length the intricacies of self-understanding of the Catholic Church during this period and the repercussions for moral theology in general. Suffice it to say that to the threat presented by the Protestant Reformation the Catholic Church responded by convening the Council of Trent in 1545. Trent sought to homogenize church teaching and to centralize church practice in an attempt to protect the Catholic church. Its disciplinary decrees were given predominance and the post-Tridentine popes vigorously carried them out. That a siege mentality was indeed developed by the post-Tridentine church is clear, for example, in the establishment of the Holy Office. Though at times difficult to understand and accept, the fact seems to be that "the motivation behind such defensive measures was often a genuine pastoral fear that the faith of the mass of the people would be endangered by 'heresy' and therefore needed to be protected from it." [22] But this positive motivation does not change the fact that the training priests received and the way the main purpose of the Sacrament of Penance was understood, in view of this need to "protect the faithful," resulted in a most legalistic understanding of the nature and role of conscience.

Catholic moral theology entered the twentieth century totally preoccupied with conscience. Its basic approach to conscience had been minimalist and legalistic, resulting in "an extrinsic understanding of morality and the moral life." [23] Conscience had been considered apart from the person. Therefore, usually no consideration has been given to the person as a whole as the doer of the action. This has meant that the understanding of conscience has been almost exclusively rationalistic with no consideration given to affectivity. It is important to note that, even though at times Catholic moral teachings about conscience have curtailed and diminished

20. Ibid., 221–22.
21. This brief explanation is based on the monumental work by Bernard Cooke, *Ministry to Word and Sacraments* (Philadelphia: Fortress, 1977), 133–53, 464–94, 591–613 passim.
22. Curran, *Directions*, 153.
23. Ibid., 226.

primacy of conscience, primacy of conscience per se—the obligation to follow conscience above anything else—has never been denied.

Beginning with the Second Vatican Council, the understanding of conscience has moved away from the minimalist and juridical approach of ages past and has attempted to be more wholistic and expansive. Most moral theologians today stay away from a concise definition of conscience and instead attempt to understand conscience by dealing with it from different perspectives. Though one can still find some theologians who define conscience as a faculty, for example Bernard Haring,[24] even in those cases the attempt is made to broaden the concept of conscience by relating it both to "the practical intellect seeking truth and the natural yearning of the will and heart of man [*sic*] for the true good."[25] Nowadays when the subject is conscience, emphasis is placed on the need to include consideration of the emotions, of affectivity.[26] As a matter of fact, conscience is seen as "the spiritual instinct for self-preservation arising from the urge for complete unity and harmony . . . which is possible only through unity with the world of the true and the good."[27] This unity with the true and the world is not to be seen as an abstraction or an ideal but rather refers to the concrete, "the order of experience in which the self is existentially implicated."[28]

Looked at from the perspective of Christianity, conscience is said to have "a voice of itself, but not a word of its own; it is the word of Christ (spoken in creation, in the Incarnation of the Word, through the influence of grace) which speaks through this voice."[29] Furthermore, the natural function of conscience is

> to make us partakers of the eternal law of God through the created nature around us and through our rational nature. Our bond with the natural moral law is an exalted participation in the eternal law of God manifested in our conscience whose natural function is to reveal our likeness to God.[30]

This results not in direct revelation by God to a particular person but rather a conferring by the Holy Spirit on conscience of "a delicacy of perception

24. Bernard Haring, *The Law of Christ* (Westminster, MD: The Newman Press, 1966), 135.

25. Ibid., 142.

26. Ronald Preston, "Conscience," in *Dictionary of Christian Ethics,* ed. James E. Childress and John Macquarrie (Philadelphia: Westminster, 1986), 116.

27. Haring, *Law of Christ*, 143.

28. Daniel Maguire, *The Moral Choice* (New York: Doubleday & Co., 1979), 371.

29. Haring, *Law of Christ*, 135.

30. Ibid., 147. Given Haring's use of natural law in his understanding of conscience, it may be helpful here to keep in mind that "the Catholic tradition in moral theology has insisted that its moral teaching is based primarily on natural law and not primarily on faith or the Scripture. The natural law is understood to be human reason reflecting on human nature. Even those teachings which have some basis in Scripture . . . were also said to be based on natural law." (Curran, *Faithful Dissent*, 61.)

and tenderness of tact so that in the light of divine revelation projected on all the circumstances in which one is involved in particular instances one readily discerns the divine will."[31]

But this does not mean that the person has nothing to contribute of her own in making a decision. On the contrary, the rational insights of the person are her responsibility; conscience as the voice of God simply impels one to act according to those rational insights. Therefore, conscience cannot "draw truth from its own obscure depth or even create it."[32] But for many centuries the church has insisted that conscience does have to conform to what the person has come to believe is true, correct, and valid. For example, Thomas Aquinas (c. 1225–1274), a key figure in all theologies, dealt with the obligatory aspect of conscience, asserting that conscience binds whether it is correct or erroneous.[33] However, it must be noted that Aquinas insisted on the fact that it is sinful to follow an erroneous conscience if it is wrong because of ignorance that is voluntary or vincible, which Aquinas calls "consequent ignorance." He indicated that there are two kinds of consequent ignorance. "First, and positively, the ignorance may be willed, as when somebody chooses not to be informed, in order to find some excuse for sin or for not avoiding it . . . this is called affected ignorance. Second, and negatively, ignorance may be voluntary . . . : it is an ignorance of what we can and should know."[34] However, if it is invincibly erroneous, conscience does excuse from guilt. One can readily see, therefore, that when there is no agreement as to what is true, correct, and valid, even if the person one is disagreeing with is in a position of authority and power, one may not obey that person in opposition to the judgment of one's conscience.

One's right to freedom of conscience is based on the absolute duty one has never to act against conscience. In this context the term *right* involves both the person claiming to have the right and the claim that such a right makes on the institutional church, on the Roman Curia. One question, then, is whether one can make such a claim on the institutional church. Rights are based on the ultimate end of the person, and "end" for *mujerista* theology is understood as the liberation of the person. The question, then, is whether the institutional church exists to help the person attain her end, or whether the end of the person is secondary to the end of the church. The institutional church is a human construct, a sociological and historical reality—just as the law of the Sabbath—created for the person and not the person for the institutional church. Therefore, the faithful have this claim

31. Ibid.
32. Ibid., 148.
33. Thomas Aquinas, *Summa Theologiae, Pars Prima Secundae*, question 19, article 5.
34. Ibid., question 6, article 8.

on the institutional church: it must recognize the right of the person to follow one's conscience. This means that the faithful must have essential, inner freedom, as well as effective, external freedom. The institutional church must not coerce anyone to act against conscience, and this means that each person must have "immunity from external force compelling one to act against one's conscience, and the 'full possession of privilege,' the faculty and freedom to perform these actions which conscience enjoins, without let or hindrance."[35]

The attempt by the hierarchy to restrict dissent contradicts the documents issued by the Second Vatican Council as well as the new Code of Canon Law, both official church documents.[36] For example, in the Vatican II Dogmatic Constitution on the Church, #25 indicates that the appropriate response to noninfallible teaching is *obsequium religiosum*.[37] This phrase has been translated as "religious assent," "submission," "due respect," "respect." With very few exceptions, regardless of how it is translated, theologians understand this phrase as not precluding dissent. This was the understanding, too, of those who wrote the document. When it was being formulated, a revision was requested that would make specific the possibility of dissent. The official response to the request was that such a revision was not necessary because the phrasing of *obsequium religiosum* meant that dissent was possible.[38]

Two issues raised here of particular interest to *mujerista* theology are the role of theologians in the magisterium of the church, and the way the hierarchy treats the laity. The magisterial function, the teaching function of the church as such, is not limited to the teaching function of the hierarchy, though that is the prevailing operating understanding of the Roman Curia. The fact is that the term *the authoritative hierarchical magisterium*, much used today, only came into existence in the nineteenth century. But more important than the "recent" date of this understanding is the fact that "history shows instances of errors in hierarchical teaching which were later corrected, at least partially due to theological dissent."[39]

All Catholics participate to a certain extent in the teaching function of the church.[40] Through Baptism all Christians receive the gifts of the Spirit

35. Eric D'Arcy, *Conscience and Its Right to Freedom* (New York: Sheed & Ward, 1961), 205. The argument presented in this paragraph is based on D'Arcy, 190–272.

36. Curran, *Faithful Dissent*, 52–62. It would be too long here to develop fully the issue of dissent from noninfallible teaching in the church. Curran's book is certainly an excellent resource on this matter.

37. Abbott, *Documents of Vatican II*, 49.

38. Joseph A. Komonchak, "Ordinary Papal Magisterium and Religious Assent," in *Readings in Moral Theology #3: The Magisterium and Morality*, ed., Charles E. Curran and Richard A. McCormick, S.J. (New York: Paulist Press, 1982), 67–90 passim.

39. Charles E. Curran, *Moral Theology: A Continuing Journey* (Notre Dame, Ind.: Univ. of Notre Dame Press, 1982), 4. See also Curran, *Faithful Dissent*, 57–58.

40. Cooke, *Ministry to Word and Sacraments*, 195–97.

and share in the prophetic and teaching office of Jesus. This does not mean that there is no hierarchical teaching function but it does mean that "there can be no absolute division between the hierarchy as the teaching church and the rest of the faithful as the learning church."[41] The role of the hierarchical teaching office of the church is to proclaim and safeguard Christian faith. The role of theology is "to understand and interpret the reality of the Christian mystery in the world in which we live."[42] Obviously these roles, though different, are not contradictory. On the contrary, they are interrelated, but distinct.

> The role of theology is not totally absorbed into or entirely subordinated to the hierarchical magisterium, but theology must give due weight to the authoritative hierarchical teachings. Yes, error and heresy are possible in theology. Yes, the hierarchical teaching office has a God-given role to protect the church from heresy. But in making such judgments the hierarchical teaching office is somewhat dependent on theology and, in all but its solemn statements, is subject to the possibility of error.[43]

What about the possibility that public dissent from noninfallible teaching causes scandal? Scandal has to do with an action or omission that might cause others to sin. Scandal also has to do with the wonderment and confusion caused by an action or omission. This great concern of the hierarchy about scandal is rooted in the paternalistic and authoritarian manner in which they view the people of God. For them, the faithful are poor and ignorant, in need of protection and guidance. But the faithful are not ignorant. Since Vatican II an increasing number of the laity have become well educated in matters of theology. The faithful are far from being poor sheep who can be easily manipulated or who cannot judge for themselves.[44]

> Too often we worry about protecting the weak and the scandal that might be given to them. What about the scandal of the strong? Many intelligent lay Catholics would be scandalized if Catholic theologians were not searching for better understandings and proposing new theories. Look at the number who have left the church because the Christian message seems to be no longer meaningful for them in their world. At the very least there are both weak and strong in the church.[45]

41. Curran, *Moral Theology*, 4. See also, Joseph A. Komonchak, "Humanae Vitae and Its Reception: Ecclesiological Reflections," *Theological Studies* 39 (June 1978): 229–30.
42. Ibid., 5.
43. Ibid., 5.
44. Ibid., 7. Here Curran quotes from an address to Catholic academics given by John Paul II in 1979 during his visit to the U.S.A. "It is the right of the faithful not to be troubled by theories and hypotheses that they are not expert in judging or that are easily simplified or manipulated by public opinion."
45. Ibid.

Instead of being so concerned about scandal, the hierarchy of the church should carry out vigorously its theological task of increasing religious education, of assisting in the formation of conscience, including imparting knowledge about what many call the best kept secret in the church: primacy of conscience. Formation of conscience must also include education about the rights of all the members of the church in all areas, including religion, and including the right to dissent from noninfallible church teaching.

Conscience in Historical Protestant, Fundamentalist, and Pentecostal Churches

Another reason why it is important for *mujerista* social ethics to argue for and defend the development of Hispanic Women's moral agency has to do with the fact that 20 percent of the Hispanics in the U.S.A. belong or relate to Protestant denominations. In the Protestant tradition, because of the emphasis on faith over works, there is a tendency to understand conscience as playing a theological rather than an ethical role. The function of conscience here has been to make people aware of their transgressions and the consequences. The emphasis has been upon guilt and damnation, reminding people that "in the life of faith they were confronted with an angry God."[46] This tendency in much of Protestant theology results, in general, in understanding conscience as having no directive role before the action takes place.[47]

This is because in Protestantism sin is peripheral to the relation of the person to God. Salvation comes through "God's imputation of righteousness to persons."[48] Therefore, to discuss the proper role of conscience or its nature is not important because an emphasis on morality could lead to legalism. Luther's and Calvin's reaction against the Catholic morality of their epoch, intent as it was on detailing sin and appropriate penance and restitution, led them to insist that persons cannot earn salvation on the basis of moral merit. Although this is not what the Catholic doctrine was or is, "the practical preoccupation with sins as deterrents to union with God" does give some basis to this Protestant understanding.[49] Such reaction led Protestantism to think of the moral life as not having the same "religious seriousness" as before. "It is serious, but it is set in a different religious and theological context. Ethics and moral theology no longer have

---

47. See Ronald Preston, "Conscience ," 116–18. See also, Walter Conn, *Conscience: Development and Self-Transcendence* (Birmingham, Ala.: Religious Education Press, 1981), 18.

48. James M. Gustafson, *Protestant and Roman Catholic Ethics* (Chicago: Univ. of Chicago Press, 1978), 10.

49. Ibid., 11.

the same theological significance,"[50] and conscience is not important since it is understood mainly in reference to sin.

In fundamentalist, Pentecostal, and storefront churches, this general Protestant theological understanding of conscience, coupled with an emphasis on discipline and obedience, greatly threatens the role of conscience as one of the main aids of self-determination for Hispanic Women. Much of what we have already said regarding an authoritarian conscience is applicable in these churches. Whether based on a fundamentalist understanding of the Bible, or on the authority of the ministers who claim to have been "baptized in the Spirit," members of these churches follow what is understood as the law because it is where authority resides and not because it reflects or embodies their own value judgment.[51]

It is important to examine the fact that the great majority of these churches have male ministers and that their so-called rules of discipline have to do much more with directing and controlling the behavior of women than that of men. Many of the rules of discipline, for example, involve dress codes for women, and forbid women to wear make-up and jewelry—something Hispanic Women find greatly restrictive. Since the main sin of an "authoritarian conscience" is disobedience, Hispanic Women in these churches often find themselves in internal turmoil at the same time that they are ostracized for such things as wearing pants or painting their lips.[52]

The fundamentalist or pietistic way in which the Bible is used in these churches also leads to an "authoritarian conscience." The fact is that fundamentalist use of the Bible denies any mediation between the Bible as the word of God, and the way the Bible is understood. Even if the way the Bible is used by Pentecostals were understood along the sacramental lines proposed by some, the fact remains that what the Bible says is equated to the way it is understood, and the Bible is considered authoritative in all areas of life.[53] Furthermore, the way the Bible is preached, what the ministers say the Bible says, is understood to be *indeed* what the word of God is by the majority of Hispanic Pentecostals and fundamentalists. In addition, what the ministers say the Bible says is directly applied to concrete situations, resulting not in responsible Christian living but in oppressive

50. Ibid., 10.

51. I am greatly indebted for these understandings and insights to the Reverend Nicanor González, D.Min., presbyter of the Hispanic District of the Assemblies of God of the South Bronx. See Nicanor González, "Hacia una teología de acción y reflexión pentecostal hispana" (D.Min. diss., New York Theological Seminary, 1991). Regarding the authority of the minister or pastor see Eldin Villafañe, *The Liberating Spirit* (Lanham, Md.: Univ. of America Press, 1992), 128.

52. I strongly disagree with the attempt of Villafañe throughout his book to find value in Hispanic male chauvinism. See Villafañe, *The Liberating Spirit*, 14–15, 118–19, 130–31.

53. Ibid., 205–6, including note 31.

situations in which "blind" obedience is demanded. Such use of the Bible in these churches promotes an exclusively deontological type of ethics which tends to diminish the moral agency of Hispanic Women.[54]

From Conscience to Moral Consciousness and Conscientization[55]

Understanding conscience in a wholistic way, as an integral part of the person and not as a faculty that can be ascertained and examined separately, focuses on the person as agent of her own life, able to determine, and responsible for, who she is and what she does. This allows seeing the moral life as other than obedience to extrinsic laws, and formation of conscience as more than a matter of learning laws. One of the important consequences of focusing on the person as agent instead of on conscience as an isolated part of the individual, is that ethical considerations are not confined just to decision making but rather focus on "the self who continues from decision through decision and who actually affirms and creates one's moral self in and through those decisions."[56] Conscience, then, should not be understood as a faculty or power but instead should be identified with the "moral consciousness" of the person.[57] Consciousness here refers to awareness of oneself as agent, experiencing oneself in one's own experiencing, understanding, judging, and deciding.[58]

Consciousness starts at the level of sensitivity at which one perceives and senses. Human beings share this level of consciousness with animals, but can transcend it. The second level transcends the first level, "presupposes, complements and incorporates it (sublation),"[59] a process that continues through all the levels. At this level human beings understand what they have sensed. The third level is the one at which we judge. The key operation of the fourth level is to choose or decide. It is at this level, therefore, that consciousness becomes moral. At the level of moral consciousness one asks questions about value; then these questions are answered in judgment of values; and finally one decides in accordance with the judgment of values. This decision is always made according to the person's—the moral agent's—"exigence for self-consistency, for making one's decisions, one's choices in accord with one's best judgment about what he or

54. Ada María Isasi-Díaz, "The Bible and *Mujerista* Theology" in *Lift Every Voice: Constructing Christian Theologies from the Underside*, ed. Susan Brooks Thistlethwaite and Mary Potter Engle (San Francisco: Harper & Row, 1990): 261–69.

55. For a somewhat different way of connecting conscience and conscientization see Antonio Moser and Bernardino Leers, *Moral Theology* (Maryknoll: Orbis Books, 1990), 112–27.

56. Curran, *Directions in Fundamental Moral Theology*, 233.

57. This concept of moral consciousness was developed by Bernard Lonergan. I have used both the work of Curran and of Conn to guide me through Lonergan's exposition. The three books in which Lonergan deals with this concept are included in the bibliography.

58. Conn, *Conscience*, 121–24.

59. Ibid., 133.

she should do."[60] And, for a Hispanic Woman, what she should do has to do with survival, and liberation.

Formation of moral consciousness has to be understood quite differently from the way formation of conscience has previously been understood, as instruction in the law. In *mujerista* moral theology conscience is understood as the agent herself as morally conscious, and since consciousness is constitutive of the human person as agent, the formation of moral consciousness has to do with enabling the process of conscientization of the person. Conscientization is an integral part of the understanding of and the struggle for liberation and involves:

> (1) recognizing the distinction between nature in its inevitability and culture in its changeability; (2) unmasking the myths that allow oppressors to dominate society by blurring this distinction; and (3) exploring the alternatives available under the fundamental "generative theme" of our epoch, namely, liberation.[61]

For *mujerista* moral theology there are two especially significant points about the process of conscientization: the importance of praxis in its relationship to liberation, and the meaning and purpose of generative themes. Insofar as praxis is concerned, conscientization is an ongoing process of critical reflection on action, which leads to critical awareness, and this in turn becomes an essential building block in deciding the next action. This reflection on action is one of the moments of praxis and it cannot be separated from action:

> One cannot change consciousness outside of praxis. But it must be emphasized that the praxis by which consciousness is changed is not only action but action and reflection. Thus there is a unity between practice and theory in which both are constructed, shaped and reshaped in constant movement from practice to theory, then back to a new practice. . . . [Conscientization] must . . . be a critical attempt to reveal reality. . . . It must . . . be related to political involvement. There is no conscientization if the result is not the conscious action of the oppressed as an exploited social class, struggling for liberation. What is more, no one conscienticizes anyone else. The educator and the people together conscienticize themselves, thanks to the dialectical movement which relates critical reflection on past action to the continuous struggle.[62]

Another element of conscientization that needs further explanation is that of the generative themes. Generative themes are the issues that are

---

60. Ibid., 138.

61. Dennis P. McCann, "Conscientization," in *The Westminster Dictionary of Christian Ethics*, ed. James F. Childress and John Macquarrie (Philadelphia: Westminster, 1986), 120.

62. Paulo Freire, "Education, Liberation and the Church," *Religious Education* 79 (Fall 1984): 527–28.

important to the person, those issues about which she feels the strongest. The deep feelings, the emotions around an issue incite the person to action; they motivate her to take the initiative and move out of her apathy.[63] The overarching generative theme for Hispanic Women is the binomial survival-liberation. In the process of conscientization, in the formation of moral consciousness, this generative theme unfolds, gaining specificity and thus becoming the basis for praxis.

At the end of the previous chapter we presented some of these specifics by elucidating how the Hispanic Women whose voices are presented in this work value themselves, and know that they must act for themselves. These two themes will always play a key role in their process of conscientization, in further enabling their own self-determination and their participation in the liberative praxis of the Hispanic community. Other themes emerging from the "translations" also have an important role to play in the process of conscientization. One very directly connected to survival-liberation is the value of life for Hispanic Women.

It was difficult for most of the women interviewed to imagine that anyone would be so cruel as to make a mother choose which one of her children would be killed. Most of them refused to choose and insisted on trying to find a way out of the situation. Women who often deal with their own survival and that of their children or their people with such determination that it seems almost effortless, could not decide in this case because they refused to think it could really happen. Likewise, for most of the women, it presented no moral dilemma to have to steal to feed a baby. But the example for them was farfetched because they take for granted that life is so important that there will always be someone to help the mother of a hungry child. In their own lives they have been so creative about survival, they have managed with the help of others to survive, why would it be different for this mother I was telling them about?

Life is life if it is linked to others, whether to their people or their children. It is not a matter of Hispanic Women denying themselves, sacrificing themselves for their children or their people. It is their sense of responsibility to their families and communities that becomes their standard for judging and doing. They do for their children and their people because that is what fulfills them, what *'me hace sentir satisfecha,"* makes me feel satisfied, as Inez says. María has found such joy and satisfaction in bringing up her children that it is difficult for her to understand mothers who take no responsibility for their children or have no time for them. She tries to be understanding and not to criticize, but she could not resist sharing how, when her daughters complain about their children, she refuses to

63. Anne Hope and Sally Timmel, *Training for Transformation*, Book 1 (Zimbabwe: Mambo Press, 1984), 40.

listen to them. One of her proudest moments was when the children were small and she went to a parent-teacher conference. When she introduced herself, the teacher said for all to hear, "You do not know how much I have been wanting to meet a mother who has twelve children and has time to help them with their homework and to play with them." For Julieta, her real concern is not that God might not have forgiven her for having had to work as a prostitute, but that her husband will tell her children. All she has done is for her children; how they think of her is most important. It is impossible to describe her tenderness with her five year-old son who hovered around us during our long conversation.

In the midst of all the comings and goings of life, there is always the presence of a God who understands, who forgives, who is on their side; there is no doubt about it. Marta knows that the church is not on her side, but that has nothing to do with her relationship with God. "I am no agnostic," she says with determination. For Inez, Eucharist happens in the people's celebration she organized in the basement of her church on Holy Thursday. That is when God is really present, not in the ceremonies of the church where the people "did not have a chance to say anything." God gives guidance to Olivia in everything, and for Adela there is no doubt that God puts her on the road she must travel. María prays to every saint anyone mentions. She says that with so many children she has many different kinds of needs and the saints are like friends who help her—a dimension of the divine in her life. Her closing words in the interview were to express her desire to serve her God and her people. Lupe has come to realize in her heart what she knew in her head, that her work with the poor people of the community, with her *viejitos*, is not separate from knowing God for it is through them that God is known.

Generative themes provide the starting place for the process of conscientization. These themes can and should be used to enable Hispanic Women to understand how they make decisions, the values those decisions reflect, how the socio-economic situation in which they live affects their decision making. Listening to Lupe, Inez, Marta, and the other women, it is clear what it is that awakens and sustains them in the development of their moral consciousness. This is why these generative words are the jumping off point into the process of conscientization.

The process of conscientization involves the totality of the person. It operates at the empirical level in which one perceives and senses, at the intellectual level of understanding, and at the rational level of judgment in which women, by defining themselves in the context of struggling to survive and judging by a standard of responsibility and community building, affirm themselves.[64] It is at this level that one becomes moral because

64. Following Curran's lead in *Directions in Fundamental Moral Theology*, 240–43, my starting

values enter the picture, in this case the values of responsibility and care. The Hispanic Women heard in this study repeatedly emphasize the centrality in their lives of responsibility and community building expressed through care. María asserts that she is very responsible perhaps because she grew up without her mother and had to start making decisions for herself at such a young age. And she readily admits to loving her children to excess—the starting point for her involvement with her community *"que me encanta,"* which enchants me, which I love, because it is so satisfying. Marta's central reason for divorce was her responsibility and care for her children. But she knows that intimately linked with her concern for her children is caring and being responsible for herself. For Lupe, care for and responsibility to the community are part of her own inward journey to know and value herself.

Therefore, for *mujerista* moral theology it is essential to understand these values of responsibility and care as the response of a moral consciousness which has at its very heart loving and caring for oneself. Authentic love of self becomes the basis for a relationship with the divine, with God transformed from one who is radically beyond the person as agent, to one radically immanent to the agent, the God who is the *"algo me lo decía dentro de mí,"* knew inside me that I had to go, of Adela, or the daily guidance from God of which Olivia speaks so readily.

The research done for this work illumines only in passing the second aspect of generative themes within the process of conscientization, the problematization of the themes themselves. The themes become issues when the Hispanic Women realize that their self-determination is thwarted by factors which they cannot control and which are unjust. The problematization of what is important to Hispanic Women is precisely one of the goals of the process of conscientization; that is the spark of suspicion that will move them to liberative praxis.[65] What this process entails and how it happens is beyond the scope of this work but needs to be indicated here in order to complete the explanation of conscientization.

The process of conscientization calls for us to accept our freedom and responsibility without which we cannot truly participate in liberative praxis. An intrinsic part of this process is the realization of the dangers involved in judging and deciding, the two basic ones being human finitude and sinfulness:

---

place for this analysis of moral consciouness was Bernard Lonergan, *Method in Theology* (New York: Herder and Herder, 1972), 103–5. I have changed his schema significantly to reflect what I have learned from the Hispanic Women whose voices are presented in this work. See also Carol Gilligan, *In a Different Voice* (Cambridge, Mass.: Harvard Univ. Press, 1982), 160.

65. See Juan Luis Segundo, *The Liberation of Theology* (Maryknoll: Orbis Books, 1982), 7–9.

Finitude is different from sinfulness. As a result of our finitude we are limited; we see only a partial aspect of reality; we cannot achieve all possible goods or values. Human sinfulness, on the other hand, stems not from creation itself but from the actions of ourselves or others and can be seen in the sinfulness both of the individual and of the society in which we live.[66]

But the process of conscientization pushes us beyond realization to the overcoming of those dangers. This requires a strong spirit of openness which presses us always to search deeper and more ardently for what is true and what is good; it impels us to a liberative praxis that has as its goal the creation of nonoppressive structures. This kind of openness is what humility is all about. Humility is not a matter of self-effacement and self-negation but of being open always to new ways of being responsible and of caring.

The process of conscientization is a personal process. For us Hispanic Women what is personal is related to the Hispanic community. Besides our own communities there are different communities that we Hispanic Women must relate to in our process of conscientization. There is the community of the "popular church," the community which lives a Christianity that brings together the tenets of Catholicism with those of Amerindian and African religions as well as with the day-to-day struggle for survival of Hispanic Women.[67] Then there are the other communities of struggle: the feminist community, the African American community—especially the Womanist community, the gay and lesbian community, the native American community, the Asian American community, and so forth. Our dialogue with these communities results in a deep praxis of solidarity which resists any attempts to engage in horizontal violence.[68]

For *mujerista* moral theology to insist on the understanding of moral consciousness presented here is imperative. Our task as *mujerista* theologians is to continue to develop such understanding and to facilitate the development of moral consciousness of Hispanic Women in all circumstances. Given the centrality of the struggle for liberation in the lives of Hispanic Women, this is perhaps the best way in which *mujerista* theology can carry on both its creative role and its critical role, central roles that each and every true theology is called upon to play.

---

66. Curran, *Directions*, 246.

67. In the term "tenets of Catholicism," I include the doctrine and dogmas of the Roman Catholic Church as well as accepting the teaching authority of the Church in its broadest sense and not exclusively to mean the hierarchical magisterium.

68. This explanation of the process of conscientization, though my own, borrows terminology used by Curran, *Directions in Fundamental Moral Theology*, 244–50.

SÍNTESIS DEL CAPÍTULO 5: Consciencia, Conscientización y Agencia Moral en la Teología *Mujerista*.

Para ayudar a desarrollar la agencia moral de las mujeres hispanas hemos investigado el significado que le damos y el papel que juega para nosotras la conciencia. La frase, "mi conciencia me dice", es usada a menudo por mujeres hispanas. Es común para nosotras recurrir a "la conciencia" aún en discusiones de poca importancia. En la cultura hispana nos referimos a la conciencia frecuentemente pero no sin respeto. Cuando aconsejamos a otros a menudo decimos, "haz lo que tu conciencia te indique"; a veces usamos la conciencia para avergonzar a otros a ver si así hacen lo que deben: "parece mentira que no te remuerda la conciencia"; e indicamos nuestro desacuerdo con alguien refiriéndonos a la conciencia: "la conciencia no le va a dejar tranquilo". Esta manera tan corriente de referirnos a la conciencia es una forma de dejarle saber a los demás que uno ha pensado seriamente lo que uno dice, que uno tiene opinión personal y toma decisiones.

El hecho de que reconocemos lo importante que es la conciencia y el papel que juega en nuestras vidas hace difícil que actuemos "a pesar de lo que mi conciencia me dice", aún en circunstancias que no controlamos. Uno de los elementos principales de la opresión de las mujeres hispanas es el saber que repetidamente estamos obligadas a actuar en contra de lo que nos dice la conciencia. Nosotras relacionamos hacer lo que nos dice la conciencia con el honor—nuestro valor como ser humano—un elemento importante de la cultura hispana. El actuar en contra de la conciencia lo lleva a uno a la destrucción personal.

Cuando las teólogas mujeristas examinamos el rol de "la conciencia", nos preocupa la influencia que tiene en ésto la iglesia católica debido a recientes episodios en los cuales la curia romana ha tratado de suprimir puntos de vista tradicionales sobre la primacía de la conciencia y ha tratado de subordinar la conciencia personal a la obediencia a Roma en materia moral tanto como en disciplina eclesiástica. Ésto impide el desarrollo de la agencia moral de mujeres hispanas, elemento central de nuestra lucha por la liberación.

En nuestros países de origen, la mayoría de las mujeres hispanas tienen poca relación con la iglesia católica "oficial". Pero aquí en los EE.UU. la iglesia católica tiene la posibilidad de ejercer mayor control sobre las hispanas principalmente por dos razones: Primero, en este país la iglesia tiene una estructura mucho más fuerte a nivel parroquial mientras que en nuetros países de origen faltan sacerdotes y no hay una organización parroquial efectiva. Segundo, en este país la iglesia católica oficial tiene considerable acceso a los medios de comunicación y las hispanas escuchamos la radio y vemos la televisión mucho más que lo hacen las mujeres en nuestros países de origen. Por lo tanto, la iglesia tiene oportunidad de ejercer mayor influencia sobre lo que pensamos y cómo actuamos. Es por eso que nuestra tarea como teólogas mujeristas de apoyar el desarrollo de la agencia moral de las mujeres hispanas es tan importante. Es más, siguiendo la tradición doctrinal de la iglesia católica, nos toca a las teólogas mujeristas defender el derecho y la obligación que tenemos de desarrollar y obedecer nuestras conciencias.

El pensar de los obispos católicos hoy día sobre la conciencia

Aunque la doctrina de la primacía de la conciencia es muy antigua, en general no es algo que los fieles sepan y hoy en día es algo no respetado por un número significativo de la jerarquía. La jerarquía hoy día tiende a pensar en la naturaleza y función de la conciencia en relación con la manera en que entiende el papel que ellos juega en determinar qué es la verdad y qué función tiene ella en hacer que su verdad sea aceptada por todos. Más y más, gran número de obispos parecen creer que la autoridad de la jerarquía es el factor decisivo en la función educativa de la iglesia. Es más, Juan Pablo II y algunos miembros de la jerarquía han dicho que lo que dice la jerarquía y la sabiduría de la Biblia tienen la misma función en cuanto a lo que tienen que hacer y creer los católicos; como dijo un delegado del Vaticano no hace mucho, "no hay diferencia sustancial entre la palabra de Dios y la palabra del Papa". Esta manera de pensar es una amplificación del dogma de la infalibilidad papal la cual se debe invocar sólo en cuestiones de fe. Esta manera de pensar no permite estar en desacuerdo con enseñanzas de la iglesia que no son infalibles y presenta a los católicos un dilema: hacer lo que nos dice la conciencia o lo que dice el Vaticano.

Restricción de la libertad de conciencia

Negar la posibilidad de estar en desacuerdo con las enseñanzas no infalibles de la iglesia tiene como resultado la restricción de la importancia y el papel de la conciencia. La insistencia por parte de la jerarquía en que hay que obedecer y la amenaza de medidas punitivas contra aquellos que no lo hacen, el énfasis que los obispos ponen en saber y obedecer las leyes de la iglesia—todo esto lleva a una "conciencia autoritaria" que internaliza la autoridad externa y la obedece en vez de hacer lo que le dice su conciencia de acuerdo a los valores morales de la persona. La "conciencia autoritaria" piensa que no tiene derecho a preguntar, a criticar; el pecado principal para ella es la desobediencia. Personas con "conciencia autoritaria" creen que deben obedecer a ciegas y se sienten culpables cuando se sienten fuertes, independientes, orgullosos de quienes son y lo qué piensan. Personas con "conciencia autoritaria" creen que aquellos en posiciones de autoridad son superiores a ellas. Y las personas con autoridad piensan que tienen el privilegio de dictar lo que los demás deben hacer, pensar, ser; las personas con autoridad piensan que son, no un medio, sino el fin en sí. Es posible que ésta sea la razón por la cual la jerarquía hoy día no quiere que los teólogos participen en la función magisterial de la iglesia: la jerarquía no puede aceptar el ser influenciada por otros, haciendo lo que otros dicen. Ésta también puede ser la razón por la cual la jerarquía hoy día parece ignorar la creencia en el *sensus fidelium*, creencia que la iglesia ha mantenido por siglos y siglos. El *sensus fidelium* es la creencia de que los fieles, desde los obispos hasta el último miembro de la feligresía, ungidos por el Espíritu Santo, no erran en sus creencias. Es verdad que los fieles no se pueden considerar en ésto aparte de la jerarquía, pero la jerarquía no se puede considerar incapaz de errar sino se considera como parte del Pueblo de Dios, sino se ve intrinsicamente ligada al resto de los fieles.

El reverso de la "conciencia autoritaria" es la "conciencia buena", que no se entiende como algo aparte del resto de la persona, sino que le ayuda a uno a ver que lo importante no es una norma externa sino la revelación del ser humano como persona. Para la "conciencia buena" lo que uno hace no sólo revela quien uno es, sino también ayuda a que uno se constituya en sujeto, se cree a sí mismo como agente moral.

Desarrollo histórico de la tradición católica

Desgraciadamente desde el siglo XVI hasta la segunda mitad del siglo XX la teología moral en la iglesia católica fue una disciplina muy práctica, preocupada mayormente con la educación de confesores en su papel de jueces. La teología moral durante este período se alejó de sus raíces dogmáticas y espirituales. Ésto se debió en gran parte a la mentalidad de sitio que prevaleció en la iglesia a partir de la Reforma Protestante. El Concilio de Trento en 1545 homogeneizó las enseñanzas de la iglesia y centralizó su autoridad tratando de proteger a la iglesia del "asedio" protestante. Fue por eso que se le dió tanta importancia a los decretos disciplinarios y que se estableció la Oficina del Santo Oficio.

Comienza el siglo XX con la teología moral católica totalmente preocupada con la conciencia a la cual veía en forma minimalista y legalista lo cual llevó a un entendimiento de la moralidad y la vida moral como algo extrínsico a la persona. El entendimiento de la conciencia ha sido durante todos estos siglos mayormente racionalista sin ninguna consideración afectiva. Pero, aún durante estos tiempos, aunque a veces se trató de restarle importancia a la primacía de la conciencia, nunca se llegó a negar que uno tiene por encima de todo la obligación de hacer lo que la conciencia dicta.

Es a partir del Concilio Vaticano Segundo que la perspectiva jurídica sobre la conciencia ha ido cambiando. Aunque de vez en cuando todavía se habla de la conciencia como una facultad humana, mayormente hoy se entiende la conciencia como una clase de instinto espiritual para la preservación de la persona que surge del deseo de unidad y armonía. Esta unidad y armonía se logran sólo a través de la inserción en el mundo de lo veraz y lo bueno a nivel de experiencias en las cuales el ser existencial esta involucrado. Desde la perspectiva cristiana se puede decir que la conciencia tiene una voz propia pero no una palabra propia; su palabra es la voz de Cristo que escuchamos en la creación, en la encarnación del Verbo. Los puntos de vista que uno tiene son responsabilidad propia, pero la voz de Dios nos impela a actuar de acuerdo con esos entendimientos racionales. Así es que la conciencia no crea la verdad pero sí tiene que actuar de acuerdo con lo que considera que es la verdad aunque uno esté equivocado.

La obligación de actuar de acuerdo a lo que dicta la conciencia va mano a mano con el derecho que tenemos al libre albedrío. Este derecho está basado en el objetivo final de toda persona, meta que para la teología mujerista no puede ser otra que la liberación de la persona. Nos preguntamos entonces, ¿existe la iglesia institucional para ayudar a la persona a lograr su meta o es la persona una consideración secundaria? La iglesia institucional es una realidad sociológica e histórica—al igual que lo fue para Jesús la ley y el sábado—creada para la persona y no al revés. Es por eso que la persona puede insistir en que la iglesia reconozca y respete el derecho que tiene a seguir los dictados de su conciencia. Ésto quiere decir que los fieles tenemos que tener libertad interna y externa, libertad de verdad. Cada uno de los fieles tiene que tener inmunidad contra fuerzas externas, tiene que poder reclamar plenamente el privilegio de obedecer su conciencia y tiene que poder actuar de acuerdo a lo que la conciencia le dicta sin estorbo ni embarazo.

En vez de la preocupación inordenada de la jerarquía por la obediencia, las teólogas mujeristas creemos que lo que la iglesia insititucional necesita es preocuparse por programas de educación religiosa que ayuden a formar conciencia y eduquen acerca de los derechos y obligaciones que tenemos los católicos en lo que se refiere a la conciencia.

La conciencia en las iglesias protestantes históricas, las iglesias fundamentalistas y las pentecostales

Veinte por ciento de los hispanos en EE.UU. pertenecen o van a iglesias protestantes. En general en la tradición protestante debido al énfasis en la fe en vez de en las obras, hay una tendencia a ver la conciencia desde una perspectiva teológica y no ética. En la tradición protestante el papel de la conciencia ha sido mayormente el de hacer que la gente sepa que ha pecado. Se ha enfatizado mayormente el rol de la conciencia en hacer que la persona se sienta culpable y condenada y no se le ha dado, en general, el papel de dirigir a la persona. Esto se debe en gran parte a que en la teología protestante el pecado tiene poco que ver con la relación que la persona tiene con Dios ya que la salvación la da Dios sin que la persona tenga mucho que ver con ello. Es por eso que usualmente se ha pensado que el discutir el papel de la conciencia pudiese llevar a un énfasis en la moralidad lo cual pudiese desembocar en legalismo.

En el fundamentalismo, las iglesias pentecostales y las iglesias no-denominacionales, esta perspectiva protestante de la conciencia junto con un énfasis en la disciplina y la obediencia hacen peligrar la auto–determinación de las mujeres hispanas que participan en ellas. Los miembros de estos tipos de iglesias obedecen lo que se les dice es la ley, ya esté basado en una lectura fundamentalista de la Biblia o en lo que dice el ministro, porque creen que es la ley lo que tiene autoridad en vez de porque la ley refleja o encarna sus propios juicios morales. Es importante hacer notar dos cosas sobre la mayoría de estas iglesias. Primero, sus ministros son, mayormente, hombres, y la gran parte de la "disciplina" regula el comportamiento de las mujeres: cómo vestirse, arreglarse. Segundo, la lectura fundamentalista de la Biblia niega que existan mediaciones entre la palabra de Dios en la Biblia y la manera en que entendemos la Biblia. Lo que la Biblia dice y cómo se entiende, especialmente por aquellos que reclaman tener autoridad, es visto como una misma cosa. Además, lo que la Biblia dice se aplica directamente a situaciones contemporáneas totalmente ajenas al mundo bíblico. El resultado no es sólo una moralidad basada exclusivamente en el obedecer leyes, sino que el obedecer es ciego. Todo ésto lo que hace es disminuir la capacidad de las mujeres hispanas como sujetos morales.

Conocimiento moral y concientización

El pensar sobre la conciencia en forma integral nos lleva a enfatizar, no la conciencia como facultad aislada de la persona, sino a la persona como sujeto de su propia vida, capaz de determinar y de ser responsable de sí misma y de lo que hace. Ésto nos permite ver la vida moral como más que un obedecer de leyes y a la formación de la conciencia como más que un aprender leyes. Cuando el enfoque es la persona como agente moral, las consideraciones éticas no se relegan sólo a tomar decisiones sino crea la capacidad de la persona como agente moral a través de esas decisiones. La conciencia, por lo tanto, tiene que ver con el conocimiento moral de la persona, el conocimiento de la persona como agente moral, que se conoce a sí misma a través de sus propias experiencias y del comprender, juzgar y decidir por sí misma.

El conocimiento moral incluye lo que percibimos a través de los sentidos, lo cual vamos entendiendo y juzgando hasta llegar al momento donde tenemos que tomar una decisión. Es entonces que entramos en un proceso de evaluación moral, analizamos valores, los juzgamos y entonces decidimos de acuerdo a cómo hemos juzgado. Cuando las decisiones son libres, el agente moral escoge lo que cree debe hacer para ser consistente con quién uno es.

Desde la perpectiva de la teología mujerista, la mejor manera de educar acerca del conocimiento moral es a través de un proceso de concientización. El proceso de concientización tiene tres elementos: a) reconocer la diferencia entre lo que es natural e inevitable y lo que es cultural y cambiable; b) desenmascarar los mitos que permiten a los opresores dominar la sociedad negando las diferencias entre lo natural y lo cultural; c) explorar las alternativas que se pueden lograr a través del proceso de liberación.

El proceso de concientización, que no se da sino en la praxis, es un proceso de análisis crítico de la acción que lleva a entendimientos claves para decidir cuál será la próxima acción liberadora. Nadie puede concientizar a otra persona. Cada cual se concientiza a sí mismo participando en el proceso de acción–reflexión–acción que revela la realidad opresora en que vivimos las mujeres hispanas. Es por eso que el tema generador principal del proceso de concientización de las hispanas, la comprensión que juega el papel central en el proceso de acción–reflexión–acción, es el binomio supervivencia–liberación. Este tema expresa tanto lo que nos motiva como nuestra meta.

Ésto lo vimos en las entrevistas con las mujeres hispanas. Para ellas lo importante es hacer lo posible, lo que tengan que hacer, para vivir ellas— pero sobretodo, para que vivan sus hijos. Éste es el valor central que afecta sus decisiones, que constituye el eje central de su conocimiento moral. Y para ellas lo que la ética moral llama una norma moral es la responsabilidad que sienten por lograr la supervivencia no sólo de sus familias, sino de toda la comunidad. Estas mujeres hispanas saben que tienen esta responsabilidad también para consigo mismas, que tienen que cuidarse, respetarse y amarse porque si no, ¿cómo van a poder tener una relación con Dios? Ellas saben que el no cuidarse a sí mismas, el no preocuparse por su supervivencia y liberación tanto como la de la sus hijos y la comunidad en general, es el pecado que expresa y genera todo otro pecado.

CHAPTER 6

Praxis and Lived-Experience in *Mujerista* Theology

AT THE HEART of all liberation theologies is precisely the struggle for the liberation of the oppressed group from which each of these theologies rises. Though at times it may not be specifically pointed out and though at times an objectifying language does creep into some writings, most liberation theologians and other liberation activists claim, or at least recognize, that liberation is a personal, self-actualizing struggle which each one must accept as one's own responsibility. Liberation is a struggle that lasts one's whole life. Personal responsibility is one of the elements at the core of the moral subject and, therefore, at the heart of moral agency. Liberation theologies insist that the poor and the oppressed must struggle consciously to be agents of our own history. They must move away from being mere objects acted upon by the oppressors and become active subjects: moral persons.

As the women who speak to the reader through the pages of chapter 4 indicate, Latinas produce practical reality as they struggle to survive. Their telling of their stories shows how their struggle to survive is a praxis: a critical reflective action. This is obvious in their decision making which is not something they sit down to do apart from their daily struggles. Their decision making, formed within the Latino cultural ethos and sharpened by the struggle for survival, provides for them the moral wisdom they need in their everyday lives—in a praxis that challenges and effectively changes, even if it is only in minute ways, the oppressive reality in which they live.

Struggle and agency, then, do not exist apart from praxis. Liberative praxis is a dominant theme in *mujerista* theology, providing a point of entry into it and into its main preoccupation: the moral agency of Latinas. This is why in this chapter I will examine the meaning of *praxis*, how it is used in *mujerista* theology, and why we consider our theological enterprise a praxis in itself.

What grounds *mujerista* theology as a praxis? It is grounded by and rises from the lived-experience of Latinas, which in turn leads to future lived-experience that enables and expresses our moral agency. We have dealt with the centrality of the lived-experience of Latinas since the beginning of this book. In the second part of this chapter we concentrate on analyzing why *mujerista* theologians insist on the lived-experience of Latinas as the source of our theology.

The collective or communal lived-experience of Latinas as oppressed people is at the heart of *mujerista* theology and leads to a preferential option for Latinas, a preferential option that constitutes the "verifying criterion" of all Christian understandings, practices, and institutions for *mujerista* theology and ethics. When this preferential option becomes the lens through which doing theology is analyzed, it becomes necessary to embrace grassroot Latinas not merely as the subject matter of *mujerista* theology and as the ones to whom we who write about *mujerista* theology are accountable. We must must also embrace grassroot Latinas engaged in liberative praxis infused with their religiosity as *mujerista* theologians themselves and their liberative praxis as *mujerista* theology. We will explore this important concept in the last section of this chapter.

Praxis in *Mujerista* Theology

From the very beginning of our attempts to articulate a *mujerista* theology, the centrality of praxis has been clear. In *mujerista* theology praxis is critical reflective action based on an analysis of historical reality perceived through the lens of an option for and a commitment to the liberation of Latinas.[1] In *mujerista* theology "life is already praxis, that is why in the praxis is included, in a condensed form, all of reality."[2] For us, praxis is a political action which seeks to change the oppressive economic-socio-cultural structures of society.[3] This political action is a liberative action which requires a historical project—a project that, as we have indicated in chapter 2, questions the established order while proposing its own perspective about a preferred future. Praxis, therefore, requires human agency, intentionality, and a political commitment to change the infrastructure in relationship to the suprastructures. It demands a keen awareness that *how* we go about changing the structures is a key element in what we will

---

1. Ada María Isasi-Díaz and Yolanda Tarango, *Hispanic Women: Prophetic Voice in the Church* (Minneapolis: Fortress, 1992), 1.

2. Leonardo Boff, "¿Qué es hacer teología desde América Latina?" in *Liberación y cautiverio*. Encuentro Latinoamericano de Teología (México, 1975), 144.

3. Political here is used not in the sense of partisan politics nor having to do directly with holding governmental positions. Political here refers to the activity we carry out in society that seeks to influence society, that has consequences for society at large.

accomplish.[4] Praxis in *mujerista* theology is always understood as liberative praxis.

In defining praxis as critical reflective action—reflective as different from mechanical, routine action—*mujerista* theology seeks to emphasize that the reflection part does not follow action nor is it "at the service of action."[5] Both action and reflection become inseparable moments though neither is reduced to the other. Praxis "combines reflection with action to create the human world of ideas, symbols, language, science, religion, art, and production."[6]

In *mujerista* theology liberative praxis is one of the main referents of *mujerista* anthropology. Praxis as a referent leads to an anthropology that departs from that of modern theology. Modern theology's anthropology revolves around a so-called bourgeois subject characterized by a freedom based on rationalism and individualism. In contrast, the anthropology of Latin American liberation theology (and perhaps of other liberation theologies as well), centers on the poor, on those who suffer, on those who have been ignored by history and are not only marginal but considered and treated by the power elites as superfluous population.[7]

An anthropology developed out of the lived-experience of Latinas centers on a subject who struggles to survive and who understands herself as one who struggles. A small but common indication of this is how to the casual question, "How are you," grassroot Latinas commonly respond just as *casually*, *"Ahí, en la lucha,"* there, in the struggle, instead of the "fine, thank you," which we are accustomed to hear. Of course the centrality of struggle as a constitutive element of the everyday lives of Latinas, of Latinas' self-construction, can be understood and grasped only against a background of oppression due to specific historical injustices that are the cause of great suffering. But in listening carefully to grassroot Latinas, one finds that what locates us in life is not suffering but *la lucha* to survive.[8] To consider suffering as what locates us would mean that we understand ourselves not as a moral subject but as one acted upon by the oppressors.[9] It would

4. Xosé Miguélez, *La Teología de la liberación y su método* (Barcelona: Editorial Herder, 1976), 49.

5. José Míguez Bonino, *Doing Theology in a Revolutionary Situation* (Philadelphia: Fortress, 1975), 72.

6. Denis E. Collins, *Paulo Freire: His Life, Works, and Thought* (New York: Paulist Press, 1977), 49.

7. Rebecca Chopp, *The Praxis of Suffering* (Maryknoll: Orbis Books, 1986), 121–26.

8. As a *mujerista* theologian I want to stay within the boundaries of this specific theological enterprise but I do believe "struggle" is what locates all oppressed people. I believe that even—or maybe precisely—in the worst of conditions, what makes a human being maintain her humanity until her last breath is her capacity to struggle to live.

9. Here I am arriving at a different conclusion than that of several Latin American liberation theologians, of Rebecca Chopp in *The Praxis of Suffering*, and of Hispanic theologians, Roberto Goizueta, *"Nosotros:* Toward a U.S. Hispanic Anthropology," *Listening* 27, no. 1

mean that what is central to ourselves is consenting and accepting a life full of opprobrium. That is the opposite of what our lives are.[10]

Though we have not received much public recognition for it, Latinas are often leaders in our communities. Latinas have been always in charge of making ends meet in our families and when we have not been able to do so any longer, we have been the ones to raise our voices in protest, to push Latino men to organize and demand more. Our exclusion from the public arena has not kept us out of struggles for justice, and we have, time and again, realized that waiting for our reward in heaven will not feed our children here on this earth. Often Latinas are seen as submissive and docile, and perhaps this is why suffering is seen by some as the main referent in our self-understanding. But most of the time submission and docility are survival tactics that make it possible to find a space to "be," to fight for our families and communities and, yes, for ourselves.

If what locates Latinas is *la lucha*, then we will be seen not only as a strategic force in history but rather as historical, moral subjects, aware of our own role in defining and bringing about a preferred future. Latinas have always been key actors in the history of our people. *Mujerista* theology recognizes this and moves on to enable the "irruption of history" into the lives of Latinas:

> When we speak of the irruption of history into the lives of women – and especially the theological expression of their faith – we do not mean the entrance of women into history; they have always been present. What we have in mind is something qualitatively different and new, that is, the irruption of historic consciousness into the lives of millions and millions of women, leading them to struggle by means of an active participation in different fronts from which they had previously been absent. . . . [Women have become] aware of history, entering into a broader meaning, in which women are also creators or increasingly want to be forgers of history.[11]

But we cannot understand *la lucha* as what locates the Latinas unless, as we have said above, we posit praxis as a referent for a *mujerista* anthropology. Only if Latinas as human subjects are reconceived through praxis can our everyday struggle be understood as having meaning in our

---

(Winter 1992): 55–69, and Samuel Solivan, "Orthopathos: Interlocutor between Orthodoxy and Praxis," *Andover Newton Review* 1, no. 2 (Winter 1990): 19–25.

10. María Pilar Aquino, *Nuestro Clamor Por La Vida* (San José, Costa Rica: Editorial D.E.I., 1992), 37.

11. Ivone Gebara, "Women Doing Theology in Latin America," in *Through Her Eyes*, ed. Elsa Tamez (Maryknoll: Orbis Books, 1989),43. I find parts of this translation, like most translations, lacking in preciseness, somewhat distorting what the original version says. Though I have made use of the book in English, I have referred to the Spanish version often, in itself a translation of Gebara's Portuguese.

lives and giving meaning to our existence, as an element of our process to become moral agents and moral subjects. [12]

To grasp better what claiming praxis as a referent for *mujerista* anthropology means, we must, first of all, understand the importance of reflection in praxis. *Mujerista* theology insists on the reflective moment of praxis, for it is precisely Latinas' ability to understand and think that is often questioned and debased. Praxis must not be equated with practice. Praxis is both intellectual enterprise as well as action; the dichotomy between intellectual activity and physical work is a fictitious one. *Mujerista* theology has insisted that Latinas are organic intellectuals because, as Gramsci stated, "one cannot speak of non-intellectuals, because non-intellectuals do not exist. . . . There is no human activity from which every form of intellectual participation can be excluded: *homo faber* cannot be separated from *homo sapiens.*" [13] We believe with Gramsci that each person who participates "in a particular conception of the world, has a conscious line of moral conduct, and therefore contributes to sustain a conception of the world or to modify it, that is, to bring into being new modes of thought." [14]

Mujerista theologians' insistence on the centrality of praxis, therefore, does not make our enterprise anti-intellectual, just as Latinas' self-construction as persons who struggle to survive does not mean that we surrender the intellectual enterprise to the dominant groups. [15] Our insistence on praxis does not put reason and intellect aside. On what grounds can oppressors claim that Latinas' style of life, a style necessary to survive, is nonrational? On the contrary, those who struggle to survive are the very ones who can question the rationality of oppressors, who themselves are not capable of understanding this basic truth: that in the long run, only what benefits all of humanity will really benefit them. Those whose daily bread is the struggle for survival are the ones who have grounds to question what is considered intelligent and reasonable by society at large.

Another reason praxis is a referent for *mujerista* anthropology is that praxis is not just any reflective action. Rather it is reflective action grounded in community, action that depends on the changing needs of the Latino community, action that is ongoing in a community responsible for itself. [16] The sense of community pervades Latinas' liberative praxis

12. Cf. Chopp, *The Praxis of Suffering*, 122.
13. Antonio Gramsci, *Prison Notebooks*, ed. and trans. Quintin Hoare and Geoffrey Nowell Smith (New York: International Publishers, 1975), 9.
14. Ibid.
15. See Roberto Goizueta, "Presidential Address," *ACHTUS Newsletter* (A publication of the Academy of Catholic Hispanic Theologians of the United States, 1050 N. Clark, El Paso, TX 79905) 2, no. 1 (Winter 1990): 4–6.
16. Chopp, *The Praxis of Suffering*, 122–23.

because for us community is not a matter of where we live or of how we work, but of who we are. In our culture, to be a person one necessarily has to relate to others. Community is not something added on, but a web of relationships constitutive of who we are. This is why our use of the word *individual* is not a positive one. Commonly, when one says *ese individuo* (that individual), one is talking about someone who is selfish, who is despicable in some way or other, someone who for some reason or other is outside the Latino community. Since community, then, is also an intrinsic element of praxis, community becomes another motive for considering praxis as the main referent in a *mujerista* anthropology.[17]

Mujerista theology not only understands liberative praxis as one of its key elements but claims that the doing of *mujerista* theology is itself a praxis. We do not believe that our theological enterprise is a "second step,"[18] or a "second reality."[19] We do not see theology as the reflection part of the "dialectic circularity of praxis-reflection [which] constitutes the unity and richness of the experience."[20] We do not see our writing of *mujerista* theology as a reflection on praxis, or mostly as "an explication of what was already present in a diffuse and a-thematic way in the praxis."[21]

In claiming the doing of *mujerista* theology as a liberative praxis, as a matter of fact, we are carrying out one of the constitutive dimensions of praxis: critiquing and denouncing oppressive structures. Simply claiming that *mujerista* theology is a liberative praxis severely critiques and protests the diminishment of Latinas portrayed by the dominant culture which does not recognize us as intellectuals capable of critical and creative thinking. This critique is precisely the motivating force behind our insistence on the reflective moment of praxis.

Second, the doing of *mujerista* theology is a liberative praxis because our enterprise has as its lens the liberation of Latinas and, therefore, it critiques oppressive structures of the dominant culture while refusing to romanticize Latino culture. We critique the oppressive understandings and practices of women inherent in Latino culture, and we refuse to keep silence in the name of "protecting" our communities against the dominant culture.

Third, *mujerista* theology is a liberative praxis because our critique extends to the attempts that are made, even by some liberation theologians, to reserve the title of "theologian" to those who are academically trained.

17. For an insightful view of the role of the Hispanic view of community in articulating a Hispanic anthropology see Goizueta, *"Nosotros,"* 55–69.

18. Gustavo Gutiérrez, *A Theology of Liberation* (Maryknoll: Orbis Books, 1988), 9.

19. Leonardo Boff, "Qué es hacer teología," 143.

20. Ibid., 144.

21. Ibid.

We believe that one of the elements at work in this reservation is the lack of acceptance of the intellectual capacity of grassroot people, of poor and oppressed people, the majority of whom—as demonstrated in the Latino community—are women.

Finally, as a liberative praxis *mujerista* theology does not shrink from the responsibility of critiquing ourselves when necessary. As we did in chapter 2 above, we critique Latinas who seek to accommodate, who want to make it in this society, no matter what the cost, who work vigorously to become part of the dominant group instead of struggling to change oppressive structures. We see their attempts as an individualistic struggle betraying the sense of community which grounds us. Those of us who do make it in this society must examine how we ourselves have become part of oppressive structures, how we maintain these structures, and how our apparent "liberation" comes at the expense of others.

For us, then, doing *mujerista* theology is not a second moment, having to do only with the reflection part of praxis. For us, reflection and practice are inseparably bound in praxis, and our doing theology is a liberative praxis. This does not mean, however, that we see the doing of *mujerista* theology as the only praxis in our struggle for liberation. But admitting that it is not the only praxis does not mean that it not a praxis and, at times, a very important one.

Our understanding of *mujerista* theology as a liberating praxis is a refusal to reduce theology to a formal, disciplinary discourse in which adequacy has to do with certain intellectual criteria formulated by those who control the cultural and academic apparatus and which are quite foreign to the day-to-day struggle of Latinas to survive.[22] *Mujeristas'* understanding of theology is indeed an attempt to deconstruct the normative, mainline, disciplinary method of theology in order to recognize that theological understandings play an important role in Latinas' daily life where the norm is *hacer lo que se puede aunque no sea siempre lo mejor*, to do what one is able to do even if it is not always the best thing to do, in order to survive.[23]

Hacer lo que se puede para sobrevivir, to do what one has to do in order to survive, points to the importance of preferring orthopraxis to orthodoxy in *mujerista* theology.[24] For *mujerista* theologians, then, "truth is at the

---

22. We are not denying the need for consistency and coherence as part of moral and theological criteria, but the way they are understood has to take into consideration, for example, the practicality and flexibility of Latinas' everyday life which is essential for their survival. Mainline intellectuals often consider practicality and flexibility to be incoherent because of what they consider inconsistencies and contradictions.

23. Pedro A. Sandín-Fremaint, "Domesticating the Theology of Liberation: A Deconstructive Reading of Clodovis Boff's *Theology and Praxis*," *Apuntes* 7, no. 2 (Spring 1987): 27–41.

24. In this we follow the lead of Latin American liberation theology and other liberation

level of history, not in the realm of ideas."[25] We do not understand *mujerista* theology as contributing primarily to an explanation of the world or to traditional, mainline understandings of questions of ultimate meaning. For us theology is a task, a doing; it is an attempt to change, in a radical way, oppressive structures. It aims to transform the world by making the voice of Latinas heard, by having our understandings impact what is normative in society. This is why our concern is with orthopraxis, with transformative action, with the ways in which religious understandings are at the heart of Latinas' struggle to survive; with how our struggle impacts religious understandings and practices; and with helping to enable the development of Latinas' moral agency. We believe that in the long run *mujerista* theology, understood and functioning as a liberative praxis, will contribute significantly to the creation of new constructs within new paradigms, paradigms that will always be in the process of being developed and that will remain open to the critique arising out of the lived-experience of Latinas and of other oppressed peoples.

The Lived-Experience of Latinas

For some, the phrase *lived-experience* may seem tautological but we use it in *mujerista* theology to differentiate it from our regular, daily experience, that is, everything we do and everything that happens to us. In *mujerista* theology, lived-experience identifies those experiences in our lives about which we are intentional. It is the sum of our experience which we examine, reflect upon, deal with specifically. In so doing we make it a building block for our personal and communal struggle for liberation. Because intentionality is required in order to reflect actively on what we experience, Latinas' lived-experience is the ground for our moral development, for our consciousness raising and conscience formation, for the discovery and development of our values. And for us Latinas, none of this can happen without an awareness of the oppression and alienation we suffer.

As we have analyzed in the first two chapters, Latinas are oppressed in our society because of our ethnicity and our sex. Most Latinas are also oppressed economically: we are poor. This means that our lived-experience is often not the same as that of other ethnic groups or even of Latino men. Even if some of our experiences are the same as others', when we reflect on those experiences we bring to that reflection understandings which are different from those of other groups. Because of cultural differences, the

---

theologies. See Gutiérrez, *A Theology of Liberation*, 8; and Juan Luis Segundo, "Two Theologies," *Journal of Theology for South Africa* 52 (1985): 321–27.

25. José Míguez Bonino, *Doing Theology in a Revolutionary Situation* (Philadelphia: Fortress, 1975), 81.

way we understand a situation and the motives and values that come into play as we live through it are different from those of the dominant culture and different, too, from those of other marginalized racial/ethnic groups. Although we often conform outwardly to society's norms in order to survive, we are under great stress—as indeed would any group which is not an integral part of society—because of differences in our values and motivations. Racial/ethnic prejudices and sexism doubly compound the stress in the lives of Latinas.

Those who are influential in society are not our models. Their reasons for success are not our reasons. In other words, we Latinas do not find our understandings and values reflected in those of society. Our values are not part of the societal norm and are not, therefore, validated by society. But our lack of participation in setting what is normative in society results in more than mere lack of validation. Not only have we been excluded from shaping and interpreting the norms as well as the principles and institutions of society according to our own experience, but those norms, principles and societal institutions have been shaped and interpreted against us, in order to exclude and to exploit us.[26]

What is worse, the very understandings and values of Latino culture and the role of women within our culture are used to justify excluding and oppressing us.[27] The cultural and androcentric bias of contemporary U.S. society not only does not allow us to participate in setting the norm but even ignores anyone who may point out our absence.[28] Therefore, in order to validate who we are and what we do, in order to keep our sanity, we have to go deep within ourselves. We have to reflect on what we do and on who we are in order to remain faithful to ourselves, in order to remain sane.

Our lived-experiences have to be the building blocks of our self-understanding and of our morality if we are not to lose ourselves in the process. We have to depend on how we understand and live the events of our daily lives. We have to consider carefully our own stories in order to bring understanding out of the chaos created in our lives by the many forces that pull us in different directions. This chaos, this uprootedness, this not-having-a-place-to-call-home—these are the main reasons why our central preoccupation in this society is and has to be survival.

The lived-experience of Latinas, which deals mainly with the struggle to survive, is not only the *locus theologicus* which situates *mujerista* theology.

---

26. Cf. Rosemary Radford Ruether, "Feminist Interpretation: A Method of Correlation," in *Feminist Interpretation of the Bible*, ed. Letty Russell (Philadelphia: Westminster, 1985), 112.

27. This is also true within Latino culture, in the Latino communities.

28. Radford Ruether, "Feminist Interpretation," 113.

Our lived-experience is also the primary source of *mujerista* theology. This understanding validates our struggle and enables the development of the moral agency of Latinas. This understanding calls into question the whole issue of "objectivity." The need for a hermeneutic of suspicion regarding "objectivity" and "validity" is intrinsic to any theological enterprise arising from oppressed communities. For too long theology done by those belonging to the dominant culture, the dominant race, the dominant sex, has claimed to be objective. Those of us who belong to marginalized, oppressed groups have come to understand that what is called "objective" is simply the understanding of a given group of people who have the power to impose that understanding as normative in society. This so-called objectivity arises from the lived-experience of dominant groups of society and ignores the lived-experience of the oppressed to the point of considering it deviant.

As *mujerista* theologians we claim that even the attempt to be objective is flawed. Though we do not deny that *the truth* does or might exist, what we are insisting on is that our theological enterprise has to do with the reality Hispanic Women create and confront every day.[29] For *mujerista* theologians it is clear that theology is not so much about God as about how we understand and relate to God. And that is precisely one of the reasons for our insistence on the lived-experience of Latinas as the source of our theology. We insist on our lived-experiences as central not because we think that our reality is necessarily unique. This insistence should not be understood either as an attempt to claim a clearer or better understanding of *the truth*. We do it because we believe that what needs to be done is to identify the perspective from which we are writing and to state clearly the goal of our theological discourse. This will make it possible for those who engage us to understand and to analyze what we are saying.

When we claim the lived-experience of Hispanic Women as the source of *mujerista* theology, we are making clear our subjectivity by identifying what it is that grounds us, what our starting point is, and where we get the material we work with.[30] Those who claim the Bible or church teaching as the source of their theology are glossing over the fact that the real source of their theology is *their* understanding of the Bible and of church teaching. Furthermore, theologians often ignore the fact that the Bible as well as church teaching are conditioned by the socio-economic-political realities of the period in which both were formulated.

29. Sheila Greeve Davaney, "The Limits of the Appeal to Women's Experience," in *Shaping New Vision: Gender and Values in American Culture*, ed. Clarissa W. Atkinson, Constance H. Buchanan, and Margaret R. Miles (Ann Arbor: U.M.I. Research Press, 1987), 41–49.

30. The bibliographical references in our work point to other sources, secondary ones, of our theology.

To use the lived-experience of Hispanic Women as the source of *mujerista* theology contributes to a reconceptualization of what is rational. Instead of thinking that only thought processes can yield rationality, we insist that lived-experience highlights the point of view that the whole mystery of existence—including what we know, conclude, and express using the senses, desires, flavor, pleasure, pain, imagination—can also contribute to and yield rational thinking and rational behavior. The totality of Latinas' lived-experience, not only our thought process, amplifies our theological language, leading it to include not only linear, logical argumentation but also prophetic denunciation, songs and poems of protest and hope, lamentations and language of consolation. And our theological language is not only a matter of written words but also of liturgical rituals, street demonstrations, and protest actions.[31]

The doing of *mujerista* theology starts by examining the lived-experience of Latinas and uses it to understand who we are, to ask questions of ultimate meaning for survival, and to answer those questions. Without this lived-experience, *mujerista* theology would have nothing to say: it could only repeat what has already been said. That is not a valid reason for any theological enterprise. Because of its source, *mujerista* theology goes beyond a reinterpretation of theological understandings. Our agenda, then, has to do with framing questions rather than providing answers, challenging religious understandings which negate our experience rather than finding ways to relate those understandings to our lives. *Mujerista* theology is more about questioning the way theology is done than making a niche for ourselves within the structures of contemporary theology and academia.

Grassroot Latinas as *Mujerista* Theologians

Since the source of *mujerista* theology is the lived-experience of Latinas, since we believe that grassroot Latinas are organic intellectuals capable of reflection, and since *mujerista* theology is a liberative praxis, we do not hesitate to call grassroot Latinas whose religious understandings and practices are an intrinsic element of their struggle to survive *mujerista* theologians.[32] In chapter 3 we argued from a sociological perspective the need to present the actual voices of Latinas in *mujerista* theology. We also indicated that if Latinas do not speak for ourselves we run the risk of once

---

31. Cf. the interview of Ivone Gebara in Elsa Tamez, *Teólogos de la liberación hablan sobre la mujer* (San José, Costa Rica: Editorial D.E.I., 1986), 121–22.

32. In Isasi-Díaz and Tarango, *Hispanic Women*, 104–9 we called those of us who facilitate the theological process, gather the wisdom of the Latinas, and do the writing, "theological technicians," and we outlined the task of these technicians. Since the first edition of our book, published in 1988, this is one of the points that has been most debated and opposed. This is why we felt it important to expand this understanding here.

again being objectified, of perhaps becoming subject matter for theology but not being the subjects of the process of theologizing.

If the title and role of theologian is reserved only for those with academic education and degrees, it would not be possible to claim that *mujerista* theology is a liberative praxis in which all Latinas can engage, and it would be impossible to have as its main goal the enablement of moral agency for Latinas. Though we realize that those who are not poor and oppressed—or those who are less poor and oppressed than Latinas—can stand in solidarity with us and use their theological enterprise to help us in our struggle for liberation, such theological enterprise still cannot be sufficient, for it might excuse us from doing *mujerista* theology.[33]

To insist that grassroot Latinas can be and are *mujerista* theologians is part of the process of conquering spaces to express our word and our being.[34] It points to a change in our consciousness: though we have earlier understood ourselves as struggling to survive, now we are conscious of our *causality*. This sense of causality in our lives is not a mere psychological development but it is also an intellectual and rational process promoting hermeneutical suspicions in all areas of our lives and leading to great creativity in the way we understand ourselves and in our day-to-day living.[35] Being conscious of the causality of our lives leads us to claim the right to speak for ourselves, for only *we* can explain how we understand ourselves and our reality.

As we have said before, *mujerista* theology as a praxis is done by the community as each one contributes to the process of doing theology according to her own gifts. At a given moment, because of a particular need, one gift may be more useful than another, but that does not make it more important. Those of us who are the "theological technicians," who generally have academic training and academic degrees, are not to be considered more fully theologians than the Latinas who lead the action component of our liberating praxis, or those who are gifted in expressing the beliefs of the community through rituals.[36] Therefore, there is no such thing as academic *mujerista* theology on one hand and grassroot *mujerista* theology on the other.[37]

33. This was already dealt with in much greater detail in chap. 3 when we talked about the issue of the theologian as insider or outsider.

34. Gebara, "Women Doing Theology," 44.

35. Aquino, *Nuestro Clamor*, 58–62.

36. Isasi-Díaz and Tarango, *Hispanic Women*, 104–10. We owe much in helping us to understand and formulate what we believe in this regard to Carlos Abesamis, "Doing Theological Reflection in a Philippine Context," in *The Emergent Gospel* (Maryknoll: Orbis Books, 1978), 112–23.

37. See Gustavo Gutiérrez, "Reflections from a Latin American Perspective," in *Irruption of the Third World*, ed. Virginia Fabella and Sergio Torres (Maryknoll: Orbis Books, 1983),

Some Latin American liberation theologians have posited different levels of liberation theology: professional, pastoral, popular. [38] Though *mujerista* theologians accept that there are different kinds of "theological jobs" to be done in the community, [39] declaring that these jobs yield different kinds of discourse, have different kinds of logic, and use different kinds of methods is not congruent with our experience. [40] But we go further and question the very understandings of *discourse, logic,* and *method* that are proposed in an attempt to differentiate different levels of liberation theology. In *mujerista* theology, for example, theological discourse cannot but be organically related to practice and that does not make it any less detailed or rigorous. Nor does being detailed and rigorous mean that it is not spontaneous, for *mujerista* theology as a discourse is not something obscure. It is, rather, something *a flor de piel* – only skin deep – which Latinas share quite readily. And when it comes to logic, can one really differentiate between a "logic of life" and a "logic of action: specific, prophetic, propulsive"? For Latinas who struggle to survive, is not our logic of life, which is necessarily a logic of action, a logic that has to be "methodical, systematic and dynamic"?

Finally, perhaps it is with the differences posited in method that we have greatest problems. For *mujerista* theologians the ongoing revelation of who God is and what God is like is to be found in our struggle for survival and justice. For us, to be a Christian is to participate in this struggle, and we participate in this struggle by doing *mujerista* theology. We do not live differently as Christians from the way we live as *mujerista* theologians. We do not accept the understanding that "contemplation and practice together constitute the *first act*; theologizing is the *second act*."[41] For us, this division is artificial not only because of our understanding of the intrinsic connection between reflection and practice in praxis but also because for us the sacred is an integral part of our daily lives. This is why our operative understanding is that our doing *mujerista* theology is our way of life.

224–31. Here Gutierrez struggles with this differentiation and we believe tends to affirm it because of understanding theology as a "second act," which in our opinion separates action from reflection.

38. Leonardo Boff and Clodovis Boff, *Introducing Liberation Theology* (Maryknoll: Orbis Books, 1987), 11–21.

39. See Isasi-Díaz and Tarango, *Hispanic Women,* 104–5 for examples of possible jobs. See also Ivone Gebara's interview in *Teólogos de la liberación hablan sobre la mujer* (San José, Costa Rica: Editorial D.E.I., 1986), 121–25. A synthesis of what she says there is included in Gebara, "Women Doing Theology."

40. We also question the other five elements that the Boff brothers indicate as being different in the three levels of liberation theology that they posit. We concentrate here on these three because they are the ones that most contradict *mujerista* theology's understandings and practices.

41. Gutiérrez, "Reflections," 226.

It seems to us that to insist that grassroot Latinas whose liberative praxis is informed by their religiosity are the same kind of and as fully *mujerista* theologians as those of us who are academically trained, is to take seriously the preferential option for the poor and the oppressed that grounds all liberation struggles. This option is grounded in the belief that from their marginality the poor and the oppressed can see a different future, a better future for themselves, and, in the long run if not in the short one, a better future for all. The option for the poor is also grounded in what we said above about Latinas coming into a new consciousness regarding our causality in history. Although we believe we have always been "one of the most decisive dynamic elements in history,"[42] up to now this dynamism has been unspecific, part of the structural forces of society. At present, however, Latinas have moved from being "a submerged conscience" to being "an emerged or critical conscience."[43]

A preferential option for the poor cannot be paternalistic, it cannot be a "doing for them," no matter how self-sacrificing that is. How can liberation theologians claim on the one hand that the preferential option of the Church for the poor entails recognizing the poor as the agents, the protagonists, of the evangelizing efforts of the Church,[44] and not recognize grassroot people as theologians? How can they insist that "the exact meaning" of the preferential option for the poor is "to recognize the privileged status of the poor as the new and emerging historical subject which will carry on the Christian project in the world,"[45] while at the same time excluding them from the theological task or severely limiting their participation by creating different levels of liberation theology?

Mujerista theologians believe that the preferential option for the poor has to be more than a conceptual claim and that in order to do so it has to yield specific praxis. A key praxis it must produce is the recognition that all Latinas engaged in the struggle to survive—the struggle for liberation—are capable of speaking our own word, naming our own reality, reflecting upon and making explicit our own religious understandings and practices.

42. Marciano Vidal García, "La Preferencia por el pobre, criterio moral," *Studia Moralia* 20 (1982): 284.

43. Ibid. Vidal here is using some of the terminology of Paulo Freire. I do not think this is the place to verify this irruption of history into Latinas' lives. Vidal verifies this in regard to the poor in Latin America in a way that we believe we can apply to Latinas. The same is true of Gutiérrez's arguments in this regard in *The Power of the Poor in History* (Maryknoll: Orbis Books, 1984), especially chaps. 4 and 7.

44. Vidal, "La Preferencia," 290.

45. Leonardo Boff, *Church: Charism and Power* (New York: Crossroad, 1986), 9.

⊡ SÍNTESIS DEL CAPÍTULO 6: Praxis y Experiencia de Vida en la Teología *Mujerista*.

Como indican las entrevistas que hicimos para este libro, las latinas producen su realidad cotidiana al luchar por sobrevivir. La manera en que viven prueba el hecho de que esa lucha es una verdadera praxis, una acción reflexiva. Vimos como ellas toman decisiones de acuerdo a los valores de la cultura latina y a lo que les ha enseñado la lucha por sobrevivir. Ésto es lo que les da la sabiduría moral que necesitan en la vida cotidiana, en la praxis liberadora que va cambiando, casi en forma imperceptible, la realidad opresiva que vivimos.

La lucha por la liberación, por ser agentes o sujetos morales no existe sino en la praxis. ¿Por qué es que la teología mujerista se considera praxis liberadora? Es porque está centrada en la experiencia cotidiana, en la experiencia colectiva–comunitaria de las latinas como grupo oprimido. Es porque la teología mujerista encarna una opción preferencial por las latinas, opción que para ellas constituye el criterio verificativo del cristianismo: de las enseñanzas, instituciones y prácticas cristianas. El que esta opción preferencial sea el lente a través del cual analizamos todo aspecto teológico hace necesario que las latinas sean no sólo el tema principal de la teología mujerista sino también sean consideradas ellas mismas teólogas: mujeres que reflexionan en forma crítica sobre sus creencias y prácticas religiosas.

La praxis en la teología mujerista

Desde el principio hemos insistido en que la teología mujerista es una praxis liberadora. En la teología mujerista entendemos praxis como la acción reflexiva basada en un análisis crítico de nuestra realidad histórica hecho a partir de una opción por y un compromiso con la liberación de las latinas. La vida de las mujeres latinas es una praxis porque nuestro sobrevivir es una acción política que busca cambiar estructuras económicas, sociales, y culturales que son opresivas. Esta praxis, al ser acción política, requiere un proyecto histórico que cuestione el orden presente y tenga su propia visión del futuro. La praxis, por lo tanto, requiere intencionalidad y un compromiso con el cambio tanto de la infraestructura como el de la superestructura. También requiere especial atención a cómo se lleva a cabo el cambio de las estructuras ya que la manera en que se hace influye en lo que se logra.

El definir la praxis como acción reflexiva la distingue de la acción rutinaria y enfatiza que la reflexión no viene después de la acción ni está al servicio de la acción. En la praxis, la acción y la reflexión son inseparables aunque no se deben confundir el uno con el otro. En la praxis, la reflexión se combina con la acción para crear el mundo humano de ideas, símbolos, lenguaje, ciencia, religión, arte y producción. Para ver la praxis como punto central de una antropología mujerista hay que insitir en la parte reflexiva de la praxis. Hemos insistido en que las latinas somos "intelectuales orgánicas" porque creemos que participamos en una concepción específica del mundo, que lleva a una cierta conducta moral, y que, por lo tanto, contribuye a sostener una concepción del mundo o la modifica introduciendo nuevas formas de pensar.

Para la teología mujerista la praxis liberadora es uno de los puntos de referencia principales para la elaboración de una antropología mujerista. Como esta praxis es parte integral de la experiencia cotidiana de las latinas, la antropología mujerista tiene como tema un sujeto histórico que lucha por sobrevivir y que se entiende como tal. Una pequeña pero muy común prueba de ésto es que a la pregunta, "¿cómo estás?" las latinas mayormente responden, "ahí, en la lucha". Claro está que el que la lucha por sobrevivir sea punto central de referencia de la manera en que las latinas nos entendemos a nosotras mismas sólo se puede comprender si se conoce la opresión que sufrimos a causa de injusticias específicas. Pero cuando se les presta atención, sobretodo a latinas de la base, lo que identifica sus vidas no es el sufrimiento sino la lucha por sobrevivir. Si fuese el sufrimiento no nos veríamos mayormente como sujetos morales sino como objetos sobre los cuales el opresor actúa infligiéndonos dolor y sería el aceptar y consentir ese dolor lo que nos daría nuestra identidad. Es precisamente lo opuesto lo que es verdad.

Lo que nos identifica es la lucha. Es por eso que somos una fuerza estrategicamente importante en la historia; es por eso que somos sujetos morales concientes del papel que tenemos en definir y hacer realidad nuestro proyecto histórico. Las latinas siempre hemos jugado un papel importantísimo en la historia de nuestros pueblos aunque la "historia oficial" lo ignora. Lo que la teología mujerista hace posible es la irrupción de la historia en la vida de las latinas en el sentido de ayudarnos a adquirir conciencia histórica, para que participemos en esferas en las cuales hemos estado ausentes, en las cuales podemos ser creadoras y forjadoras de la historia.

Otra razón por la cual uno de los puntos principales de referencia de una antropología mujerista es la praxis liberadora porque dicha praxis está enraizada en nuestras comunidades y sus necesidades. La comunidad no es algo que se añade sino que es parte constitutiva de quienes somos, es parte de nuestro ser personas.

Nosotras consideramos la teología mujerista como una praxis liberadora ya que a través de ella criticamos y denunciamos las estructuras que nos oprimen. Es una denuncia, primero porque critica en sí el hecho que la sociedad no reconoce a las latinas como intelectuales capaces de un pensar creativo. Segundo, debido a que nuestro lente es la liberación de las mujeres nuestra crítica no es parcial sino que incluye una crítica de la cultura latina y aún de nosotras mismas. Tercero, criticamos el que aún teólogos de la liberación no quieran reconocer a las personas de la base como teólogos, queriendo reservar ese título para aquellos que tenemos una educación académica.

El que entendamos a la teología mujerista como una praxis liberadora, nos lleva a rehusar la reducción de la teología a un discurso formal y disciplinado, en el cual lo adecuado es lo que se puede encasillar en criterios intelectuales formulados por los que controlan aparatos culturales y académicos que tienen muy poco que ver con la lucha cotidiana de las latinas por sobrevivir. La manera en que las teólogas mujeristas entendemos la teología sin duda lleva a deconstruir lo normativo, lo que es aceptado como lo principal en los métodos de la disciplina teológica. Esto es imprescindible para poder reconocer que, lo que es lo principal en la teología mujerista, en la ética mujerista, es la experiencia cotidiana de las latinas, expresada en algo que se escucha repetidamente en la comunidad, "hacer lo que se puede aunque no sea siempre lo mejor" para poder sobrevivir. Es por eso que en nuestro quehacer teológico preferimos enfatizar la ortopraxis en vez de la ortodoxia. La verdad para nosotras se encuentra al nivel de la historia, de la experiencia de lucha diaria, no en el ámbito de las ideas. No nos preocupa si la teología mujerista contribuye a una "explicación" del mundo o de lo tradicional o a la manera en que se "piensa" acerca de cuestiones de significado trascendental. Para nosotras la teología es un quehacer; es un tratar de cambiar las estructuras opresivas del mundo, de lo tradicional, un tratar de transformar el mundo.

La experiencia cotidiana de las latinas

En la teología mujerista la frase "experiencia cotidiana" se refiere a esas experiencias que son intencionales, a la suma de las experiencias que examinamos, sobre las que reflexionamos y con las que lidiamos. Estas experiencias cotidianas son los ladrillos con los que construímos nuestra lucha personal y comunitaria en contra de la opresión. Como hemos dicho ya en el capítulo 2, en esta sociedad las latinas sufrimos opresión étnica y sexista y la mayoría también sufrimos opresión económica. La multiplicidad de elementos en nuestra opresión lleva a una especificidad que sólo nosotras podemos apreciar y comprender por completo. Esta opresión nos lleva a menudo a vivir bajo gran presión sicológica ya que nuestras motivaciones y valores son ajenos a los que la sociedad valora. Por lo tanto, la sociedad no valida ni a nuestros valores culturales ni a nosotras mismas. No solamente se nos excluye de darle forma a los principios y las instituciones de la sociedad en la que vivimos, sino que muchas

veces éstas son interpretadas y usadas en contra de las latinas, para ex-
cluírnos y oprimirnos.

Lo que es aún peor es que los valores y las costumbres de nuestra propia cultura latina son a menudo usadas en contra de nosotras. Los prejuicios étnicos y androcéntricos no sólo nos oprimen sino que también
hacen posible el que se ignore aún a aquellos que hacen notar nuestra ausen-
cia. Es por eso, que para validar quiénes somos y lo que hacemos, para
no volvernos locas, las latinas tenemos que continuamente reflexionar profundamente, tenemos que saber por qué es que actuamos como lo hacemos.
Tenemos que reflexionar sobre quienes somos para saber hacia donde
vamos o sino nuestras vidas se disuelven en nada. El caos, la falta de raíces,
este no tener un lugar en el que nos podamos sentir en casa: éstas son
las razones principales por las cuales decimos que nuestra preocupación
principal en esta sociedad es la supervivencia.

La experiencia cotidiana de las latinas, esta lucha diaria por sobrevivir,
no sólo es el *locus theologicus*, sino además es el lugar teológico desde el
cual funciona la teoría mujerista. Esta lucha es también la fuente de nuestra
teología—entendimiento que reconoce el valor de nuestra lucha, ayuda
en el desarrollo de nuestra agencia moral y cuestiona lo que dice ser "objetivo". Las latinas tenemos una hermenéutica de sospecha en lo que se
relaciona con la "objetividad" y la "validez"; Esta sospecha es elemento
intrínseco de toda teología que surge de comunidades oprimidas. Los miembros de estas comunidades sabemos que lo que se dice es "objetivo" es sen-
cillamente la manera de ver y entender la realidad de aquellos que tienen
el poder para hacer que su punto de vista sea el normativo. Lo "objetivo"
en realidad surge de la experiencia cotidiana de los grupos dominantes e
ignora la experiencia cotidiana de las latinas y otros grupos minoritarios
o los clasifica como aberrantes.

Las teólogas mujeristas creemos que aún el pensar que se pueda ser objetivo es una equivocación. Aunque no negamos que "la verdad" existe
o pudiese existir, en lo que insistimos es que nuestro quehacer teológico
tiene que ver no con eso sino con la realidad que las latinas construímos
y confrontamos día a día. Para la teología mujerista es obvio que la teología
no es tanto acerca de Dios como acerca de lo que los humanos creemos
de Dios. Y una de las mayores influencias en el pensar es la experiencia
en nuestras vidas. Lo importante entonces, en vez de insistir en que somos
objetivas, es reclamar, identificar nuestra subjetividad: dejar saber cuál es
nuestra perspectiva en nuestro quehacer teológico. Y eso es precisamente
lo que hacemos cuando reclamamos la experiencia cotidiana de las latinas
como fuente teológica.

El usar la experiencia cotidiana de las latinas como fuente de la teología
mujerista lleva a una reconceptualización de qué es lo racional. En vez

de pensar que sólo los procesos intelectuales producen racionalidad, la insistencia en la experiencia cotidiana hace resaltar que es todo el misterio de nuestra existencia, incluyendo lo que nos enseñan y expresan los sentidos, los deseos, los placeres, las penas, la imaginación–que todo ésto también contribuye a lo racional. La totalidad de la experiencia cotidiana de las latinas, no solamente nuestra manera de pensar, amplifica nuestro lenguaje teológico, llevándonos a incluir no sólo argumentos que responden a una lógica lineal, sino también incluyendo denuncias proféticas, cantos y poesías de protesta y esperanza, lamentaciones y el lenguaje de la verdadera consolación. Nuestro lenguaje teológico no se circunscribe sólo a la palabra escrita sino que también usamos rituales litúrgicos, protestas callejeras, etcétera.

Latinas de la base como teólogas mujeristas

En el capítulo 3 indicamos la necesidad desde una perspectiva sociológica de usar las voces de las latinas de la base en el quehacer teológico. Ya también indicamos que si las latinas no hablamos, otros hablarán por nosotras convirtiéndonos en objetos de su reflexión en vez de ser nosotras sujetos de nuestro pensar teológico. Si el título de "teóloga" se reserva sólo para aquellas y aquellos que tengan educación formal y grados académicos, no podríamos decir que el hacer teología mujerista es una praxis para todas aquellas latinas que luchan por la liberación. El insitir en que latinas de la base son teólogas mujeristas es parte del proceso de conquistar espacios en los cuales podemos expresar nuestra palabra y nuestro ser. Ésto señala un cambio en nuestra manera de concebirnos: hasta ahora nos entendíamos como latinas luchando por sobrevivir; ahora estamos consciente de que además de eso también somos causa de nuestra lucha, de nuestra supervivencia. Este sentido de ser causa no es meramente un desarrollo sicológico sino también un proceso intelectual y racional que nos lleva a aplicar la sospecha hermenéutica a todas las áreas de nuestras vidas y nos hace posible tener gran creatividad en nuestra auto–comprensión. El estar concientes de que somos causa de nuestras propias luchas nos ayuda a reclamar el derecho que tenemos a hablar en nombre propio, ya que sólo nosotras sabemos explicar cómo es que nos entendemos y entendemos nuestra realidad.

Como la teología mujerista es un quehacer comunitario, no todas las teólogas mujeristas de una comunidad realizamos las mismas tareas teológicas. Las "teólogas técnicas", que hemos dedicado tiempo al entrenamiento académico y tenemos diplomas académicos, no somos más teólogas, por ejemplo, que las que se encargan de programar actos de protesta o de organizar rituales litúrgicos. Tampoco creemos que haya distintas categorías de teología mujerista que tienen a diferentes quehaceres teológicos y diferentes clases de lógica. A lo que más nos oponemos es a pensar que el quehacer teológico viene después de la acción. Para las teólogas mujeristas ésta es una división artificial que no sólo ignora la conexión intrínseca que hay entre la acción y la reflexión en la praxis, sino que tampoco respeta la unión que existe en la cultura latina entre lo sagrado y todo lo demás. Es por eso que para las teólogas mujeristas el quehacer teológico es nuestra manera de vivir, nuestra vocación.

Finalmente, el reconocer que todas las latinas que luchan por la liberación y así se entiendan son teólogas mujeristas, reconoce el hecho de que son los pobres y oprimidos los que hoy en día constituyen la dinámica decisiva de nuestra historia. En realidad, esto ha sido así siempre; pero es ahora que los oprimidos nos hemos dado cuenta de ésto. El pensar que los que tenemos diplomas académicos podemos liberar a los demás desemboca necesariamente en un paternalismo opresivo o nos lleva a traicionar una idea clave en la teología mujerista: la teología mujerista en sí es una praxis liberadora.

CHAPTER 7

Mestizaje: Symbol of Hispanic Women's Moral Truth-Praxis

AT THE BEGINNING of this book *mestizaje* was examined as one of the key elements of Hispanic Women's self-understanding, an integral aspect of our racial/ethnic cultural reality. In chapter 2 we saw that there is a *mestizaje* that has to do with the mingling of sixteenth-century Spanish Catholicism and Amerindian and African religious understanding resulting in the practices and rituals of a *religiosidad popular*. There we analyzed how this *mestizaje* has yielded a theologically rich *religiosidad popular* empowering to us in our everyday struggles. In this chapter we return to *mestizaje* in order to analyze the challenges it presents to Hispanic Women.

Many of us doing Hispanic theology understand and use *mestizaje* as a hermeneutical tool and a paradigm. As a hermeneutical tool, *mestizaje* helps us interpret the complex and rich reality of our community; as a paradigm, it is a way of representing, of talking about who we are as a community. Some of us *mujerista* theologians, however, fear that the use of *mestizaje* in Hispanic theology may lead to a romanticizing of our culture, and of the way we understand community. In meeting with Hispanic Women throughout the U.S.A., in reflecting with them on their lived-experiences, on their struggles for self-definition and survival, it becomes obvious and important that in the elaboration of *mujerista* theology we have to insist on two things if we are not to fall into an idealization of *mestizaje*. First, there is a need for in-depth analysis not only of differences among Hispanics, but of the way we deal with differences, because if we do not embrace differences there is no possibility of *mestizaje*. Second, we acknowledge that because ethnicity is a social construct, a heuristic device that includes not only biological and cultural characteristics but also social and economic elements of the Hispanic community in the U.S.A., Hispanics have a choice: we must choose to be or not to be Hispanics, and this includes choosing *mestizaje* as a way of understanding and interpreting ourselves.

The need to *choose* to be Hispanic became obvious to me as I talked with the women the reader has heard from in this book. Though I continue to find a pattern of cultural similarities in their religious and ethical understandings and practices, it is very obvious that these similarities do not yield sameness but rather a continuum of characteristics punctuated by particularity, specificity, diversity. As I heard them talk about themselves as Cubans, Puerto Ricans, Mexican-Americans, or Mexicans—not as Hispanics—I could not help but remember my own journey from *being* exclusively Cuban to an understanding of being Cuban-Hispanic, or, as I always introduce myself in this country and abroad, as "a Cuban who lives in the U.S.A." This journey has led me to understand and appreciate that the insistence on particularity and specificity is not antithetical to *mestizaje*, but, on the contrary, is required for *mestizaje* to exist.

Another issue that has made it important for *mujeristas* to consider differences has been the need to challenge European-American feminists' way of conceptualizaing all women as the same. Though many of them nowadays acknowledge this failing, the majority of their writings do not go beyond that: differences among women do not seem to impact their practice or theories. In the first part of this chapter, I want to capitalize on what we have learned from dealing with European-American feminists in order to examine differences, diversity, specificity, and particularities.[1]

The second part of the chapter contains a short discussion on the need we have as Hispanic Women to learn for our own community much of what we have said to European-American feminists. The third part explains how we are using *mestizaje* as a symbol of *mujerista* moral truth-praxis.

Understanding and Valuing Difference

One of the easiest ways of approaching the understanding of difference in the U.S.A. is to analyze the way people react to Hispanic Women.[2] These reactions manifest the significance that difference has for the dominant culture. The way those in power—those from the dominant culture—respond in general to Hispanic Women indicates that difference is not

---

1. I will use these four words interchangably in this chapter because I think they throw light on the issue here discussed from different sides, thus giving a richness to the discussion that it would lack if I used only one of these terms.

2. Of course, by doing this I am focusing on Hispanic Women, on how we experience the way people relate to us. The complexities of difference for theories of feminism as well as for the politics of feminism are dealt with at length in Elizabeth V. Spelman, *Inessential Woman* (Boston: Beacon Press, 1988). Also important is the work of María C. Lugones. See María C. Lugones and Elizabeth V. Spelman, "Have We Got a Theory for You! Feminist Theory, Cultural Imperialism, and the Demand for the 'Woman's Voice,'" *Women's Studies International Forum* 6, no. 6 (1983): 573–81; María C. Lugones, "On the Logic of Pluralist Feminism," in *Feminist Ethics,* ed. Claudia Card (Lawrence: Univ. of Kansas Press, 1991), 35–44; María C. Lugones, "Playfulness, 'World'-Travelling, and Loving Perception," in *Hypatia* 2, no. 2 (Summer 1987): 3–19.

appreciated or embraced in this culture. Difference breeds at best a competitiveness that has to end in someone's losing. And at its worst, difference breeds a destructive contempt commonly defined as racism and ethnic prejudice. As we have already examined, this destructive contempt, which results in oppression, depends on domination and works by subjugating, exploiting, and repressing.[3]

One reaction to Hispanic Women is to ignore us totally. Elsewhere I have referred to this as "invisible invisibility."[4] "Invisible invisibility" questions the very existence of Hispanic Women; it makes us question not only the value of our specificity but the very reality of it. Most of those who totally ignore us do not even know they are doing so; they are not even capable of acknowledging our presence. Their only point of reference seems to be themselves, their reality, their world, and this is often why they can insist that who they are, the way they understand reality, and the way they deal with it is what should be and is therefore normative in society. Those for whom Hispanic Women are "invisibly invisible" usually react with shock when one points out what they are doing. Their reaction is generally, "Well, I never think of you as Hispanic." And when we let them know how offensive that is, they cannot understand why we feel that way. Many of those who react to Hispanic Women this way consider themselves as people committed to doing away with group difference. To them this is what justice is about. In doing this, however, they are espousing a model of assimilation that excludes diversity and specificity and allows "norms expressing the point of view and experience of the privileged groups to appear neutral and universal," and, ultimately, normative.[5]

A second kind of reaction to Hispanic Women that we experience is that of *respect*. This kind of respect is not the profound awe that makes one value and give importance to someone else. No, the "respect" we experience is the quick-nod-of-the-head-acknowledgment, the politically correct response that one gets from those in control when they do not want to take Hispanic Women seriously. This is the reaction we also get from well meaning people of the dominant culture who believe they recognize and accept differences. Those who respond to Hispanic Women with respect are aware of the *problem* of differences but are not willing to take difference into consideration. Though they do acknowledge that there are other understandings than their own and that of the dominant culture, these well

---

3. See above, chapter 1, pages 6–7.
4. Ada María Isasi-Díaz, "Toward an Understanding of *Feminismo Hispano*," in *Women's Consciousness, Women's Conscience*, ed. Barbara Hilkert Andolsen, Christine Gudorf, and Mary D. Pellauer (Minneapolis: Winston-Seabury, 1985), 51–61.
5. Iris Marion Young, *Justice and the Politics of Difference* (Princeton: Princeton Univ. Press, 1990), 165.

meaning people proceed as if the only understanding is their own. They obviously fail to recognize that if they really respected Hispanic Women, their very identity and their theories and practices would have to be different.[6]

What is missing in the respect some of us Hispanic Women receive is engagement. The respect we are given does not seem to include being taken seriously. It does not allow what we say to affect the other. It does not recognize that what one says about oneself cannot ignore others and their struggles. That is precisely what engagement is all about. For engagement to happen, difference has to be recognized as an asset and not as a problem. Difference is truly an asset because those who are different

> are mirrors in which you can see yourselves as no other mirror shows you. . . . It is not that we are the only faithful mirrors, but I think we *are* faithful mirrors. Not that we show you as you *really* are; we just show you as one of the people who you are. What we reveal to you is that you are many—something that may in itself be frightening to you. But the self we reveal to you is also one that you are not eager to know for reasons that one may conjecture.[7]

For difference to be seen as a positive factor making engagement possible, the person who is different has to be allowed to be herself. Hispanic Women cannot be required to act or present ourselves first and foremost in a way intelligible to those of the dominant culture. Engagement requires that we enter into each other's worldview as much as possible and help others open up to new perspectives. If there is no willingness to enter into the world of the other, the self presented to people who are different from us is a "pretend self." We will hide our real selves in order to protect ourselves from others' projection of us. Respectful engagement requires honesty and a willingness to risk on the part of the Hispanic Women as well. But we are not called to lose ourselves in engagement; rather we are called to grow and effectively contribute to our liberation and that of our community. For this to happen, those who are willing to engage us must embrace our difference instead of making us a reflection of who they are.

Engagement and interaction are not a matter of including Hispanic Women in the dominant culture. It is not a matter of adding us to the melting pot as a way of avoiding guilt or accusations of being either noninclusive or falsely inclusive. It is a matter of embracing the other because she is important, and not because of how much she can be used. This requires a commitment to know Hispanic Women and our struggles,

---

6. María Lugones, "On the Logic of Pluralist Feminism," in *Feminist Ethics,* 35–44.
7. Ibid., 41–42.

and to recognize that our oppression is related to the privileges which the dominant culture enjoys.[8] Honest engagement ultimately leads to and demands that we understand that the "self requires self-conscious inter-action"[9] to the point that without such interaction we cannot be our own selves.

Finally, engagement and interaction require more than applauding diversity and romanticizing it. For pluralism to be part of the construction of our everyday reality we need an analysis of power as part of our commitment. Because of the way those in power have oppressed us, Hispanic Women—as well as women in general—have been reticent to speak about power, to analyze power, and to claim power. But unless we analyze who has the power and how it is being used, unless we are willing to understand power as an intrinsic element of our struggle to be self-determining women, difference will not be embraced. Engagement and interaction will succumb to manipulation.

Having Hispanic Women around the table does not guarantee engagement and interaction. These will become a reality when Hispanic Women are not always having to adapt to the way meetings are conducted, groups are run, businesses operate, U.S.A. society is organized, and the public interest is administered. For engagement and interaction actually to happen, my claim as a Hispanic Woman to participate in defining what is normative must be attended to. But this means that Hispanic Women will have a share of power. This, I suggest, will not happen as long as power is understood as a closed quantum instead of as a dynamic interaction that is rooted in and belongs to the community. Therefore, those who have power need to be accountable to the community. They need to understand power not as something to possess but as a dynamism to be shepherded for the good of the whole community.

Differences among Hispanic Women

What has been said about differences between Hispanic Women and persons of the dominant culture applies also to differences between Hispanic Women and Hispanic men as well as to differences between Hispanic Women and persons, women and men, of other marginalized groups. Furthermore, it also applies to differences among Hispanic Women

---

8. I am here referring mostly to how people of the dominant culture relate to Hispanic Women. But of course we also have to deal with difference among communities of struggle. Much of the same dynamics are operative, and we unfortunately tend to see the other and her struggles in view of ours instead of respecting each other's specificity and building together a "new heaven and a new earth."

9. Lugones, "On the Logic of Pluralist Feminism," 43.

ourselves, differences that must be analyzed and acknowledged if we are really to claim and embrace *mestizaje.*

Intrinsic to *mujerista* theology's method is not only an acceptance of differences among Hispanic Women but an insistence on pointing out such differences.[10] From the very beginning of our attempts to articulate Hispanic Women's religious understandings and practices and our conscious practice of it as a liberative praxis, *mujerista* theologians have welcomed and not just tolerated expressions of diversity. We have attempted repeatedly not to tailor the perspectives and experiences of other Hispanic Women to fit our own. This is one of the reasons we have insisted that the voices of Hispanic Women, as diverse as possible, be an integral part of our articulation of *mujerista* theology. It is also important to make clear that we have not done this in an attempt to be politically correct but because we have felt and known what our own incompleteness would be if we were to listen and reflect theologically only with Hispanic Women in our communities who are similar to us or who agree with us.

The challenge of diversity among Hispanic Women and the role that such a diversity plays in this liberative praxis that we call *mujerista* theology is not one we feel we have resolved. Perhaps we will never resolve it. Our awareness that there is not a universal Hispanic woman-ness pushes us to deal more and more with particularity and specificity and to stay away from universal claims regarding Hispanic Women. While we embrace the similarities among ourselves, we understand that these similarities exist within the context of specificities and particularities, in a continuum of diversity. Our challenge always will be to recognize "the particularity and multiplicity of practices, cultural symbols, and ways of relating," while resisting unifying them in distinct categories.[11] The attempt to set up unifying categories would result in doing to each other what the dominant culture does to us. It would result in defining those of us who do not have those similarities as totally other, and this would lead in turn to exclusion and opposition.

This is something that those of us who wield the pen, who publish books, and have access to public forums will always have to be on guard against. We must acknowledge that we do have more of an opportunity at least to set parameters about the meaning of Hispanic woman-ness.[12] We must indeed be constant in our efforts to see Hispanic Women as distinct

---

10. For example, see above the analysis of what the women whose voices we present in this book said in chapter 4. The section of that chapter entitled, "Latinas' Understanding of Themselves," which starts on p. 112, points out not only the similarities but also the differences.

11. Young, *Justice and Politics of Difference,* 169.

12. See Spelman, *Inessential Woman,* 159.

persons with historical specificity and particularity. We must understand the *mestizaje* of Hispanic Women as a dynamic concept that is always welcoming diversity and, therefore, always reworking what we consider our similarities to be. In other words, the fact that we are Hispanic Women means that we share those characteristics and struggles we discussed in the first two chapters of this book instead of claiming a common nature or a given essentialness.

One of the leads we need to follow here is the understanding that in rejecting differences as substantive categories and attributes what we are doing is welcoming our diversity as relational.[13] Therefore, what we need to do to embrace diversity is to engage each other respectfully and to integrate each other's understandings of reality into our own. We must require of each other as Hispanic Women what we require of non-Hispanic Women. To briefly restate what has been said above: we must acknowledge and live in ways that recognize that Hispanic Women from whom I am different are important in themselves, and that who I am—for better or for worse—depends on them and vice versa, and further we must elucidate the power dynamics among us.

The understanding of difference prevalent in the U.S.A. that creates minority groups, I believe both hinders and helps Hispanic Women to recognize diversity and to embrace it as something precious. How and why does it hinder? First, the use of the term *Hispanic* in the U.S.A. by government agencies, the media, and the public at large shows that the dominant culture thinks of us as a homogeneous group. Grouping us under the label *Hispanic* also helps the dominant group in society to conceive of us and maintain us as totally other. This makes it possible to use Hispanic as a label with mostly negative connotations: it identifies a certain kind of people who are poor, uneducated, stealing jobs from Americans, who do not speak English, and so forth. Second, seeing us as a *minority* group makes the process of marginalization, oppression, and discrimination possible and viable. Third, because it ignores the variety of backgrounds and conditions of individual persons as well as the myriad of reasons why different ones of us find ourselves in the U.S.A., the term *Hispanic* makes it more difficult for us to have a positive sense of self and often leads to an internalized devaluation that is very difficult to overcome.[14] Fourth, being seen as totally *other* means that Hispanic Women are caught in a dilemma: to participate in this society means to accept and adopt an identity that is not

13. Ibid., 171.
14. Suzanne Oboler, "The Politics of Labeling—Latino/a Cultural Identities of Self and Other," *Latin American Perspectives* issue 74, vol. 19, no. 4 (Fall 1992): 18–36. This is of course most obvious in the identity crisis suffered by Hispanic youth.

ours, and to participate means to remember and be reminded constantly of what we are not. [15]

Being thrown together into a pile labeled Hispanic, however, can also be helpful for us in our process of self-definition and self-determination. I content that being other in this society provides for us an opportunity to embrace diversity, to affirm differences, to engage each other, and to interact self-consciously. Experiencing what is means to be considered total-ly other helps us to understand and reject the dynamics of cultural im-perialism. Being considered a homogeneous group in a way forces us to face up to our own prejudices: our own racism, classism, and sexism. That we are looked upon as all being the same, as a homogeneous group, can become an opportunity for us to make a conscious choice of what it does mean that we are Hispanics living in the U.S.A. as well as the role we want to have in this society. In a word, we have the opportunity of defining ourselves, of opting to be *mestizos*, opting to be *for* Hispanics, opting to be Hispanics. [16]

Hispanic Women Opting for Hispanic Women

Much has been written in the last decade about the option for the poor. Most of what has been said on this subject has to do with calling the rich, the oppressors, to conversion. I used this concept of the option for the poor in the previous chapter in a somewhat different fashion. It is my con-tention that option for the poor demands of us to embrace grassroot Hispanic Women not merely as the subject matter of *mujerista* theology and as the ones to whom those of us who publish writing about *mujerista* theology are accountable. It also calls us to recognize Hispanic Women who are engaged in liberative praxis because of their religious understand-ings as *mujerista* theologians themselves and to acknowledge their liberative praxis as doing *mujerista* theology. I now look at the option for the poor from the underside and across, instead of from the top and down. I look at the need for the poor to choose the poor, for Hispanic Women to choose Hispanic-ness and *mestizaje* as an expression of their option for the poor and the oppressed, an option to which I believe the poor and the oppressed are also called.

The term "preferential option for the poor" appears in the "Message to the Peoples of Latin America," written by the Latin American Bishops during the 1979 Puebla Conference. [17] There the bishops took up once

15. Young, *Justice and the Politics of Difference,* 165.

16. Oboler rightly indicates that this option is a political decision that includes a social justice advocacy stance. Oboler, "The Politics of Labeling," 29–92.

17. Third General Conference of Latin American Bishops, *Puebla – Evangelization at Pres-ent and in the Future of Latin America* (Washington, D.C.: National Conference of Catholic

again the position they had taken at Medellín ten years earlier when they "adopted a clear and prophetic option expressing preference for, and solidarity with, the poor."[18] The bishops saw having a preferential option for the poor within the context of a conversion that they believe the whole Church needs. This preferential option is aimed at the "integral liberation" of the poor. The bishops also made clear that this option is not an exclusive option. Among the reasons the bishops give for such preferential option is the fact that poverty dims and defiles the image and likeness of God in human beings. The bishops make explicit that the preferential option for the poor remains regardless of "the moral or personal situation in which they [the poor] find themselves."[19]

The preferential option for the poor does not rest on their being morally better, or more innocent, or purer in their motives. It exists because the poor can see and understand what the rich and privileged cannot, because power and richness are self-protective and, therefore, distort reality. The poor have no vested interest in maintaining their present situation. It is that the poor,

> pierced by suffering and full of hope are able, in their struggles, to conceive another reality. Because the poor suffer the weight of alienation, they can conceive a hope-filled project and they can provide dynamism to a new way of organizing human life *for all*.[20]

These reasons for a preferential option for the poor can very well be the same reasons why we Hispanic women should choose Hispanic-ness, *mestizaje*. These are the reasons we must welcome and embrace diversity. Because Hispanic Women embody a diversity of races and cultures, of socio-economic strata and political ideologies, failure to affirm our *mestizaje* will definitely dim and defile the image and likeness of God in us. Only if we choose to be Hispanic Women within the U.S. society can we see different possibilities for our communities and for all those living here. We must choose an integrating liberation that demands changes of structures rather than participation in present oppressive structures. For us to choose *mestizaje* means that as Hispanic Women we have to be committed to making our *proyecto histórico* a reality.[21]

Bishops Secretariat, Committee for the Church in Latin America, 1979).

18. Ibid., 178.

19. Ibid.

20. José Míguez Bonino, "Nuevas Tendencias en Teología," *Pasos* (Departamento Ecuménico de Investigaciones, San José, Costa Rica, 1987): 22.

21. I hope this paragraph makes it clear that I have amplified significantly the meaning of *mestizaje*. Originally referring to the mixing of Spanish and Amerindian blood, I use *mestizaje* to mean and embracing of all sorts of diversity among Hispanics as an intrinsic element of our struggle for liberation.

Hispanic Women opting for Hispanic Women entails struggling to make a reality our *proyecto histórico.* [22] To opt for Hispanic Women means, first of all, being self-identifying, risking whatever it takes to enhance our moral agency, to be agents of our own history by not allowing others to act upon us, to treat us as objects. Second, opting for Hispanic Women means that we, as Hispanic Women, engage in the difficult and painful task of getting rid of the oppressor within, of the internalized oppressor. Although we have few other models than the oppressor's, and although everything in society invites us to be like the oppressor in order to be successful, we must withstand such pressure. Becoming the image and likeness of the oppressor will only assure us of a continuation of the status quo, which necessitates that a group always be at the bottom of the social-economic-political ladder. Third, to opt for Hispanic Women means that we renounce vengeance, that we realize that our task is to work to make a reality a *proyecto histórico* that benefits not only us, but everyone. As Hispanic Women, we have a preferential option for Hispanic Women not because we are better but because, we hope, our struggle makes us see different possibilities and a reality different from the present one in which we can hardly survive.

In having a preferential option for Hispanic Women we are engaging in liberative praxis, which, as such, has to be an intentional, effective struggle against oppression. In other words, a preferential option of Hispanic Women for Hispanic Women is for us a moral imperative, a key element of our moral truth-praxis. Without such an option we cannot claim to embrace *mestizaje.* And if we do not do that, we will be betraying who we are and what we understand we should be about.

Mestizaje and Hispanic Women's Moral Truth-Praxis

For Hispanic Women *mestizaje* is not only a paradigm and a hermeneutical tool for our theological praxis, but, because it is a symbol of our communities, it also is a symbol of Hispanic Women's moral truth-praxis. In *mujerista* theology we understand *mestizaje* as happening now, being experienced now, in many different ways. By using *mestizaje,* therefore, as a symbol of our moral truth-praxis, we once again claim the experience of Hispanic Women as the source of our theology. In claiming *mestizaje* as a symbol of our moral truth-praxis we are saying that we do not believe in abstract notions of truth. We are using the binomial *truth-praxis* to indicate that we deal with our own experience in a critical way and look at it in light of the histories of our own communities and of other

22. See chapter 2.

communities of struggle, and in light of what has been passed down to us by our forebears, particularly our mothers, our *tías*, and our *abuelitas.*[23]

Hispanic Women's communities, like all communities, are moral communities. Specific norms and behaviors based on the values of Hispanic culture are set by our communities. Communities as a whole are expected to hold specific values and to function accordingly. Each member of our communities, of course, is expected to act according to the values and norms of the community to which she belongs. In our communities, Hispanic Women are important and active moral laborers. Hispanic Women are the main transmitters of moral norms. But we do not transmit moral standards in an acritical fashion. On the contrary, as the women we have heard speaking in the pages of this book show, Hispanic Women in their daily lives are vitally involved in a process of evaluating existing moral norms of our communities, adapting them, and producing new ones in order to survive. Although most Hispanic Women might not be aware of this, their daily struggle to survive challenges the dominant culture and its moral claims, denouncing the racism/ethnic prejudice characteristic of U.S. society. And our embracing of *mestizaje* is a clear expression of this denunciation.[24]

As symbol of our truth-praxis, then, our embracing of *mestizaje* is, first of all, a call to re-create moral standards according to our daily struggle for survival, and it is a call for social change so we can embrace diversity and live according to our own moral values norms. This means that one of the characteristics of *mestizaje* as a symbol of our moral truth-praxis is that it has to be an effective praxis. That is to say, we judge our morality and our commitment to *mestizaje* by how effective we are in welcoming diversity and in engaging each other. We cannot continue to talk positively about *mestizaje* without denouncing the prejudices that exist among us as Hispanic Women and without working to make those prejudices disappear.

Another characteristic of *mestizaje* is that it is not an abstraction or something that happened in the past. *Mestizaje* is a present historical reality being elaborated in our very lives. This is why it must be affirmed and chosen repeatedly in all aspects of our lives. As a symbol of Hispanic Women's truth-praxis, *mestizaje* concretizes and makes public a fundamental option that helps define us as historical agents. It must be clear that to choose *mestizaje* means that we reject hierarchical understandings that set some over others. It also means that we reject a competitive individualism that

---

23. See the interpretation Susan B. Thistlethwaite has given to my words and her own elaboration of truth-in-action in her book *Sex, Race and God* (New York: Crossroad, 1989), 24–26.

24. For a most insightful exposition of moral labor and women's role in it, see Janet R. Jakobsen, "The Gendered Division of Moral Labor and the Possibilities for a Responsible Feminist Ethic," unpublished dissertation, Emory University, 1992.

destroys our sense of community and makes us see life as a win-lose situation.

Finally, as a symbol of Hispanic Women's moral truth-praxis, *mestizaje* is an expression of our responsibility to each other. Responsibility to others—and not for others—means that we allow other Hispanic Women to hold us accountable for who we are and what we do. To be responsible to others is to respect them for who they are and what they do while at the same time challenging them. To be responsible to others means that we welcome diversity and embrace it because we respect each other. That requires that we take each other seriously, that we engage and challenge each other to be ever more committed to the liberation of Hispanic Women.

SÍNTESIS DEL CAPÍTULO 7: Mestizaje: Símbolo de Moral, Verdad y Praxis de las Mujeres Hispanas.

Al comienzo de este libro vimos cómo "mestizaje" es uno de los elementos principales en la realidad étnica, racial y cultural de las mujeres hispanas. En el capítulo 2 analizamos cómo "mestizaje" también se puede referir a la mezcla del catolicismo español del siglo XVI con las religiones africanas y amerindias que ha resultado en nuestra religiosidad popular. En este capítulo vamos a analizar los desafíos que el mestizaje presenta a las mujeres hispanas.

En la teología hispana en general se usa "mestizaje" en forma paradigmática para hablar sobre la comunidad hispana y como instrumento hermenéutico para ayudarnos a interpretar nuestra rica y compleja, realidad. Algunas de nosotras, teólogas mujeristas, tememos que el uso de "mestizaje" en la teología hispana puede resultar en un romantizar la cultura hispana y nuestra comunidad. Al entrevistar a mujeres hispanas en diferentes partes de este país, nos dimos cuenta de que para no "idealizar" mestizaje tenemos que hacer dos cosas: Primero, tenemos que hacer un análisis profundo no sólo de las diferencias entre hispanos, sino también de cómo lidiamos con las diferencias entre nosotros porque, si no abrazamos nuestras diferencias, no hay posibilidad de mestizaje. Segundo, como la etnicidad es una construcción social que incluye no sólo características culturales y biológicas sino también elementos socio–económicos de la comunidad hispana en los EE.UU., los hispanos podemos—tenemos—que escoger ser o no ser hispanos y ésto significa que tenemos que decidir si queremos que uno de los elementos de nuestra identidad sea el mestizaje.

El tener que escoger ser hispanos fue algo que ví claramente cuando realicé las entrevistas para este libro. Aunque continué encontrando similitudes culturales en los entendimientos y prácticas religiosas y éticas de las mujeres hispanas, es obvio que las similitudes no producen uniformidad sino un continuo de características, puntualizado por particularidades, especificidad, y diversidad. Tenemos que entender que el mestizaje requiere esta diversidad.

Otra razón por la cual las mujeristas hemos tenido que prestarle atención a las diferencias es porque hemos tenido que desafiar la manera en que las feministas euro-americanas hablan de las mujeres como si todas fuéramos idénticas. Esto nos ha llevado a examinar en la primera parte de este capítulo cómo es que las mujeres hispanas entienden diversidad y diferencias. En la segunda parte discutiremos qué creemos que las hispanas tenemos que hacer en cuanto a diversidad y diferencias. En la tercera parte explicaremos cómo es que usamos "mestizaje" como símbolo de nuestra verdad–praxis moral.

Entendiendo y valorizando diferencia

La manera cómo las personas del grupo dominante reaccionan ante las mujeres hispanas indica lo poco que se aprecia en esta sociedad el ser diferente. Parece que lo mejor que la diferencia engendra es una clase de competencia que termina siempre con alguien perdiendo; y lo peor que engendra es un despecho destructivo al que comunmente nos referimos por el nombre de racismo y prejuicio étnico. Como ya hemos dicho, este despecho destructivo es lo que lleva a la dominación que depende de la subyugación, la explotación y la represión.

Una manera de reaccionar a la presencia de las hispanas es ignorarnos. La mayoría de las personas que nos ignoran no saben ni que lo están haciendo; es como si no fuesen capaces de aceptar nuestra presencia. Para ellas su punto de referencia es exclusivamente ellas mismas, su mundo y es por eso que a menudo insisten en que quiénes ellas son, la manera en que entienden la realidad y la manera en que lidian con ella es lo que debe ser la norma en la sociedad.

Muchos de los que reaccionan en esta forma ante la presencia de las mujeres hispanas son personas que se consideran comprometidas con eliminar diferencias, porque eso es lo que la justicia requiere. Al hacer esto, sin embargo, lo que están haciendo es abrazando la asimilación, lo cual excluye la diversidad y especificidad y permite que hayan normas que expresen el punto de vista y las experiencias de los grupos privilegiados lo cual se ve como normal, universal y normativo y a las cuales el resto nos tenemos que adaptar.

Una segunda reacción ante las hispanas que encontramos es el "respeto". Pero este respeto no es esa reverencia profunda que reconoce el valor y la importancia de la persona. No, el respeto que se nos tiene es ese reconocimiento superficial, la reacción politicamente correcta de quienes controlan y no nos prestan verdadera atención. Esta gente sabe que existe un problema en esta sociedad en cuanto a diferencias, pero no lo considera cosa seria. Lo que le falta a este tipo de respeto es la interacción. El respeto que se nos tiene no incluye el tomarnos en cuenta seriamente, no reconoce que lo que uno dice sobre uno mismo no puede ignorar a otros y a sus luchas. Para que de verdad haya interacción, lo diferente se tiene que reconocer como algo positivo porque las personas diferentes a nosotras son espejos en los cuales nos podemos ver en una forma que no nos podemos ver en ningún otro espejo. Las personas diferentes a nosotras no son nuestro único espejo, pero sí son espejos que nos reflejan fielmente. Estos espejos no nos reflejan exactamente cómo somos, pero sí nos muestran una de las maneras como somos.

Para que la diferencia sea un factor positivo, haciendo posible la interacción, se les tiene que permitir a las personas que son diferente, a las mujeres hispanas, ser quienes somos, como somos. La interacción requiere respeto, honestidad y arriesgarse. Pero no estamos llamadas a disolvernos en la interacción, sino a crecer y a contribuir en forma efectiva a nuestra liberación y la de nuestra comunidad. La interacción no es un añadir a las mujeres hispanas a la olla—al *melting pot*—para no sentirse culpable o para evitar acusaciones de no ser inclusivo. En vez, la interacción es un abrazar a las demás porque son importantes y no porque las podemos usar. Esto requiere conocer a las mujeres hispanas y a nuestras luchas y reconocer que nuestra opresión tiene una relación directa con los privilegios de la cultura dominante.

Finalmente, la interacción requiere más que aplaudir y romantizar la diversidad. Para que la pluralidad sea parte de la construcción de nuestra vida cotidiana necesitamos analizar quién tiene poder. Si las mujeres hispanas no tienen poder, no podremos influenciar lo que es normativo. Y nosotras no tendremos poder mientras que el poder se entienda como algo cuantitativo en vez de una interacción dinámica que sucede en la comunidad y "pertenece" a la comunidad. Es por eso que la gente con poder tiene que rendir cuentas a la comunidad. Esas personas necesitan entender que el poder no es una posesión sino un dinamismo que se tiene que pastorear en vistas al bien común.

Diferencias entre las mujeres hispanas

Lo que hemos dicho acerca de las diferencias entre las hispanas y las personas de la cultura dominante se debe aplicar a las diferencias entre las mujeres y los hombres hispanos, entre nosotros y personas de otros grupos marginados y entre las mismas mujeres hispanas. Si no analizamos y aceptamos las diferencias que existen entre nosotras, no podemos reclamar y abrazar el mestizaje.

Un elemento intrínseco del método de la teología mujerista no es sólo aceptar diferencias entre las mujeres hispanas sino el hacerlo en forma consciente. Es por eso que hemos insistido en incluír las voces de las mujeres hispanas respetando su diversidad. Hemos hecho ésto porque sentimos, sabemos, que estaríamos incompletas si sólo escucháramos e incluyéramos en nuestra teología a hispanas que fueran como nosotras o que estuviesen de acuerdo con nosotras.

La diversidad entre las mujeres hispanas y el papel que esa diversidad tiene en este proceso liberador que llamamos teología mujerista continúa siendo un desafío. El que estemos conscientes de que no existe una sola clase de mujer hispana, nos lleva más y más a reconocer y señalar particularidades y a alejarnos de dictámenes universales acerca de las mujeres hispanas. Al abrazar las similitudes que existen entre nosotras, entendemos que estas similitudes existen en un contexto de lo específico y lo particular que forman un continuo de diversidad. El desafío siempre consistirá en reconocer las particularidades y multiplicidad de prácticas, símbolos culturales y maneras de relacionarnos, resistiendo el deseo de unificarlos en categorías discretas. El insistir en establecer categorías que unifiquen las particularidades y diferencias sería hacer lo mismo que la cultura dominante hace con nosotras. El resultado sería que las que no comparten las similitudes serían consideradas como personas ajenas y ésto es lo que lleva a la exclusividad.

Al rechazar el categorizar las diferencias y verlas como atributos, lo que estamos haciendo es entender nuestra diversidad como algo relacional. Lo que tenemos que hacer para abrazar la diversidad es establecer una interacción respetuosa y tratar de integrar en nuestra manera de ser la manera en que otros entienden y lidian con la realidad.

Pero la manera en que esta sociedad entiende diferencias es muy distinta y lleva a que hayan lo que llaman "grupos minoritarios". Yo creo que esto ayuda y obstaculiza a que las mujeres hispanas reconozcamos y aceptemos la diversidad como algo precioso. ¿Cómo obstaculiza? Primero, el que se refieran a todas con la etiqueta "hispanos" ayuda al grupo dominante a vernos como totalmente ajenas. Esto lleva a que lo hispano tenga connotaciones mayormente negativas: somos pobres, sin educación, robándoles empleo a los americanos, no hablamos inglés, etcétera. Segundo, el vernos como grupo minoritario hace posible marginalizarnos, oprimirnos y discriminar contra nosotras. Tercero, el que se nos reduzca a una sóla clase de personas llamadas hispanas hace que se nos haga difícil el tener un sentido positivo de nosotras mismas y a menudo lleva a internalizar la devaluación personal que nos tiene la clase dominante. Cuarto, el ser totalmente "ajenas" nos causa un dilema: el participar en esta sociedad quiere decir aceptar y adoptar una identidad que no es la nuestra y a la vez nos lleva a que tengamos que recordar constantemente que no somos de la sociedad en la que estamos tratando de participar.

¿Cómo nos ayuda? Yo creo que el que se nos considere seres ajenos nos da la oportunidad de abrazar diversidad, afirmar diferencias, tomar a las demás en cuenta e interactuar con ellas conscientes de las diferencias que existen. Experimentar lo que es ser considerada totalmente ajena nos ayuda a entender y rechazar el imperialismo cultural. El ser visto como un grupo homogéneo nos hace enfrentarnos con nuestros propios prejuicios: nuestro racismo, clasismo y sexismo. El que se nos vea a todas las hispanas como si no existieran diferencias y particularidades entre nosotras puede darnos la oportunidad de hacer una opción conciente: nos da la oportunidad de definirnos a nosotras mismas, de escoger el ser mestizas, de escoger el ser hispanas y el optar siempre por las hispanas.

Mujeres hispanas optando por mujeres hispanas

Se ha escrito mucho en los últimos diez años acerca de la opción por los pobres. La mayor parte de lo que se ha dicho tiene que ver con llamar a los ricos, a los opresores, a que se conviertan. Ya he dicho que para nosotras la opción por los pobres requiere que aceptemos a las mujeres hispanas no sólo como el tema de la teología mujerista sino también las tenemos que aceptar como teólogas mujeristas. Y si examinamos la opción por los pobres no de arriba para abajo pero desde abajo y horizontalmente ¿qué vemos? Yo creo que lo que vemos es la necesidad que tienen los pobres de optar por los pobres, las mujeres hispanas de optar por la hispanidad y el mestizaje.

Las mujeres hispanas conllevan una gran diversidad de razas y culturas, de ideologías políticas y posiciones socio–económicas. Si no afirmamos nuestro mestizaje en esta sociedad, profanamos y obscurecemos la imagen y semejanza de Dios que hay en nosotras. Y si no afirmamos nuestro mestizaje de culturas, perspectivas políticas y económico-sociales, razas, variedades culturales, no podremos implementar nuestro proyecto histórico, no podremos luchar por la liberación. Esto hace obvio que "mestizaje" para la teología mujerista quiere decir más que mezcla de razas; "mestizaje" la integración de la diversidad que existe entre los hispanos como elemento de nuestra lucha la liberación.

El optar por las mujeres hispanas quiere decir, primero, que tenemos que ser auto–determinantes, corriendo todo riesgo necesario para fortalecer nuestra agencia moral, nuestro ser sujetos de nuestra propia historia y para no dejar que nos traten como si fuéramos objetos. Segundo, el optar por las mujeres hispanas quiere decir que tenemos que librarnos del opresor que hemos internalizado. Aunque tenemos pocos otros modelos que nuestros opresores y aunque todo en la sociedad nos invita a imitar a los opresores si es que queremos "salir adelante", tenemos que resistir esa tentación. Ser la imagen y semejanza del opresor sólo asegura el que las cosas continúen como están y eso necesita que siempre haya un grupo oprimido, un grupo en el último escalón de la escalera socio–politico–económica. Tercero, el optar por las mujeres hispanas implica que renunciemos a la venganza, que nos demos cuenta de que lo que tenemos que hacer es luchar por implementar nuestro proyecto histórico, el cual nos beneficia no sólo a nosotras sino a toda nuestra sociedad.

Mestizaje: símbolo de nuestra verdad-praxis moral

El mestizaje puede ser símbolo de nuestra verdad-praxis moral porque es símbolo de la comunidad hispana. En la teología mujerista reconocemos que hay un nuevo mestizaje que se está llevando a cabo en el presente, en esta sociedad, de muchas maneras diferentes. Por lo tanto al usar el mestizaje como símbolo de nuestra verdad–praxis reclamamos una vez más que la fuente de la teología mujerista sea la experiencia de las mujeres hispanas. Usamos el binómio verdad–praxis para indicar que lidiamos con nuestra experiencia en forma crítica, a la luz de las historias de nuestras comunidades y de otras comunidades de lucha y tomando en consideración lo que nos han legado nuestros antepasados: en especial nuestras madres, abuelitas y tías.

Al igual que toda otra comunidad, las comunidades de mujeres hispanas son comunidades morales. Nuestras comunidades tienen normas y maneras de actuar específicas basadas en los valores de nuestra cultura y se espera que los miembros de nuestras comunidades las observen. En nuestras comunidades las mujeres hispanas somos "trabajadoras morales" muy importantes. Somos las mujeres hispanas las que transmitimos las normas morales. Pero no transmitimos esas normas en forma a–crítica. Al contrario, como han demostrado las mujeres cuyas voces hemos escuchado en estas páginas, las mujeres hispanas en su vivir cotidiano están involucradas en forma vital en el proceso de evaluar las normas morales de nuestras comunidades, en adaptarlas y en producir nuevas normas que nos ayuden en nuestra lucha por sobrevivir. Aunque muchas no se den cuenta de ésto, la lucha cotidiana de las mujeres hispanas por sobrevivir es un reto a la cultura dominante y a sus normas morales. Esa lucha es una denuncia del racismo–prejuicio étnico que caracteriza la sociedad de los EE.UU. Y nuestro abrazar al mestizaje es una clara expresión de esta denuncia.

Como símbolo de nuestra verdad–praxis el mestizaje nos llama, primero de todo, a re–crear las normas morales de acuerdo a nuestra lucha por sobrevivir y es un llamado a implementar los cambios necesarios en la sociedad, para que podamos abrazar la diversidad y vivir de acuerdo a nuestros propios valores morales. Esto lleva a que el mestizaje sea en sí una praxis efectiva. O sea, tenemos que juzgar nuestra moralidad y nuestro compromiso con el mestizaje de acuerdo a cuán efectivo es en ayudarnos a abrazar nuestra diversidad. No podemos continuar elogiando el mestizaje sin denunciar los prejuicios que existen entre las mujeres hispanas y sin hacer todo lo posible para que esos prejuicios desaparezcan.

Otra característica del mestizaje es que no es una idea abstracta o algo que sucedió en el pasado. El mestizaje es una realidad presente, algo que elaboramos día a día en nuestras vidas. Como símbolo de la verdad–praxis de las mujeres hispanas, el mestizaje concretiza y da a conocer nuestra opción fundamental por nosotras mismas y esto nos ayuda a definirnos como sujetos históricos. Tenemos que entender claramente que el optar por el mestizaje significa rechazar una mentalidad jerárquica que nos pone a unos por arriba de los otros. También quiere decir que rechazamos la competencia individualista que destruye nuestro sentido de comunidad y nos hace ver la vida como un ganar o un perder.

Finalmente, como símbolo de la verdad–praxis de las mujeres hispanas, el mestizaje es una expresión de nuestra responsabilidad para con los demás. Somos responsables para con los demás y no por los demás. Esto quiere decir que le pedimos a otras mujeres hispanas que nos hagan rendir cuentas por quienes somos y lo qué hacemos; esto quiere decir que respetamos a las demás pero que las desafiamos a ser mejores; quiere decir que aceptamos la diversidad porque nos respetamos las unas a las otras. Eso requiere que nos tomemos seriamente las unas a las otras y que nos desafiemos a estar más y más comprometidas con la liberación de las mujeres hispanas.

◱ BIBLIOGRAPHY

I. Hispanics in the United States

Abalos, David. *Latinos in the United States: The Sacred and the Political.* Notre Dame, Ind: University of Notre Dame Press, 1986.

Anzaldúa, Gloria, and Cherrie Moraga. *This Bridge Called My Back: Writings by Radical Women of Color.* Watertown, Maine: Persephone Press, 1981.

Archdiocese of New York, Office of Pastoral Research. *Hispanics in New York: Religious, Cultural, and Social Experiences.* New York: Archdiocese of New York, 1980.

Carlson, Marifran. *Feminismo.* Chicago: Chicago Publishers, 1988.

Carter, Deborah J., and Reginald Wilson. *Eighth Annual Status Report on Minorities in Higher Education.* Washington, D.C.: American Council on Education, Publication Department, December 1989.

Conferencia Episcopal Cubana. *Documento Final e Instrucción Pastoral de Los Obispos.* Roma: Tipografía Don Bosco, 1986.

Consulta del Proyecto Hispano: Teología en las Américas. "Documento Final." New York: Theology in the Americas, 1979.

Cortes, Carlos, ed. *Protestantism and Latinos in the U.S.* New York: Arno Press, 1980.

Deck, Allan Figueroa. *The Second Wave.* New York: Paulist Press, 1989.

Díaz, Rey. "La liberación hispana en U.S.A." *Apuntes* 9, no. 1 (Spring 1989): 13–19.

Elizondo, Virgilio. *Galilean Journey– The Mexican-American Promise.* Maryknoll, N.Y.: Orbis Books, 1983.

_____ . *La Morenita.* Liguori, Mo.: Liguori Publications, 1981.

Elsasser, Nan, Kyle MacKenzie, and Yvonne Tixier y Vigil, eds. *Las Mujeres: Conversations from a Hispanic Community.* Old Westbury, N.Y.: Feminist Press, 1980.

Espín, Orlando O. and Sixto J. García. "Sources of Hispanic Theology." Notes handed out at a workshop conducted at the Catholic Theological Society of America, Toronto, 1988.

_____ . "Toward a Hispanic-American Theology." Notes handed out at a workshop conducted at the Catholic Theological Society of America Convention, Philadelphia, 1987.

Espinoza, Marco A. "Pastoral Care of Hispanic Families in the United States: Socio–Cultural, Psychological, and Religious Considerations." D.Min. diss., New York, Union Theological Seminary, 1982.

Extension. Chicago: The Catholic Church Extension Society of the United States of America (July 1985).

Figueroa Deck, Allan, ed. *Frontiers of Hispanic Theology in the United States.* Maryknoll, N.Y.: Orbis Books, 1992.

Fitzpatrick, Joseph P. "The Hispanic Poor in a Middle-Class Church." *America,* 2 July 1988.

_____ . *Hispanoamericanos y la iglesia en el Nordeste.* New York: Centro de Pastoral Hispana para el Nordeste, 1977.

Galilea, Segundo. *Religiosidad popular y pastoral hispano-americana.* New York: Centro Católico de Pastoral para Hispanos del Nordeste, 1981.

García, Alma M. "The Development of Chicana Feminist Discourse, 1970–1980." *Gender and Society* 3, no. 2 (June 1989): 217–38.

García, Sixto J., and Orlando Espín. " 'Lilies of the Field': A Hispanic Theology of Providence and Human Responsibility." *Catholic Theological Society of America Proceedings* 44 (1989): 70–90.

Goizueta, Roberto. "*Nosotros*: Toward a U.S. Hispanic Anthropology." *Listening* 27, no. 1 (Winter 1992): 55–69.

_____. *We are a People!* Minneapolis: Fortress Press, 1993.

Gómez, Alma, Cherrie Moraga, and Mariana Romo Carmona, eds. *Cuentos: Stories by Latinas*. New York: Kitchen Table, Women of Color Press, 1983.

González, Justo L. *The Theological Education of Hispanics*. New York: The Fund for Theological Education, 1988.

_____. *Mañana: Christian Theology from a Hispanic Perspective*. Nashville, Tenn.: Abingdon, 1990.

_____. ed. *Voces: Voices from the Hispanic Church*. Nashville, Tenn.: Abingdon, 1992.

González, Nicanor. "Hacia una teología de acción y reflexión pentecostal hispana." D.Min. diss., New York Theological Seminary, 1991.

González, Roberto O., and Michael La Velle. *The Hispanic Catholic in the United States: A Socio-Cultural and Religious Profile*. New York: Northeast Catholic Pastoral Center for Hispanics, 1985.

Guerrero, Andrés. *A Chicano Theology*. Maryknoll, N.Y.: Orbis Books, 1987.

Hawkins, Wayne R. "Hispanic and Anglo Christians: A Model of Shared Life." *Pacific Theological Review* 19, no. 2 (Winter 1986): 39–42.

Huitrado-Rizo, MCCJ, Juan José. "Hispanic Popular Religiosity: The Expression of a People Coming to Life." *New Theology Review* 3, no. 4 (November 1990): 43–54.

Information Systems Development. *The Chicana Feminist*. Austin, Tex., 1977.

Isasi-Díaz, Ada María. "The Bible and *Mujerista* Theology." In *Lift Every Voice: Constructing Christian Theologies from the Underside*, edited by Susan Brooks Thistlethwaite and Mary Potter Engel, 261–69. San Francisco: Harper and Row, 1990.

_____. "A Hispanic Garden in a Foreign Land." In *Inheriting Our Mothers' Gardens*, edited by Letty M. Russell, Kwok Pui Lan, Ada María Isasi-Díaz, and Katie Geneva Cannon, 91–106. Philadelphia: Westminster, 1988.

_____. "La mujer hispana: voz profética en la iglesia de los Estados Unidos." Informes de Pro Mundi Vita, América Latina 28 (1982).

_____. "*Mujeristas*: A Name of Our Own," in *The Future of Liberation Theology*, edited by Marc H. Ellis and Otto Maduro (Maryknoll, N.Y.: Orbis Books, 1989): 410–19.

_____. "Solidarity: Love of Neighbor in the 1980s." In *Lift Every Voice: Constructing Christian Theologies from the Underside*, edited by Susan Brooks Thistlethwaite and Mary Potter Engel, 31–40. San Francisco: Harper and Row, 1990.

_____. "Toward an Understanding of *Feminismo Hispano* in the U.S.A." In *Women's Consciousness, Women's Conscience*, edited by Barbara Hilkert Andolsen, Christine E. Gudorf, Mary D. Pellauer, 51–61. Minneapolis: Winston Press, 1985.

_____. "*¡Viva La Diferencia!*" *Journal of Feminist Studies in Religion* 8, no. 2 (Fall 1992): 98–102.

Isasi-Díaz, Ada María, Elena Olazagasti-Segovia, Sandra Mangual-Rodríguez, María Antonietta Berriozábal, Daisy L. Machado, Lourdes Arguelles, and Raven-Anne Rivero. "*Mujeristas*: Who We Are and What We Are About." *Journal of Feminist Studies in Religion* 8, no. 1 (Spring 1992): 105–25.

Isasi-Díaz, Ada María, and Yolanda Tarango. *Hispanic Women: Prophetic Voice in the Church*. San Francisco: Harper and Row, 1988. Reprint, Minneapolis: Fortress Press, 1992.

Lachaga, José María de. *El Pueblo Hispano en U.S.A.: minorías étnicas y la iglesia católica*. Bilbao: Desclee de Brouwer, 1982.

Lucas, Isidro. *The Browning of America*. Chicago: Fides/Claretian, 1981.

Lafaye, J. *Quetzalcoatl et Guadalupe*. Paris: Gallimard, 1974.

Lara-Braud, Jorge. "Hispanic Ministry: Fidelity to Christ." *Pacific Theological Review* 19, no. 2 (Winter 1986): 5-14.

Lugones, María. "*Hablando Cara a Cara*/Speaking Face to Face." In *Making Face, Making Soul–Haciendo Caras*, edited by Gloria Anzaldúa, 46-54. San Francisco: An Aunt Lute Foundation Book, 1990.

_____ . "On the Logic of Pluralist Feminism." In *Feminist Ethics*, edited by Claudia Card, 35-44. Lawrence: Univ. of Kansas Press, 1991.

_____ . "Playfulness, 'World'-Travelling, and Loving Perception." *Hypatia* 2, no. 2 (Summer 1987): 3-19.

Lugones, María, and Elizabeth V. Spelman, "Have We Got a Theory for You! Feminist Theory, Cultural Imperialism, and the Demand for the 'Woman's Voice.'" *Women's Studies International Forum* 6, no. 6 (1983): 573-81.

Martínez, Jill. "In Search of an Inclusive Community." *Apuntes* 9, no. 1 (Spring 1989): 3-9.

Mirande, Alfredo. *La Chicana*. Chicago: Univ. of Chicago Press, 1979.

_____ . *The Chicano Experience: An Alternative Perspective*. Notre Dame, Ind.: Univ. of Notre Dame Press, 1985.

Montoya, Alex D. *Hispanic Ministry in North America*. Grand Rapids, Mich.: Zondervan Publishing, 1987.

Moore, Joan, and Harry Pachón. *Hispanics in the United States*. Englewood Cliffs, N.J.: Prentice-Hall, 1985.

Mosqueda, Lawrence J. *Chicanos, Catholicism, and Political Ideology*. Lanham, Md.: Univ. of America Press, 1986.

New Catholic World. New York: Paulist Press, July/August, 1980.

Nieto, Leo D. "Toward a Chicano Liberation Theology." In *Liberation Theologies in North America and Europe*. Mission Trends, no. 4, edited by Gerald H. Anderson and Thomas F. Stransky, 277-82. New York: Paulist Press, 1979.

Oboler, Suzanne. "The Politics of Labeling–Latino/a Cultural Identities of Self and Other." *Latin American Perspectives* issue 74, 19, no. 4 (Fall 1992): 18-36.

Ponce, Frank. "Los católicos hispanos en los Estados Unidos." Informes de Pro Mundi Vita, América Latina 23 (1981).

Recinos, Harold J. *Hear the Cry! Latino Pastor Challenges the Church*. Louisville, Ky.: Westminster/John Knox Press, 1989.

"Recovery Fails Latinos." *Dollars and Sense*, November 1989.

Rodríguez, Richard. *Hunger of Memory*. New York: Bantam, 1982.

Romero, C. Gilbert. "On Choosing a Symbol System for a Hispanic Theology." *Apuntes* 1, no. 4 (1981): 16-20.

Rosado, Caleb. "Thoughts on a Puerto Rican Theology of Community." *Apuntes* 9, no. 1 (Spring 1989): 10-12.

Rossing, John P. "*Mestizaje* and Marginality: A Hispanic-American Theology." *Theology Today* 45 (October 1988): 293-304.

Sandín-Fremaint, Pedro A. "Hacía una teología feminista puertorriqueña." *Apuntes* 4, no. 2 (1984): 27-37.

Sandoval, Moisés. "A Four-Part Series on Hispanic Catholics." Washington, D.C.:
National Catholic News Service, July 1985.
_____. "Hispanic Challenges to the Church." Washington, D.C.: Secretariat of
Hispanic Affairs, 1978.
_____, ed. *Fronteras: A History of the Latin American Church in the USA Since 1513.*
San Antonio: The Mexican American Cultural Center, 1983.
_____, ed. *The Mexican American Experience in the Church.* New York: William
H. Sadlier, 1983.
Secretariat for Hispanic Affairs, National Conference of Catholic Bishops/United
States Catholic Conference. *Proceedings of the II Encuentro Nacional Hispano
de Pastoral.* Washington, D.C.: Secretariat for Hispanic Affairs/USCC, 1978.
Segovia, Fernando. "Two Places and No Place on Which to Stand: Mixture and
Otherness in Hispanic American Theology," *Listening* 27, no. 2 (Winter 1992):
26–40.
Segunda Consulta Ecuménica de Pastoral Indígena. *Aporte de los pueblos indígenas
de América Latina a la Teología Cristiana.* Quito, Ecuador, 1986.
Sepúlveda, Juan. "Pentecostalism as Popular Religiosity." *International Review of
Mission* 78 (January 1989): 80–88.
Solivan, Samuel. "Orthopathos: Interlocutor between Orthodoxy and Praxis." *An-
dover Newton Review* 1, no. 2 (Winter 1990): 19–25.
Sosa, Juan J. "Religiosidad popular y sincretismo religioso: santería y espiritualismo."
Documentación Sureste, no. 4 (March 1983).
Stevens Arroyo, Antonio, ed. *Prophets Denied Honor.* Maryknoll, N.Y.: Orbis
Books, 1980.
Tafolla, Carmen. *To Split a Human: Mitos, Machos y la Mujer Chicana.* San Antonio,
Tex.: Mexican American Cultural Center, 1985.
Vasconcelos, José. *La Raza Cósmica.* 11th ed., Colección Austral. México:
Espasa-Calpe Mexicana, 1948.
Vázquez, Edmundo E. "Toward a Multicultural Church: A Future for the
Presbyterian Church in the Southwest." *Pacific Theological Review* 19, no. 2
(Winter 1986): 15–23.
Vidal, Jaime. "Popular Religion Among the Hispanics in the General Area of the
Archdiocese of Newark." In *Presencia Nueva,* edited by Office of Research and
Planning, 241–347. Newark: Office of Research and Planning, 1988.
Villafañe, Eldin. *The Liberating Spirit.* Lanham, Md.: Univ. of America Press, 1992.
Weyr, Thomas. *Hispanic U.S.A.: Breaking the Melting Pot.* New York: Harper and
Row, 1988.
Yankelovich, Skelly & White. *Spanish USA—A Study of the Hispanic Market in the
United States.* New York: Yankelovich, Skelly & White, 1981.
Zavala Martínez, Iris. "*En la lucha:* Economic and Socioemotional Struggles of Puerto
Rican Women in the United States." In *For Crying out Loud,* edited by Rochelle
Lefkowitz and Ann Withorn, 111–24. New York: Pilgrim Press, 1986.

II. Latin American

Aldunate, J. "Poder político, ciencia económica y moral." *Moralia* 4, no. 1-2 (1982):
83–100.
Alves, Rubem. "Thoughts on a Program for Ethics." *Union Seminary Quarterly
Review* 26 (1970): 43–58.
Anjos, M. F. dos, ed. *Articulacão da teologia moral na América Latina.* Teologia
Moral na América Latina, 2. Aparecida, São Paulo: Editora Santuario, 1987.

_____. *Temas Latino-Americanos de Etica.* Teologia Moral na América Latina, 3. Aparecida, São Paulo: Editora Santuario, 1987.

Aquino, Pilar. *Nuestro Clamor Por La Vida.* San José, Costa Rica: Editorial D.E.I., 1992.

Arriaga, P. "Los pobres ante la moral cristiana." *Christus* 39 (1974): 33–40.

Boff, Clodovis. "The Social Teaching of the Church and the Theology of Liberation: Opposing Social Practices?" In *Christian Ethics: Uniformity, Universality, Pluralism,* edited by Jacques Pohier and Dietmar Mieth, 17–22. Concilium 150. New York: Seabury, 1981.

_____. "The Poor of Latin America and Their New Ways of Liberation." In *Changing Values and Virtues,* edited by Dietmar Mieth and Jacques Pohier, 33–44. Concilium 191. Edinburgh: T & T Clark, 1987.

_____. *Theology and Praxis.* Maryknoll, N.Y.: Orbis Books, 1987.

Boff, Leonardo. *Church: Charism and Power.* New York: Crossroad, 1986.

_____. "¿Qué es hacer teología desde América Latina?" In *Liberación y cautiverio,* Encuento Latinoamericano de Teología, 129–54. México, 1975.

_____. "Método teológico. Problemática actual en Europa y en América Latina: Epistemología y Análisis." In *Liberación y cautiverio,* 566–68. México, 1975.

_____. *Salvation and Liberation.* Maryknoll, N.Y.: Orbis Books, 1984.

_____. *When Theology Listens to the Poor.* San Francisco: Harper and Row, 1988.

Boff, Leonardo, and Clodovis Boff. *Introducing Liberation Theology.* Maryknoll, N.Y.: Orbis Books, 1987.

_____. *Liberation Theology.* San Francisco: Harper and Row, 1986.

Bonnin, E., ed. *Espiritualidad y liberación en América Latina.* San José de Costa Rica, 1982.

Candelaria, R. Michael. *Popular Religion and Liberation.* Albany: State Univ. of New York Press, 1990.

Carreras de Bastos, Laura. *Feminismo Cristiano: Conferencia.* Montevideo, 1907.

Castro Rocha, Patricia. *Jesús liberador de la mujer, la sociedad y el mundo.* Managua, Nicaragua: Departamento de Publicaciones del Centro Inter-Eclesial de Estudios Teológicos y Sociales, 1987.

Cavalcanti, Tereza. "Produzindo Teologia No Feminino Plural." *Perspectiva Teológica* 20, no. 52 (September/December 1988): 359–70.

Chao, X. "Da autonomia a libertasão. Tres etapas do pensamiento etico." *Encrucilhada* 8 (1984): 316–27.

II Consulta Ecuménica de Pastoral Indígena. *Aporte de los Pueblos Indígenas de América Latina a la Teología Cristiana.* Ecuador, Documento de Circulación Interna, 1986.

Couch, Beatriz Melano. "Estudio bíblico: el reino de Dios y la ética." *Cuadernos de Teología* 7, no. 3 (1986): 177–96.

Crespo Garduno, Joaquín. "Métodos y condicionamientos de la teología moral latinoamericana." *Humanidades Anuario* 4 (1976): 151–58.

De Zan, Julio D. "Para una filosofía de la cultura y una filosofía política nacional." In *Cultura popular y filosofía de la liberación,* 89–139. Buenos Aires: Fernando García Cambeiro, 1975.

Dussel, Enrique D. *Ethics and Community.* Maryknoll, N.Y.: Orbis Books, 1988.

_____. "An Ethics of Liberation: Fundamental Hypotheses." In *The Ethics of Liberation—The Liberation of Ethics,* edited by Dietmar Mieth and Jacques Pohier, 54–63. Concilium 172. Edinburgh: T & T Clark, 1984.

_____. *Ethics and the Theology of Liberation.* Maryknoll, N.Y.: Orbis Books, 1978.

_____ . "One Ethics and Many Moralities?" In *Christian Ethics: Uniformity, Universality, Pluralism*, edited by Jacques Pohier and Dietmar Mieth, 54–61. Concilium 150. Edinburgh: T & T Clark, 1981.

_____ . *Para una ética de la liberación latinoamericana.* Tomo I. Buenos Aires: Siglo Ventiuno Argentina Editores, 1973.

_____ . *Philosophy of Liberation.* Maryknoll, N.Y.: Orbis Books, 1985.

Echegaray, Hugo. *La Práctica de Jesús.* Lima, Perú, 1980.

Encuentro Latinoamericano de teología. *Liberación y cautiverio.* México, 1975.

Fabella, Virginia, and Mercy Oduyoye, eds. *With Passion and Compassion.* Maryknoll, N.Y.: Orbis Books, 1988.

Ferre, Alberto Methol. "Itinerario de la Praxis." *Víspera* 29 (November 1972): 40–44.

Foster, Theodora Carroll. *Women, Religion and Development in Third World Countries.* New York: Praeger Publishers, 1983.

Frei Betto, "The Church, Ideology and Popular Culture." *Barricada Internacional*, July 1989.

Galilea, Segundo. *Religiosidad Popular y Pastoral.* Madrid: Ediciones Cristiandad, 1979.

García, Ismael. *Justice in Latin American Liberation Theology.* Atlanta, Ga.: John Knox Press, 1987.

Gebara, Yvone. "Option for the Poor as an Option for the Poor Woman." In *Women, Work and Poverty*, edited by Elisabeth Schüssler Fiorenza and Anne Carr, 110–17. Concilium 194. Edinburgh: T & T Clark, 1987.

Gibellini, Rossino. *The Liberation Theology Debate.* London: SCM, 1987.

Giménez, Gilberto. "De la doctrina social de la Iglesia a la ética de liberación." In *Panorama de la Teología.* 2: 45–62. Equipo Seladoc. Salamanca: Ediciones Sígueme, 1975.

Goizueta, Roberto. *Liberation, Method and Dialogue: Enrique Dussel and North American Theological Discourse.* Atlanta, Ga.: Scholars Press, 1988.

Golden, Renny. *The Hour of the Poor, The Hour of Women.* New York: Crossroad, 1991.

González Martínez, José Luis. "La ética popular y su autonomía relativa." *Allpanchis* 20, no. 31 (Primer Semestre, 1988): 125–62.

_____ . "Teología de la liberación y religiosidad popular." *Páginas* 7, no. 49–50 (November–December 1982): 4–13.

González, L. J. *Etica latinoamericana.* Bogotá (Segunda Edición), 1983.

Grupo de Investigación "Teología de la Praxis." *Sólo los cristianos militantes pueden ser teólogos de la liberación.* Documento no. 9 (1977): 4–32 y Documento no. 10 (1977): 3–37.

Gutiérrez, Gustavo. *El Dios de la vida.* Lima, Perú: Departamento de Teología, Pontificia Universidad Católica del Perú, 1983.

_____ . *On Job.* Maryknoll, N.Y.: Orbis Books, 1987.

_____ . *The Power of the Poor in History.* Maryknoll, N.Y.: Orbis Books, 1983.

_____ . *Sobre el trabajo humano.* Lima, Perú: Centro de Estudios y Publicaciones, 1982.

_____ . *A Theology of Liberation.* Maryknoll, N.Y.: Orbis Books, 1988.

_____ . *La verdad los hará libres.* Lima, Perú: Centro de Estudios y Publicaciones, 1986.

_____ . *We Drink from Our Own Wells.* Maryknoll, N.Y.: Orbis Books, 1984.

Hinkelammert, Franz J. "La Crisis del Socialismo y el Tercer Mundo." *Pasos* 30 (July–August 1990): 1–6.

Idígoras, J. L. *Vocabulario teológico para América Latina.* São Paulo: Ediciones Paulinas, 1983.

Junges, José Roque. "Moral especial: Princípio Organizativo das Suas Diferentes Áreas e Conteudos." *Perspectiva Teológica* 20, no. 52 (September/December 1988): 371-77.

Koh, Jae Sik. "A Comparison of Walter George Muelder's Christian Social Ethics of the Responsible Society and José Míguez Bonino's Liberation Ethics." Ph.D. diss., Northwestern University, Ill., 1979.

Lepargneur, Francois Huber. *Demografia, etica e igreja.* São Paulo: Editora Ática, 1983.

Lora, Carmen, Cecilia Barnechea, and Fryne Santisteban. *Mujer: víctima de opresión; portadora de liberación.* Lima, Perú: Instituto Bartolomé de las Casas, 1985.

Lozano, Itziar, and Maruja Gonzáles. *Feminismo y Movimiento Popular.* Cuadernos para la Mujer. Serie: Pensamiento y Luchas, no. 8. (México), October 1986.

Manzanera, Miguel. *Teología, salvación y liberación en la obra de Gustavo Gutiérrez.* Bilbao: Univ. de Deusto, 1978.

Marzal, Manuel. "Evangelio y mitos populares. ¿Es posible una iglesia indígena en el Perú?" *Panorama de la teología latinoamericana.* 2:143-60. Equipo Seladoc. Salamanca: Ediciones Sígueme, 1975.

———. "La religiosidad popular en el Perú." *Panorama de la teología latinoamericana.* 1:27-42. Equipo Seladoc. Salamanca: Ediciones Sígueme, 1975.

Mieth, Dietmar. "Autonomy or Liberation—Two Paradigms of Christian Ethics?" In *The Ethics of Liberation—The Liberation of Ethics,* edited by Dietmar Mieth and Jacques Pohier, 87-93. Concilium 172. Edinburgh: T & T Clark, 1984.

Miguelez, Xosé. *La Teología de la liberación y su método.* Barcelona: Herder, 1976.

Míguez Bonino, José. *Doing Theology in a Revolutionary Situation.* Philadelphia: Fortress Press, 1975.

———. "Historical Praxis and Christian Identity." In *Frontiers of Theology in Latin America,* edited by Rosino Gibellini, 260-83. Maryknoll, N.Y.: Orbis Books, 1979.

———. "Nuevas Tendencias en Teología." *Pasos* 9 (1987): 18-23.

———. *Toward a Christian Political Ethics.* Philadelphia: Fortress Press, 1983.

Mino G., Cecilia. "Algunas reflexiones sobre pedagogía de género y cotidianidad." *Tejiendo Nuestra Red,* 1, no. 1 (October 1988): 10-15.

Miranda, A. A. de. *Moral, consciência e pecado.* São Paulo, 1983.

Misfud, Tony. *Moral de discernimiento.* Tomo 1. *Hacia una moral liberadora. Ensayo de una teología moral fundamental desde América Latina.* Santiago de Chile: CUIDE, 1983.

———. "El tema ético en Puebla: visión panorámica." *Moralia* 4, no. 1-2 (1982): 115-33.

Moreno Rejón, Francisco. "Bibliografía latinoamericana sobre moral fundamental (1984-1986)." *Moralia* 9 (1987): 157-64.

———. "Información bibliográfica sobre la moral fundamental desde América Latina." *Moralia* 7 (1985): 213-31.

———. "Perspectivas para una ética de la liberación." *Moralia* 4 (1982): 135-50.

———. *Salvar la vida de los pobres.* Lima, Perú: Centro de Estudios y Publicaciones, 1986.

———. "Seeking the Kingdom and Its Justice: The Development of the Ethic of Liberation." In *The Ethics of Liberation—The Liberation of Ethics,* edited by Dietmar Mieth and Jacques Pohier, 35-41. Concilium 172. Edinburgh: T & T Clark, 1984.

———. *Teología moral desde los pobres. La moral en la reflexión teológica desde América Latina.* Madrid: PS Editorial, 1986.

____. "La teología moral en América Latina a partir de Medellín." *Páginas* 92 (August 1988): 29–38.

Moser, Antonio. "Ciencias sociales y teología moral." *Páginas* 94 (December 1988): 75–99.

____. "Como se faz teologia moral no Brasil hoje." *Revista Eclesiástica Brasileira* 44 (1984): 242–64.

____. "The Representation of God in the Ethics of Liberation." In *The Ethics of Liberation—The Liberation of Ethics*, edited by Dietmar Mieth and Jacques Pohier, 42–47. Concilium 172. Edinburgh: T & T Clark, 1984.

Moser, Antonio, and Bernardino Leers, *Moral Theology*. Maryknoll, N.Y.: Orbis Books, 1990.

Mujeres Para el Diálogo. *Mujer Latinoamericana—Iglesia y Teología*. México, DF, 1981.

Munera, Alberto. "Conciencia moral y pecado." *Teología Xaveriana* 35 (1985): 157–85.

Myscofski, Carole A. "Women's Religious Roles in Brazil: A History of Limitations." *Journal of Feminist Studies in Religion* 1, no. 2 (Fall 1985): 43–57.

Paredes, Tito. "Popular Religiosity: A Protestant Perspective." *Missiology* 20, no. 2 (April 1992): 205–20.

Parker, C. "Popular Religion in Latin America." *Popular Religions*. Pro Mundi Vita Studies (November 1988): 18–26.

Pixley, Jorge, ed. *La mujer en la construcción de la iglesia*. San José, Costa Rica: Editorial D.E.I., 1986.

Portugal, Ana María, and Amparo Claro. "Virgin and Martyr." *Conscience*, July/August 1988.

Pravera, Kate E. "The Primacy of Orthopraxis: Theological Method in the Nicaraguan Church of the Poor." Ph.D. diss., Garrett–Northwestern University, Ill., 1984.

Quade, Quentin, ed. *The Pope and Revolution*. Washington, D.C.: Ethics and Public Policy Center, 1982.

Richard, Pablo. "La ética como espiritualidad liberadora en la realidad eclesial de América Latina." *Moralia* 4, 1–2 (1982): 101–14.

____. "La Teología de la Liberación en la Nueva Coyuntura." *Pasos* 34 (March/April 1991): 1–8.

Rivera Pagán, Luis N. *Evangelización y Violencia—La Conquista de América*. San Juan, Puerto Rico: Editorial Cemi, 1991.

Ruiz García, Samuel. "Condicionamientos eclesiales de la reflexión teológica en América Latina." In *Liberación y cautiverio*, 83–89. México, 1975.

Scannone, Juan Carlos. *Teología de la liberación y praxis popular*. Salamanca: Ediciones Sígueme, 1976.

____. "Trascendencia, praxis liberadora y lenguaje. Hacia una filosofía de la religión postmoderna y latinoamericana situada." *Panorama de la teología latinoamericana*. 2:83–115. Equipo Seladoc. Salamanca: Ediciones Sígueme, 1975.

Segundo, Juan Luis. "Condicionamientos actuales de la reflexión teológica en Latinoamerica." In *Liberación y cautiverio*, 91–101. México, 1975.

____. *Teología de la liberación*. Madrid: Ediciones Cristiandad, 1985.

____. "Two Theologies of Liberation." *Journal of Theology for South Africa* no. 52 (1985): 321–27.

Segundo, Juan Luis. *The Liberation of Theology.* Maryknoll, N.Y.: Orbis Books, 1982.

Sepúlveda, Juan. "Pentecostalism as Popular Religiosity." *International Review of Mission* 78 (January 1989): 80–88.

Snoek, C. J. "La teología moral en el Brasil de hoy." *Moralia* 4, 1–2 (1982): 67–81.

Tamez, Elsa, ed. *Against Machismo.* Oak Park, Ill.: Meyer Stone, 1987.

_____, ed. *El rostro femenino de la iglesia.* San José, Costa Rica: Editorial D.E.I., 1986.

_____, ed. *Teólogos de la liberación hablan sobre la mujer.* San José, Costa Rica: Editorial D.E.I., 1986.

_____, ed. *Through Her Eyes.* Maryknoll, N.Y.: Orbis Books, 1989.

Torre, Julio de la. "Movimientos de liberación y liberación cristiana." *Moralia* 4, 3 (1982): 265–73.

Trapasso, Rose Dominic. "Poverty, Gender and Justice in Peru." *Christianity and Crisis,* 6 February 1989.

"Una ética liberadora." *Misión Abierta* 4 (1985):11–112.

Valentín, Dora. "El Cristianismo y la Mujer." *Heraldo Cristiano* 24, nos. 11–12 (1979): 2–9.

Vidal García, Marciano. "Is Morality Based on Autonomy Compatible with the Ethics of Liberation? In *The Ethics of Liberation – The Liberation of Ethics,* edited by Dietmar Mieth and Jacques Pohier, 80–86. Concilium 172. Edinburgh: T & T Clark, 1984.

_____. "La preferencia por el pobre, criterio de moral." *Studia Moralia* 20 (1982): 277–306.

_____. "Teología de la liberación y ética social cristiana." *Studia Moralia* 15 (1977): 207–18.

III. Feminism

Amott, Teresa L., and Julie Matthaei, *Race, Gender & Work.* Boston: South End Press, 1991.

Andolsen, Barbara Hilkert, Christine E. Gudorf, and Mary D. Pellauer, eds. *Women's Consciousness, Women's Conscience.* San Francisco: Harper and Row, 1985.

Beneria, Lourdes, and Gita Sen. "Class and Gender Inequalities and Women's Role in Economic Development – Theoretical and Practical Implications." *Feminist Studies* 8, no.1 (Spring 1982): 157–76.

Benhabib, Seyla. "The Generalized and the Concrete Other: The Kohlberg–Gilligan Controversy." In *Feminism as Critique,* edited by Sylvia Benhabib and Drucilla Cornell, 77–95. Minneapolis: Univ. of Minnesota Press, 1987.

Bettenhausen, Elizabeth. "The Concept of Justice and a Feminist Lutheran Social Ethics." *The Annual of the Society of Christian Ethics* (1986): 163–82.

_____. "Three Dimensions of Conviction and Conflict in Morality." *Nexus* 23, no. 2 (Summer 1980).

Brubaker, Pamela K. "The Pauperization of Women: A Proposal for Feminist Ethical Theory." Presentation at the American Academy of Religion. Chicago, 20 November 1988.

_____. "Rendering the Invisible Visible: Methodological Constraints on Economic Ethics in Relation to Women's Impoverishment." Ph.D. diss., Union Theological Seminary, New York, 1989.

Bunch, Charlotte. *Passionate Politics.* New York: St. Martin's, 1987.

Card, Claudia. *Virtues and Moral Luck.* Series 1, Institute for Legal Studies, Working Papers. Madison, Wis.: Univ. of Wisconsin–Madison, Law School, November 1985.

Carr, Anne E. "Is a Christian Feminist Theology Possible?" *Theological Studies* 43, no. 2 (June 1982): 279–97.

_____. *Transforming Grace: Christian Tradition and Women's Experience.* San Francisco: Harper and Row, 1988.

Cheatham, Annie, and Mary Clare Powell. *This Way Daybreak Comes: Women's Values and the Future.* Philadelphia: New Society Publishers, 1986.

Chopp, Rebecca. *The Praxis of Suffering.* Maryknoll, N.Y.: Orbis Books, 1986.

Christ, Carol P. *Diving Deep and Surfacing.* Boston: Beacon Press, 1980.

Christ, Carol P., Ellen M. Umansky, and Anne Carr. "What Are the Sources of My Theology?" *Journal of Feminist Studies in Religion* 1, no. 1 (Spring 1985): 119–32.

Chung, Hyun Kyung. "Opium of the Seed for Revolution? Shamanism: Women Centered Popular Religiosity in Korea." Paper given at the Ecumenical Association of Third World Theologians, New Delhi, 1–5 December 1987.

_____. *Struggle to be the Sun Again—Introducing Asian Women's Theology.* Maryknoll, N.Y.: Orbis Books, 1990.

Code, Lorraine, Sheila Mullett, and Christine Overall. *Feminist Perspectives: Philosophical Essays on Methods and Morals.* Toronto: Univ. of Toronto Press, 1988.

Culpepper, Emily Erwin. "New Tools for Theology: Writings by Women of Color." *Journal of Feminist Studies in Religion* 4, no. 2 (Fall 1988): 39–50.

_____. "Philosophia: Feminist Methodology for Constructing a Female Train of Thought." *Journal of Feminist Studies in Religion* 3, no. 2 (Fall 1987): 7–16.

Daly, Mary. *Gyn/Ecology—The Metaethics of Radical Feminism.* Boston: Beacon Press, 1978.

Donovan, Josephine. *Feminist Theory.* New York: Frederick Ungar Publishing Co., 1985.

Farley, Margaret A. "Feminist Ethics in the Christian Ethics Curriculum." *Horizons* 11 (Fall 1984): 361–72.

_____. "Feminist Ethics." In *Dictionary of Christian Ethics,* edited by James E. Childress and John Macquarrie. Philadelphia: Westminster, 1986.

_____. "Moral Imperatives for the Ordination of Women." In *Women and Catholic Priesthood: An Expanded Vision,* edited by Anne Marie Gardiner, 35–51. New York: Paulist Press, 1976.

_____. *Personal Commitments.* San Francisco: Harper and Row, 1988.

Fiorenza, Elisabeth Schüssler. *In Memory of Her.* New York: Crossroad, 1983.

_____. "The Will to Choose or to Reject: Continuing Our Critical Work." In *Feminist Interpretation of the Bible,* edited by Letty M. Russell, 124–36. Philadelphia: Westminster, 1985.

Fiorenza, Elisabeth Schüssler, Karen McCarthy, Anne Llewellyn Barstow, Cheryl Townsend Gilkes, and Mary E. Hunt. "On Feminist Methodology." *Journal of Feminist Studies in Religion* 1, no. 2 (Fall 1985): 73–88.

Gilligan, Carol. *In a Different Voice: Psychological Theory and Women's Development.* Cambridge: Harvard Univ. Press, 1982.

_____. "Remapping the Moral Domain: New Images of the Self in Relationship." In *Reconstructing Individualim,* edited by Thomas C. Heller, Morton Sosna, and David E. Wellbery, 237–351. Stanford, Calif.: Stanford Univ. Press, 1986.

Gilligan, Carol, Janie Victoria Ward, and Jill McLean with Betty Bardige. *Mapping the Moral Domain.* Cambridge: Harvard Univ. Press, 1989.

Grimshaw, Jean. *Philosophy and Feminist Thinking.* Minneapolis: Univ. of Minnesota Press, 1986.

Haney, Eleanor Humes. "What Is Feminist Ethics?" *Journal of Religious Ethics* 8, no. 1 (1980): 115–24.

Harrison, Beverly W. "A Feminist Perspective on Moral Responsibility." *Conscience*, Winter 1984/1985.

———. *Making the Connections*. Boston: Beacon Press, 1985.

———. *Our Right to Choose*. Boston: Beacon Press, 1983.

Hartsock, Nancy. *Money, Sex and Power*. Boston: Northeastern Univ. Press, 1983.

Heyward, Isabel Carter. *Our Passion for Justice*. New York: Pilgrim Press, 1984.

———. *The Redemption of God*. Washington, D.C.: Univ. Press of America, 1982.

———. *Speaking of Christ*. New York: Pilgrim Press, 1989.

———. *Touching Our Strength*. San Francisco: Harper and Row, 1989.

Hoagland, Sarah Lucia. *Lesbian Ethics: Toward New Value*. Palo Alto, Calif.: Institute of Lesbian Studies, 1988.

Hunt, Mary E. "Beyond the Academy Gates." *Center for Women and Religion Journal* 3, no. 1 (1983): 7–16.

———. "Feminist Liberation Theology: The Development of Method in Construction." Ph.D. diss., Graduate Theological Union, Berkeley, Calif., 1980.

Hunter College Women's Studies Collective. *Women's Realities, Women's Choices*. New York: Oxford Univ. Press, 1983.

Jay, Nancy. "Sacrifice as Remedy for Having Been Born of Woman." In *Immaculate and Powerful*, edited by Clarissa W. Atkinson, Constance H. Buchanan, and Margaret R. Miles, 283–309. Boston: Beacon Press, 1985.

Kittay, Eva Feder, and Diana T. Meyers, eds. *Women and Moral Theory*. Totowa, N.J.: Rowman & Littlefield, 1987.

Morstein, Petra von. "A Message from Cassandra." In *Feminist Perspectives*, edited by Lorraine Code, Sheila Mullett, and Christine Overall, 46–63. Toronto: Univ. of Toronto Press, 1988.

Mullett, Sheila. "Shifting Perspective: A New Approach to Ethics." In *Feminist Perspectives*, edited by Lorraine Code, Sheila Mullett, and Christine Overall, 109–26. Toronto: Univ. of Toronto Press, 1988.

Nelson, Lou. "What's So Feminist about Feminist Ethics?" *Canadian Journal of Feminist Ethics* 2, no. 1 (Spring 1987): 29–34.

Nicholson, Linda. "Women, Morality, and History." *Social Research* 50, no. 3 (Autumn 1983): 514–36.

Noddings, Nell. *Caring: A Feminine Approach to Ethics and Moral Education*. Berkeley: Univ. of California Press, 1984.

O'Connor, June. "On Doing Religious Ethics." *Journal of Religious Education* (1979): 81–96.

Parsons, Kathryn Pyne. "Moral Revolution." In *The Prism of Sex*, edited by Julia A. Sherman and Evelyn Torton Beck, 189–227. Madison, Wis.: Univ. of Wisconsin Press, 1979.

Patrick, Anne E. "Conscience and Community: Catholic Moral Theology Today." The Warren Lecture Series in Catholic Studies. Univ. of Tulsa, Okla., 13 February 1989.

———. "Narrative and the Social Dynamics of Virtue." In *Changing Values and Virtues*, edited by Ditmar Mieth and Jacques Pohier, 69–80. Concilium 191. Edinburgh: T & T Clark, 1987.

Plaskow, Judith. *Sex, Sin, and Grace.* New Haven, Conn.: Yale Univ. Press, 1975.

Raymond, Janice. *A Passion for Friends.* Boston: Beacon Press, 1986.

Reineke, Martha J. "The Politics of Difference: A Critique of Carol Gilligan." *Canadian Journal of Feminist Ethics* 2, no. 1 (Spring 1987): 3–20.

Robb, Carol. "A Framework for Feminist Ethics." *Journal of Religious Ethics* 9, no. 1 (Spring 1980): 48–68.

Ruether, Rosemary Radford. "Feminist Interpretation: A Method of Correlation." In *Feminist Interpretation of the Bible*, edited by Letty M. Russell, 111–24. Philadelphia: Westminster, 1985.

_____ . "A Feminist Perspective." In *Doing Theology in a Divided World*, edited by Virginia Fabella and Sergio Torres, 65–71. Maryknoll, N.Y.: Orbis Books, 1985.

_____ . *New Woman/New Earth: Sexist Ideologies and Human Liberation.* New York: Seabury Press, 1985.

Russell, Letty M. "Authority and the Challenge of Feminist Interpretation." In *Feminist Interpretation of the Bible*, edited by Letty M. Russell, 137–46. Philadelphia: Westminster, 1985.

_____ . *Human Liberation in a Feminist Perspective.* Philadelphia: Westminster, 1984.

Schaef, Anne Wilson. *Woman's Reality: An Emerging Female System in the White Male Society.* Minneapolis: Winston Press, 1981.

Sherif, Carolyn Wood. "Bias in Psychology." In *The Prism of Sex*, edited by Julia A. Sherman and Evelyn Torton Beck, 93–133. Madison, Wis.: Univ. of Wisconsin Press, 1979.

Smith, Dorothy E. "A Sociology for Women." In *The Prism of Sex*, edited by Julia A. Sherman and Evelyn Torton Beck, 135–87. Madison, Wis.: Univ. of Wisconsin Press, 1979.

_____ . *The Everyday World as Problematic—A Feminist Sociology.* Toronto: Univ. of Toronto Press, 1987.

Smith, Ruth. "Moral Transcendence and Moral Space in the Historical Experiences of Women." *Journal of Feminist Studies in Religion* 4, no. 2 (Fall 1988): 21–37.

_____ . "Morality and Perceptions of Society: The Limits of Self–Interest." *Journal for the Scientific Study of Religion* 26 (Fall 1987): 279–93.

Spelman, Elizabeth V. *Inessential Woman.* Boston: Beacon Press, 1988.

Vaughn, Judy. *Sociality, Ethics, and Social Change.* Boston: Univ. Press of America, 1983.

Welch, Sharon D. "A Genealogy of the Logic of Deterrence: Habermas, Foucault and a Feminist Ethic of Risk." *Union Seminary Quarterly Review* 41, no. 2 (1987): 1–12.

IV. Womanism

Cannon, Katie Geneva. *Black Womanist Ethics.* Atlanta: Scholars Press, 1988.

_____ . "Hitting a Straight Lick with a Crooked Stick: The Womanist Dilemma in the Development of a Black Liberation Ethic." In *The Annual of the Society of Christian Ethics*, edited by D. Yeager (1987): 100–12.

_____ . "Resources for a Constructive Ethic in the Life and Work of Zora Neale Hurston." *Journal of Feminist Studies in Religion* 1, no. 1 (Spring 1985): 37–54.

Grant, Jacquelyn. *White Women's Christ and Black Women's Jesus: Feminist Christology and Womanist Response.* Atlanta: Scholars Press, 1989.

Hooks, Bell. *Feminist Theory: From Margin to Center.* Boston: South End Press, 1974.

_____ . *Talking Back.* Boston: South End Press, 1989.

Stack, Carol B. *All Our Kin: Strategies for Survival in a Black Community.* New York: Harper and Row, 1975.

Walker, Alice. *In Search of Our Mothers' Gardens: Womanist Prose.* San Diego, Calif.: Harcourt Brace Jovanovich, 1983.

Weems, Renita. *Just a Sister Away: A Womanist Vision of Women's Relationships in the Bible.* San Diego, Calif.: Lura Media, 1988.

Williams, Delores. "Black Women's Literature and the Task of Feminist Theology." In *Immaculate and Powerful*, edited by Clarissa W. Atkinson, Constance H. Buchanan, and Margaret R. Miles, 88–110. Boston: Beacon Press, 1985.

_____. "Rumbling and Rambling with Sustenance." *Probe*, September/October 1988.

_____. "Theological and Ethical Themes *Christianity and Crisis* Ought to Address." Unpublished presentation at the Advisory Board of *Christianity and Crisis*, 25 September 1987.

_____. "Womanist Theology: Black Women's Voices." *Christianity and Crisis*, 2 March 1987.

_____. "Women's Oppression and Life-Line Politics in Black Women's Religious Narratives." *Journal of Feminist Studies in Religion* 1, no. 2 (Fall 1985): 59–72.

V. Sociological Method

Benhar, Ruth. "Rage and Redemption: Reading the Life Story of a Mexican Marketing Woman." *Feminist Studies* 16, 2 (Summer 1990): 223–58.

Bureau of Rural Workers. *Rural Women Selected Coconut and Sugar-Tenanted Farms.* Philippines: Ministry of Labor and Employment, 1986.

Cannon, Lyn Weber, Elizabeth Higginbotham, and Marianne L.A. Leung. "Race and Class Bias in Qualitative Research on Women." *Gender and Society* 2, no. 4 (December 1988): 449–62.

de Certeau, Michel. *Heterologies–Discourse on the Other. Theory and History of Literature.* 17. Minneapolis: Univ. of Minnesota Press, 1986.

Geertz, Clifford. *The Interpretation of Culture.* New York: Basic Books, 1973.

Garfinkel, Harold. *Studies in Ethnomethodology.* Cambridge: Polity Press, 1984.

Gorden, Deborah. "The Politics of Feminist Ethnography: On Women Representing Other Women." Unpub. manuscript.

Griffen, Joyce. "Inside and Outside: The Moebius Strip of Oral History." Paper presented at the Conference "Methodologies and Strategies for Women's Oral History in the Rocky Mountains/Southwest," Denver, Colo., 13–14 November 1981. Tucson, Ariz.: Southwest Institute for Research on Women, 1982.

Jameson, Elizabeth. "May and Me: Relationships with Informants and the Community." Paper presented at the Conference "Methodologies and Strategies for Women's Oral History in the Rocky Mountains/Southwest," Denver, Colo., 13–14 November 1981. Tucson, Ariz.: Southwest Institute for Research on Women, 1982.

Kirk, Jerome, and Marc L. Miller. *Reliability and Validity in Qualitative Research.* Beverley Hills: Sage Publications, 1986.

Light, Linda and Nancy Kleiber. "Interactive Research in a Feminist Setting: The Vancouver Women's Health Collective. In *Anthropologists at Home in North America*, 167–84. Cambridge, Mass.: Harvard Univ. Press, 1981.

Miller, Delbert C. *Handbook of Research Design and Social Measurement.* New York: Longman, 1983.

Noblit, George W., and R. Dwight Hare. *Meta-Ethnography: Synthesizing Qualitative Studies*. Beverley Hills: Sage Publications, 1988.

Riessman, Catherine Kohler. "When Gender Is Not Enough: Women Interviewing Women." *Gender and Society* 1, no. 2 (June 1987): 172–207.

Silman, Janet. "In Search of Liberation Methodology." Unpub. paper, 7 May 1985.

Spradley, James R. *The Ethnographic Interview*. New York: Holt, Rinehart & Winston, 1979.

_____. *You Owe Yourself a Drunk*. Boston: Little, Brown & Co., 1970.

Stanley, Liz, and Sue Wise. *Breaking Out: Feminist Consciousness and Feminist Research*. London: Routledge & Kegan Paul, 1983.

Watts, Dale. "Ethnomethodology: A Consideration of Theory and Research." *Cornell Journal of Social Relations* 9, 1 (Spring 1973): 99–115.

Williamson, John B., David A. Karp, and John R. Dalphin. *The Research Craft*. Boston & Toronto: Little, Brown & Co., 1977.

Zavella, Patricia. "Recording Chicana Life Histories: Refining the Insider's Perspective." Paper presented at the Conference "Methodologies and Strategies for Women's Oral History in the Rocky Mountains/Southwest," Denver, Colo., 13–14 November 1981. Tucson, Ariz.: Southwest Institute for Research on Women, 1982.

VI. Additional Resources

Agirrebaltzategi, Paulo. *Configuración eclesial de las culturas*. Bilbao: Univ. de Deusto, 1976.

Amirtham, Samuel, and John S. Pobee. *Theology by the People*. Geneva: World Council of Churches, 1986.

Birch, Bruce C., and Larry L. Rasmussen. *Bible and Ethics in the Christian Life*. Rev. ed. Minneapolis: Fortress, 1989.

Centre "Cultures and Religions." *Effective Inculturation and Ethnic Identity*. Rome: Pontifical Gregorian University, 1987.

Clark, David. *The Liberation of the Church: The Role of Basic Christian Groups in a New Re-formation*. Birmingham (West Midlands): National Centre for Christian Communities and Networks, 1984.

Collins, Denis E. *Paulo Freire: His Life, Works, and Thought*. New York: Paulist Press, 1977.

Cone, James. *A Black Theology of Liberation*. New York: Lippincott, 1970.

Conn, Walter. *Conscience: Development and Self-Transcendence*. Birmingham, Ala.: Religious Education Press, 1981.

Cooke, Bernard. *Ministry to Word and Sacraments*. Philadelphia: Fortress Press, 1977.

Costa, Ruy O., ed. *One Faith, Many Cultures: Inculturation, Indigenization, and Contextualization*. Maryknoll, N.Y.: Orbis Books, 1988.

Curran, Charles E. *Directions in Catholic Social Ethics*. Notre Dame, Ind.: Univ. of Notre Dame Press, 1985.

_____. *Directions in Fundamental Moral Theology*. Notre Dame, Ind.: University of Notre Dame Press, 1985.

_____. *Faithful Dissent*. Kansas City: Sheed and Ward, 1986.

_____. *Moral Theology, A Continuing Journey*. Notre Dame, Ind.: Univ. of Notre Dame Press, 1982.

_____. *Themes in Fundamental Moral Theology*. Notre Dame, Ind.: Univ. of Notre Dame Press, 1977.

Curran, Charles, and Richard McCormick. *Readings in Moral Theology No. 6: Dissent in the Church.* New York: Paulist Press, 1988.

———. *Readings in Moral Theology No. 5: Official Catholic Social Teaching.* New York: Paulist Press, 1986.

———. *Readings in Moral Theology No. 4: The Use of Scripture in Moral Theology.* New York: Paulist Press, 1984.

D'Arcy, Eric. *Conscience and Its Right to Freedom.* New York: Sheed and Ward, 1961.

"Declaration on Religious Freedom." *The Documents of Vatican II*, edited by Walter M. Abbott, S.J., 14–101. New York: America Press, 1966.

Dehavenon, Mary Lou. "Cultural Anthropology and the Values of Community, Diversity, Poverty, Femininity, Peace, and Change in the United States in 1984." Lecture delivered at the Leadership Conference of Women Religious, Kansas City, Mo., August 1984.

"Dogmatic Constitution on the Church." *The Documents of Vatican II*, edited by Walter M. Abbott, S.J., 14–101. New York: America Press, 1966.

Driver, Tom F. *Christ in a Changing World.* New York: Crossroad, 1981.

Ellwood, Robert S. *Religion and Spiritual Groups in Modern America.* Englewood Cliffs, N.J.: Prentice-Hall, 1973.

Emmet, Dorothy. "Ethical Systems and Social Structures." In *International Encyclopedia of the Social Sciences*, edited by David L. Sills. New York: Macmillan and Free Press, 1968.

———. *The Moral Prism.* New York: San Martin's, 1979.

Fabella, Virginia. *Asia's Struggle for Humanity.* Maryknoll, N.Y.: Orbis Books, 1980.

Fabella, Virginia, and Sergio Torres, eds. *Doing Theology in a Divided World.* Maryknoll, N.Y.: Orbis Books, 1985.

———. *Irruption of the Third World.* Maryknoll, N.Y.: Orbis Books, 1983.

Fishman Joshua A. "Language Maintenance." In *Harvard Encyclopedia of Ethnic Groups*, edited by Stephan Thernstrom, 629–38. Cambridge, Mass.: The Belknap Press of Harvard Univ., 1980.

Franklin, Robert Michael. "An Ethic of Hope: The Moral Thought of Martin Luther King, Jr." *Union Seminary Quarterly Review* 40, no. 4 (1986): 41–51.

Freire, Paulo. *La Educación como práctica de la libertad.* Madrid: Siglo Ventiuno de España Editores, 1976.

———. "Education, Liberation and the Church." *Religious Education* 79 (Fall 1984): 527–28.

———. *The Politics of Education: Culture, Power and Liberation.* Hadley, Mass.: Bergin & Garvey, 1985.

———. *Cultural Action for Freedom.* Cambridge, Mass.: Harvard Educational Review, 1970.

Fromm, Erich. "Conscience." In *Moral Principles of Action: Man's Ethical Imperative*, edited by Ruth Nanda Anshen, 176–98. New York: Harper and Row, 1952.

Gottwald, Norman. *The Bible and Liberation.* Maryknoll, N.Y.: Orbis Books, 1983.

Gramsci, Antonio. *Prison Notebook.* Edited and translated by Quintin Hoare and Geoffrey Nowell Smith. New York: International Publishers, 1975.

Green, James W. *Cultural Awareness in the Human Services.* New York: Prentice-Hall, 1982.

Gustafson, James M. *Theology and Ethics.* Oxford: Blackwell, 1981.

Haring, Bernard. *The Law of Christ.* Westminster, Md.: The Newman Press, 1966.

———. "La teología moral después del Vaticano II y la contribución de América Latina." *Páginas* 97 (June 1989): 95–111.

Harrod, Howard L. *The Human Center: Moral Agency in the Social World.* Philadelphia: Fortress Press, 1981.

Hauerwas, Stanley. *A Community of Character.* Notre Dame, Ind.: Univ. of Notre Dame Press, 1981.

Herkovits, Melville J. *Cultural Relativism: Perspectives in Cultural Pluralism.* New York: Vintage Books, 1973.

Holland, Joe, and Peter Henriot. *Social Analysis: Linking Faith and Justice.* Maryknoll, N.Y.: Orbis Books, 1983.

Hope, Anne, and Sally Timmel. *Training for Transformation.* Zimbabwe: Mambo Press, 1984.

Johnston, William B. *Workforce 2000: Work and Workers for the 21st Century.* Indianapolis, Ind.: Hudson Institute, 1987.

Jones, Major J. *Christian Ethics for Black Theology.* Nashville, Tenn.: Abingdon Press, 1975.

Kammer, Charles. *Ethics and Liberation.* Maryknoll, N.Y.: Orbis Books, 1988.

Kelly, Matthew. "St. Thomas and the Moral Agent." *The Thomist* 46 (April 1982): 307–12.

Komonchak, Joseph. "Moral Pluralism and the Unity of the Church." In *Christian Ethics: Uniformity, Universality, Pluralism,* edited by Jacques Pohier and Dietmar Mieth, 89–94. Concilium 150. New York: Seabury Press, 1981.

_____. "Ordinary Papal Magisterium and Religious Assent." In *Readings in Moral Theology No. 3: The Magisterium and Morality,* edited by Charles E. Curran and Richard A. McCormick, 67–90. New York: Paulist Press, 1982.

Lebacqz, Karen. *Six Theories of Justice.* Minneapolis: Augsburg Press, 1986.

Lafaye, J. *Quelzalcoatl et Guadalupe.* Paris: Gallimard, 1974.

Langan, John, S.J. "Roman Catholic Theological Anthropology as a Basis for Human Rights." Paper presented at the 24th Annual Meeting of the Society of Christian Ethics. Indianapolis, Ind., 14–16 January 1983.

Linton, Ralph. "Universal Ethical Principles: An Anthropological View." In *Moral Principles of Action: Man's Ethical Imperative,* edited by Ruth Nanada Anshen, 645–60. New York: Harper and Row, 1952.

Lonergan, Bernard J.F. *Insight: A Study of Human Understanding.* New York: Philosophical Library, 1970.

_____. *Method in Theology.* New York: Herder and Herder, 1972.

_____. *The Subject.* Milwaukee, Wis.: Marquette Univ. Press, 1968.

McCann, Dennis. *Christian Realism and Liberation Theology.* Maryknoll, N.Y.: Orbis Books, 1981.

_____. "Conscientization." In *The Westminster Dictionary of Christian Ethics,* edited by James F. Childress and John Macquarrie. Philadelphia: Westminster, 1986.

Macmurray, J. *The Self as Agent.* London: Faber and Faber, 1957.

McGovern, Arthur F. *Liberation Theology and Its Critics.* Maryknoll, N.Y.: Orbis Books, 1990.

Maguire, Daniel C. "The Feminization of God and Ethics." *Christianity and Crisis,* 15 March 1982.

_____. *The Moral Choice.* New York: Doubleday & Co., 1979.

Mahoney, John. "The Spirit and Moral Discernment in Aquinas." *Heythrop Journal* 13 (1972): 291–94.

McErlane, M. J. "El tratamiento de la moral católica actual. Acercamiento a la teología moral de Ch. E. Curran." *Moralia* 4, 4 (1982): 421–38.

Morgan, John H. "The Concept of 'Meaning' in Religion and Culture: A Dialogue Between Theology and Anthropology." In *Understanding Religion and Culture*, edited by John H. Morgan. Washington, D.C.: Univ. of America Press, 1979.

Mueller, J. J. *What Are They Saying About Theological Method?* New York: Paulist Press, 1984.

Murray, John Courtney, ed. *Freedom and Man.* New York: P. L. Kennedy, 1965.

Mveng, Engelbert. "A Cultural Perspective." In *Doing Theology in a Divided World*, edited by Virginia Fabella and Sergio Torres, 72–75. Maryknoll, N.Y.: Orbis Press, 1985.

Neal, Maria Augusta. *The Just Demands of the Poor: Essays in Socio-Theology.* New York: Paulist Press, 1987.

Nelson, Paul. *Narrative and Morality: A Theological Inquiry.* University Park, Pa.: Pennsylvania State Univ. Press, 1987.

Niebuhr, H. Richard. *Christ and Culture.* New York: Harper and Row, 1951.

———. *The Responsible Self.* New York: Harper and Row, 1963.

O'Connell, Timothy. *Principles for a Catholic Morality.* New York: Seabury Press, 1978.

Oglesby, Enoch Hammond. *Ethics and Theology from the Other Side: Sounds of Moral Struggle.* Washington, D.C.: Univ. Press of America, 1979.

Ogletree, Thomas W. *The Use of the Bible in Christian Ethics.* Philadelphia: Fortress Press, 1983.

Parker, C. "Popular Religion in Latin America." *Popular Religions.* Pro Mundi Vita Studies. (November 1988): 18–26.

Paris, Peter. "The Task of Religious Social Ethics in the Light of Black Theology." In *Liberation and Ethics*, edited by Charles Amjad-Ali and W. Alvin Pitcher, 135–43. Chicago: Center for the Scientific Study of Religion, 1985.

Pfeifer, Michael. "Thoughts on Freedom, Conscience and Obedience." *Conscience*, July/August 1987.

Pieris, Aloysius. "Place of Non-Christian Religions." In *Irruption of the Third World*, edited by Virginia Fabella and Sergio Torres, 113–39. Maryknoll, N.Y.: Orbis Books, 1983.

Piper, Otto A. *Christian Ethics.* London: Thomas Nelson & Sons, 1970.

Preston, Ronald. "Concience." In *The Westminster Dictionary of Christian Ethics*, edited by James E. Childress and John Macquarrie, 116–18. Philadelphia: Westminster, 1986.

Proudfoot, Wayne. *Religious Experience.* Berkeley: Univ. of California Press, 1985.

———. *The Pope and Revolution.* Washington, D.C.: Ethics and Public Policy Center, 1982.

Rahner, Karl. *Concern for the Church.* 2, *Theological Investigations.* New York: Crossroad, 1981.

———. *Grace in Freedom.* New York: Herder and Herder, 1969.

———. *Theological Investigations.* Vol. 6. Baltimore: Helicon Press, 1969.

Rasmussen, Larry. "New Dynamics in Theology." *Christianity and Crisis*, 16 May 1988.

Reich, Alice Higman. "Ethnicity as a Cultural System." In *Understanding Religion and Culture*, edited by John H. Morgan. Washington, D.C.: Univ. of America Press, 1979.

Rosaldo, M. Z. "The Use and Abuse of Anthropology: Reflections on Feminist and Cross-Cultural Understanding." *Signs* 5, no. 3 (Spring 1980): 389–417.

Sano, Roy I. "Ethnic Liberation Theology: Neo-Orthodoxy Reshaped or Replaced?"

In *Liberation Theologies in North America and Europe,* edited by Gerald H. Anderson and Thomas F. Stransky. Mission Trends, 4, 247–58. New York: Paulist Press, 1979.

Scheman, Naomi. "Individualism and the Objects of Psychology." In *Discovering Reality,* edited by Sandra Harding and Merrill B. Hintikka. Dordrecht, Holland: D. Reidel Publishing Co., 1983.

Schneewind, J. B. "The Use of Autonomy in Ethical Theory." In *Reconstructing Individualism,* edited by Thomas C. Heller, Morton Sosna, David E. Wellbery, 64–75. Stanford, Calif.: Stanford Univ. Press, 1986.

Schreiter, Robert J. *Constructing Local Theologies.* Maryknoll, N.Y.: Orbis Books, 1985.

Smith, Erwin. *The Ethics of Martin Luther King, Jr.* Lewiston, N.Y.: Edwin Mellen Press, 1981.

Spaeth, Robert L. *The Church and a Catholic's Conscience.* Minneapolis: Winston Press, 1985

Sprio, M. E., and Roy D'Andrade. "A Cross–Cultural Study of Some Supernatural Beliefs." *American Anthropologist* 60 (1958).

Third General Conference of Latin American Bishops. *Evangelization at Present and in the Future of Latin America.* Washington, D.C.: National Conference of Catholic Bishops, 1979.

Tillich, Paul. *Sytematic Theology.* Vol. 1. Chicago: Univ. of Chicago Press, 1951.

Tracy, David. *Blessed Rage for Order.* New York: Seabury Press, 1978.

U.S. Bishops' Committee for Social Development and World Peace. "Beyond the Melting Pot: Cultural Pluralism in the United States." *Origins* 10, no. 31 (15 January 1981).

Verhey, Allen. *The Great Reversal: Ethics and the New Testament.* Grand Rapids, Mich.: Eerdmans, 1984.

Vidal, Marciano. *El Discernimiento ético.* Madrid: Ediciones Cristiandad, 1980.

West, Charles. "Culture, Power and Ideology in Third World Theologies." *Missiology* 12, no. 4 (October 1984): 405–20.

West, Cornell. "Marxist Theory and the Specificity of Afro–American Oppression." In *Marxism and the Interpretation of Culture,* edited by Carry Nelson and Lawrence Grossberg. Chicago: Univ. of Chicago Press, 1988.

_____ . *Prophesy Deliverance!* Philadelphia: Westminster, 1982.

_____ . *Prophetic Fragments.* Grand Rapids, Mich.: Eerdmans, 1988.

INDEX